Orientation to College Learning

The Wadsworth College Success™ Series

College Study Skills: Becoming a Strategic Learner, by Dianna L. Van Blerkom (1994)

Orientation to College Learning, by Dianna L. Van Blerkom (1995)

I Know What It Says... What Does It Mean? Critical Skills for Critical Reading, by Daniel J. Kurland (1995)

Integrating College Study Skills: Reasoning in Reading, Listening, and Writing, Third Edition, by Peter Elias Sotiriou (1993)

Mastering Mathematics: How to Be a Great Math Student, Second Edition, by Richard Manning Smith (1994)

Merlin: The Sorcerer's Guide to Survival in College, by Christopher F. Monte (1990)

The Adult Learner's Guide to College Success, Revised Edition, by Laurence N. Smith and Timothy L. Walter (1995)

Right from the Start: Managing Your Way to College Success, by Robert Holkeboer (1993)

Toolkit for College Success, by Daniel R. Walther (1994)

Your Transfer Planner: Strategic Tools and Guerrilla Tactics, by Carey Harbin (1995)

Turning Point, by Joyce D. Weinsheimer (1993)

The Freshman Year Experience℠ Series

College Is Only the Beginning: A Student Guide to Higher Education, Second Edition, by John N. Gardner and A. Jerome Jewler (1989)

Create Your College Success: Activities and Exercises for Students, by Robert A. Friday (1988)

The Power to Learn: Helping Yourself to College Success, by William E. Campbell (1993)

Step by Step to College Success, by A. Jerome Jewler and John N. Gardner (1987)

Your College Experience: Strategies for Success, Second Edition, by John N. Gardner and A. Jerome Jewler (1995)

Your College Experience: Strategies for Success, Concise Edition, by A. Jerome Jewler and John N. Gardner with Mary-Jane McCarthy (1993)

The Senior Year Experience℠ Series

Ready for the Real World, by William C. Hartel, Stephen W. Schwartz, Stephen D. Blume, and John N. Gardner (1994)

Orientation to College Learning

Dianna L. Van Blerkom
University of Pittsburgh at Johnstown

WADSWORTH PUBLISHING COMPANY
Belmont, California
A Division of Wadsworth, Inc.

To my husband,

MAL

With love

Senior and Managing Editor: Angela Gantner-Wrahtz
Assistant Editor: Lisa Timbrell
Editorial Assistant: Kate Peltier
Production Services Coordinator: Vicki Friedberg
Production: Cecile Joyner, The Cooper Company
Print Buyer: Barbara Britton
Permissions Editor: Robert M. Kauser
Interior Designer: Christy Butterfield
Copy Editor: Francesca Busch
Cover Designer: Bruce Kortebein, Design Office
Cover Photograph: Jason Jones, courtesy of Azusa Pacific University
Compositor: Thompson Type
Printer: Malloy Lithographing

This book is printed on acid-free recycled paper.

International Thomson Publishing
The trademark ITP is used under license.

Printed in the United States of America

1 2 3 4 5 6 7 8 9 10 — 99 98 97 96 95

Library of Congress Cataloging-in-Publication Data
Van Blerkom, Dianna L.
Orientation to college learning / Dianna L. Van Blerkom.
p. cm.
Includes index.
ISBN 0-534-24528-5
1. College student orientation. 2. Study skills. 3. Note-taking. 4. College students — Time management. I. Title.
LB2343.3.V36 1994 94-9682
378.1′98 — dc20

Brief Contents

Detailed Contents

To the Instructor

One of the most difficult tasks that instructors in orientation courses must face is helping students succeed in college. This task includes such things as helping students develop independence, improve relationships, and learn their way around campus, just to name a few. Although all of these are important first steps in helping students succeed, once they feel comfortable living away from home and learning to balance their time between home, work, and campus, they must begin to focus their attention on their course work. Many orientation texts do a good job of preparing students to meet the social challenges ahead of them; however, few of them prepare students to meet the academic challenges that they must face in order to succeed in college. I wrote this text in order to fill that gap — to provide students with a solid foundation of study skills and strategies that will help them succeed in college.

During the past ten years, I've had the opportunity to work with freshmen at several different colleges. I found that they were often as unaware of the level of work that would be expected of them in college as they were lacking in the skills and strategies that would help them succeed. By combining the traditional orientation topics with study-skills instruction, I found a formula that led to success for many of them. This combination provided for a good transition for students both socially and academically. I have tried to share this formula with others in the field through writing *Orientation to College Learning*.

Why is study-skills instruction important? Many college students say that no one ever really taught them how to study. Although they probably did learn some study skills during their twelve years of schooling, they may not have learned the study strategies that were necessary for college success. College courses are often more difficult, more intensive, cover more material at a faster pace, and focus on topics that are completely unfamiliar to new college students. Some or all of these differences may contribute to the difficulties that some students have during their first year in college. As a result, some students are dissatisfied with their grades or their performance in their courses, but they don't know what to do to correct this problem. Often, they experience anxiety and frustration and may even begin to doubt whether they have the ability to succeed in college. For many of these students, simply learning how to study and how to learn strategically in college makes the difference between failure and success. Other students benefit by improving their grades, boosting their self-esteem, or learning better ways to study so that they can enjoy their college experience more.

In this text, I have also provided a wide variety of active learning strategies that have proven to be successful with many students. Not all of them will work for every student. In fact, most students will find that, although one strategy may work well in one course, they may need to use different strategies for other courses. When students have an opportunity to try a number of different strategies, they will be able to find the ones that work best for them.

In order to succeed in college, students must learn to apply the strategies that they are learning to real course material. Practicing these strategies on psychology, history, biology, and sociology material, for example, will help students learn to modify and adapt the strategies to the lectures, texts, exams, and assignments that they have in their other courses. This transfer experience can be achieved through the activities at the end of each chapter or by having students complete specific activities in the Activities Packet.

UNIQUE FEATURES OF THE TEXT

You would expect to find many of the important aspects of this book in any orientation text. However, I feel that there are many features unique to this text:

- Clear, in-depth explanations for each of the skills presented
- A step-by-step approach to success in college
- Down-to-earth suggestions that really work
- Emphasis on strategic learning
- Excellent student examples based on other college courses
- Exercises and activities for immediate practice of new skills
- Excerpts from other college textbooks in many content areas (available in the Instructor's Manual and Activities Packet)
- Longer text passages for more realistic application to other content work (available in the Instructor's Manual and Activities Packet)

IMPORTANT ASPECTS OF THE BOOK

This text provides a step-by-step approach to college study skills. By breaking each of the topics down into smaller units, students will be able to master each of the steps before moving on to the next. Each chapter includes instruction in the skill, student examples, exercises for practice, and activities for self-evaluation.

Instruction

This text provides clear, easy to read explanations of how to study. Strategies for adjusting to college, setting goals, managing time, improving concentration, taking notes, reading and understanding textbooks, preparing for and taking tests, and writing college papers are included. Because every student learns differently, a number of different strategies for taking text notes, preparing "To Do" lists, and preparing study sheets (just to name a few) are described in the text. Students are encouraged to try all of the strategies and are then permitted to select the ones that work best for them. But, learning to study effectively and efficiently requires more than just knowing a new skill; it also requires using that skill. In many cases, understanding why particular strategies work helps motivate students to use them in their other courses. Reasons and rationales for using these strategies are also presented so that students understand why one strategy may work in particular situations while others may not.

Examples

A large number of examples, most of them prepared by students, have been included in the text to show students how to use the strategies that are presented. For many students, seeing an example of what they have to do makes it much easier to do it right the first time. Since there are many ways to develop a study sheet, take notes, or even keep track of assignments, a number of different examples are shown for each of the different strategies discussed in the text. These models help students understand how to use the strategies and may also motivate them to complete their assignments.

Practice

One of the most important goals of any successful orientation course is getting students to transfer what they learn to their other course work. In order to help students achieve this goal, well over 100 activities have been designed so that students can practice what they have learned. Many of these activities are included at the end of each of the text chapters. In addition, an Activities Packet containing additional exercises is available to accompany this text. Some of these activities are based on excerpts from other college textbooks. In this way, students are afforded practice with material that is similar to the course material they are currently using. Finally, many of the activities require students to practice the strategies using their own course materials. In this way, students transfer the skills they have learned to their other courses while at the same time increasing their understanding of the material for their other courses. In many cases, this leads to higher grades in all their courses, something that helps them see the real value of their orientation course.

Self-evaluation

Many of the activities are designed to help students monitor their own learning. The pre- and posttest "Where are you now?" activities provide a quick check of how many effective strategies students have prior to beginning each unit and how many they have made a part of their repertoire at the end of the unit. In addition, activities at the end of the chapter and in the Activities Packet ask students to evaluate many of the strategies that are presented in the text. It is only through self-evaluation that students can actually prove to themselves that one method of study is working for them. Once students know that a strategy is effective, they will continue to use it.

ACKNOWLEDGMENTS

I am especially thankful to all of my students for allowing me to use their examples in the text and for their encouragement and excitement throughout the development of this book. Thank you, Mal, for all of your support in making this book possible. Without your constant encouragement and help, this book (especially Chapter 10) never would have been possible. I also thank Angie Gantner-Wrahtz for encouraging me to write this book and for all of her support and assistance during the development of the manuscript, Vicki Friedberg and Cecile Joyner for making the production process run incredibly smoothly, Lisa Timbrell for her suggestions and encouragement in the development of the Activities Packet and Instructor's Manual, the rest of the Wadsworth team for all of their assistance in producing the book, and Dean Paul Strzempka for all of his personal and professional support. I also thank the following reviewers for their insight and excellent suggestions, which helped turn a manuscript into a textbook: Elaine Byrd, Utah Valley State College; Jim Johnson, Essex County College; Kathie Lorentz, Southern Illinois University; Donna Plank, University of Mary Hardin-Baylor; Corinne Plotkin, University of Wisconsin, Milwaukee; and Judi Repman, Texas Tech University.

To the Student

As you are reading this preface, you are probably feeling excited about beginning your college career. You should be — being in college is an exciting opportunity. Recently, I heard someone talking about how foolish some people are to put so much emphasis on their college years. After all, the person said, it's only a few years out of an entire lifetime. But many students remember their college years as being a very important and very special time of their lives — perhaps because they are extremely important years. These years open many new doors — both socially and professionally — and, in many ways, shape your entire future.

Many students begin college unsure of themselves. Some of their uncertainties involve living away from home and being on their own. However, other concerns often involve how well they will do academically. As you will learn in Chapter 1, college is very different from high school. Many of the study strategies that worked for you in high school may not be as useful in college. In order to make the transition from high school to college as smooth as possible, you may need to learn more about how to study. This text introduces and explains many study strategies that will help you achieve your academic goals. If you are using this text before or during your first semester in college, you should be well prepared for the challenges ahead of you. By learning and applying new strategies for dealing with college courses, you can improve your academic performance.

Once you put your newly learned strategies into practice, you should see your grades improve in each of your courses. This kind of improvement does not result from just being told what to do differently but rather from hard work and persistence in applying effective study strategies to your own course material. Becoming a successful student takes time and effort — there are no miracles involved. If you are willing to learn new skills and strategies and are also motivated to practice them and use them when doing your other course assignments, you, too, can achieve your goals.

Speaking of goals — I have four goals for you in your use of this text. First, I want you to learn new strategies that will make learning and studying much more effective. Second, I want you to improve your performance in your courses. Third, I want you to feel better about yourself both as a student and as a person — I want you to have self-confidence. Fourth, I want you to learn to actually enjoy school. Instead of dreading a class, an assignment, or even an exam, I'd like you to look forward to them because you will know how to be successful in taking notes, writing that report, and preparing for and taking that exam. If you apply what you are learning, you should see an improvement in your grades, have more time for leisure activities, feel less stressed about your academic work, feel better about yourself, and perhaps even begin to enjoy learning.

It is always exciting and rewarding when students tell me that the strategies in this book helped them. I am especially delighted to hear about their success in their freshman year. I am often as happy as they are, I think, when they make the Dean's List. If you are successful during your first semester, first year, or at any time during your college career because of your use of this text, I'd love to hear from you. Please drop me a note and let me know how *Orientation to College Learning* helped you. Also, if you have any suggestions for how this book can be improved in order to help other students succeed in college, please let me know. Perhaps the survey questionnaire at the end of this text will help you to respond to some aspects of this text in a more formal way. You can contact me by writing to:

Dianna Van Blerkom
Wadsworth Publishing Company
10 Davis Drive
Belmont, California 94002

CHAPTER 1

Adjusting to College

"In the beginning of the semester, I was dead set against changing my ways. I thought my study methods were tried and true and would work in college the same as they did in high school. I was wrong. With the increased workload of college, I needed to change practically everything that I did academically. I was studying, taking notes, and writing papers the wrong way. Now that I've learned new study methods, I've changed my habits, and I am getting higher grades in college than I ever did in high school."

Carlos Becerra

WHAT'S SO DIFFERENT?

Attending college requires a certain amount of adjustment for most students. If you are going on to college immediately after high school graduation, you may experience many changes in your life. You may be on your own for the first time—you may have to take on many of the responsibilities that your parents or teachers previously handled. College life offers many exciting new experiences, and many

PRETEST

Where Are You Now?

Take a few minutes to answer *yes* or *no* to the following questions.

	YES	NO
1. Do you know how to set up a budget and stick to it?	_____	_____
2. Do you know where to go on your campus to get financial aid, a tutor, and information on clubs and organizations?	_____	_____
3. If you miss class, do you expect your professor to go over the material with you at a later date?	_____	_____
4. Do you know who your advisor is?	_____	_____
5. Do you plan to take a lighter course load during your first semester in college?	_____	_____
6. Do you attend class regularly and stay up-to-date with your assignments?	_____	_____
7. Do you cut back on your sleep in order to get your assignments done for the following day?	_____	_____
8. Do you maintain regular contact with your family?	_____	_____
9. Have you really thought about why you are in college?	_____	_____
10. Do you expect college to be the same as high school?	_____	_____

Give yourself one point for each *yes* answer to all questions except 3, 7, and 10, and one point for each *no* answer to questions 3, 7, and 10. Now total up your points. A low score indicates that you need some help adjusting to college. A high score indicates that you are already using good strategies.

new freshmen want to join in on the activities. Learning to balance your priorities in college is one of the most important adjustments that you will have to make. If you remember to make academics your first priority, you can still have time for friends, extracurricular activities, and relaxation.

If you are a commuter or a non-traditional college student, you will have to make adjustments, too. Although learning to juggle both work and school or home and school responsibilities is a challenging task, many students do it every day. Making friends and developing a new peer group is another change you will face. As a commuter, you may need to make a special effort to get involved in campus life. Joining one club or organization at the beginning of the year will help you feel like you are a part of things.

Finally, many non-traditional students enter college unsure of their ability to succeed. Because they have been out of school for a number of years, they are afraid that they won't be able to compete with the traditional students. Once they get over the initial adjustment, most non-traditional students tend to do very well in college.

TAKING RESPONSIBILITY

There's a lot more to living on your own than doing your own laundry; however, even that added responsibility is a challenge for some students. Many high school seniors spend the summer before college learning how to sort, wash, and iron their clothing. But few students practice scheduling their time, budgeting their money, or learning to set priorities. These new responsibilities are also critical to college success. It's important to set up a schedule for the week so that you can accomplish all of your goals. Chapters 2 and 3 will help you establish realistic goals and learn how to manage your time.

Keeping track of your expenses can help you stay financially solvent throughout the year. Take some time to work out a realistic budget for each semester and then stick to it. If you write down the amount of money you spend and the reason for each expenditure every day for the first few weeks of school, you should be able to get a realistic picture of your fixed expenses and your discretionary ones. If you don't have a checking account, set one up. When you have to keep track of where your money goes, it's easier to monitor it when it's in writing. You can look back at your check register and see exactly how much you spent. You also can allot a certain amount for pocket money and still stay on your budget.

Learning to set priorities is one of the most difficult tasks you will face. Everything seems so interesting, exciting, and new when you begin college. Just getting your room set up the way you want it can occupy hours and hours of your time. College life offers many opportunities to get involved in social, organizational, and sporting events. All of these activities are appealing and interesting to new college students, and all of them take time—some a great deal of time. Although you should get involved in campus life, you need to start out slowly. Join one or two clubs instead of every club that your roommate or next-door neighbor joins. If you become too involved in campus activities, you won't have enough time to complete your academic tasks.

If you have to work in order to finance your education, you need to balance your time and priorities, too. Don't think of school as your first or your second priority. Think of work as your first priority during work hours and school as your first priority during school hours. Since you need the income from your job to pay for your education, you can't let things slide at work. In order to do both your job and your school work well, you may temporarily have to give up many of your other activities. You will need to spend your evenings and weekends studying rather than partying or spending time with family members. By carefully scheduling your time, you can excel on the job and in the classroom.

As a new college student, you will have new responsibilities in the classroom, too. In college, you're expected to be an independent learner. This involves taking responsibility for attending class, doing assignments, taking notes, and preparing for exams. You may be thinking that you did the same things in high school. You did, but the teacher often took the responsibility of making sure that you completed each of these tasks. In college, no one is there to make you do these things; in fact, your professors may not even mention the assignments or exams after handing you the syllabus on the first day. *You* are responsible for your education. If *you* don't take the initiative, *you* will lose out.

DRABBLE reprinted by permission of UFS, Inc.

GETTING TO KNOW THE TURF

One of the most important steps in adjusting to college is feeling comfortable in your new environment. One way that you can speed up this process is by getting to know your campus and the resources that are available to you. You may have already taken a tour of the campus during a college visit or during an orientation program, but that tour was probably one of many that you took. During the first week of school, take your own tour. Walk through buildings and check out some of the offices, such as the Dean's office, the financial aid office, and health services. Make a special point of visiting the computer labs on campus, and sign up for a tour of the library. (You will be expected to use library resources throughout your college career.) Find out whether you have a campus learning center. If there is one, take a few minutes and check out the services that are available to you.

Another way to get to know the college campus is by reading about it. Pull out the college catalog that you received and reread it. This time, though, read it as a student rather than as a prospective student. The catalog includes information about what services you can expect from the college and what the college expects from you if you wish to stay in good academic standing. Many colleges also prepare student handbooks that detail your rights as well as college rules and regulations. You should be aware of this information but may find some of it confusing. In that case, ask your resident assistant or your advisor to clarify those points. The more that you know about your campus, the more comfortable you will feel, and the more easily you will become a part of the college landscape.

USING YOUR COLLEGE LIBRARY

Learning to use your college library or library system is another important step in achieving college success. After you take the library tour, go back several times to get acquainted with the resources that you may need to use. Most college libraries have shifted from traditional card catalogs to computerized listings of their holdings. If you've never used a computer or a computerized card catalog before, you may find your first experience challenging or even frustrating. Some libraries provide instruction sheets next to each computer terminal while others "walk you through" the instructions right on the computer screen. Of course, you may want to save yourself a lot of time and effort and ask one of the librarians to show you how to use the computerized catalog or database. I did.

Select a topic, title, or author that interests you and search the catalog or database to see what books and periodicals are available. Don't stop there — select one or two of the books or periodicals and print out the information that is on the screen.

You will be amazed at what you can learn just from this printout. The author, title, copyright date, and Library of Congress call number will all be included. Your printout may also contain the book's location in the stacks, whether or not it is checked out, and an abstract (short summary) of the book. Just for practice, locate the book in the stacks and check it out. Going through this process even once will make you feel more comfortable the next time you need to use the library. After you've read some or all of the book, return it to the library.

On your next trip to the library, you may want to focus on using some of the reference materials. Set up an appointment with one of the reference librarians to learn more about using the various indexes, abstracts, and databases that you may be required to use when completing assignments for your major. Knowing how to use these resources will save you a great deal of time when you are ready to do research for a paper or project. You may already be familiar with indexes such as the *Reader's Guide to Periodical Literature*; however, college libraries have specialized indexes in a number of areas. Some of these include the *Humanities Index*, the *Social Science Index*, the *General Science Index*, *Applied Science and Technology Index*, *Education Index*, and *Book Review Digest.*

College libraries also contain many types of abstracts, such as *Psychological Abstracts* and *ABI Inform*, a business abstract. Many libraries now have many of these indexes and abstracts on line (available through computer terminals), which makes searching for sources much faster and much easier. Although each database requires specialized commands and keywords, it is well worth your effort to learn them. Once you know how to search the database, you'll use this service much more often. The best resource, though, is your library staff. Feel free to ask them for help — they welcome your questions and your interest in using the library's resources. Using the library should become a regular part of your academic plan.

Once you become familiar with the resources available in your college library, check to see what other resources outside your library are available to you. Many students don't realize that they have access to books and journal articles that are not available in their own library. Interlibrary loan agreements allow you to request materials that you need from other libraries, often at no charge. You should also check to see if you can access your library databases and card catalog from other locations. Many colleges provide computer terminals in residence halls, study lounges, and academic offices. You may even find that you can do your searches using a modem right in your own home.

Finally, your college library is an excellent location for study. Whether you're a commuter with time to kill between classes or a resident student looking for a quieter study environment, your college library is often the best place to study.

Take a few minutes to find the study rooms or locate a study carrel tucked away in a remote corner; then make it a regular stop in your daily travels.

GETTING ALONG WITH YOUR PROFESSORS

Learning your way around campus and learning to use the library are important, but learning to get along with your professors is critical to your academic success. College professors are different from your high school teachers, but they are not inhuman or superhuman. Many college students are terrified of or in awe of their college professors. They don't know how to interact with them, so they avoid any contact. Although some college professors appear to be unapproachable in the classroom, they are often very different in the less formal settings outside of the lecture hall. At many colleges, graduate students may teach or may assist the professor in teaching the course. Even though they may not differ much in age from their students, they should be approached in the same way as other professors. All professors and teaching assistants have office hours. These hours are set aside to meet with students on an individual basis. Your professor, however, is not likely to ask you to meet with him or her. Instead, you must take the initiative and set up an appointment. If you have questions about the course content or any of the assignments, schedule an appointment during office hours. You may also want to stop in to see your professors just to introduce yourself and chat about the course. Making this initial contact will help you feel more comfortable about seeing your professor when you do have a question or problem.

Many students are afraid to talk in class because some professors appear to be annoyed by interruptions during class. It won't take too long to get to know each of your professors and their particular teaching styles. Although many of your professors use the lecture format, some try to develop a dialogue with the class. Most professors tend to invite questions at the end of the lecture or at the end of a particular topic. If you have a question, ask it. If you are afraid, ask the question after class or during office hours. Professors like students who are interested in the class and are well prepared. They generally are willing to answer reasonable or thoughtful questions. They don't, however, respond well to questions that clearly show that you, the student, didn't read the assignment or missed the previous lecture.

If you miss class, *you* are responsible for the material and the assignment. Don't expect your professor to repeat the lecture for you privately at your convenience. Instead, you should ask another student for the notes. In the same way, you should not call the professor and ask, "Did I miss anything important?" To college professors, each class is important, and that question is an insult. Even though you were absent, you should get the assignment from a classmate or check your syllabus so that you are prepared for the next class. Your professors expect you to take the responsibility for your education.

If you fail a quiz or exam, you need to see your professor to talk about your performance. Don't, however, expect your professor to call you in for a conference. Instead, you need to take the initiative and schedule the appointment. Just because your professors don't constantly remind you about your academic performance, it doesn't mean that they don't care. They do care, but they believe that you have to take the responsibility for your education.

YOUR COLLEGE ADVISOR

Most college students are assigned an advisor during their first year. Your advisor, generally a professor in your major field of study, is the person who will help you monitor your progress toward your degree. You are still the one responsible, however, for completing all of the degree requirements. Be sure to obtain a copy of the check sheet that your department uses and record each of the courses that you take, the grade you receive, and the semester during which you completed the course. Ask your advisor for suggestions about course offerings and discuss your career plans honestly and openly. Don't expect your advisor, however, to tell you what you should take each semester — you should plan your schedule, and then your advisor will approve your selections or make suggestions about alternative courses.

Your advisor may also serve as a mentor or counselor at your college. Most colleges try to match up new college students with a professor who will help them over the hurdles of that first year. If you need someone to talk to, go to your advisor. If your advisor can't help you, he or she will know where on campus to send you for assistance. Think of your advisor as your link to all of the other faculty and staff on campus. Don't expect your advisor to schedule appointments to see you; you need to take the first step. If you didn't meet with your advisor to prepare your current schedule, make an appointment just to get acquainted. Again, this initial contact will make it easier to take the next step when you have a question or just need someone with whom to talk.

PLANNING YOUR SCHEDULE

Although you probably have already completed your schedule for this semester, you may want to consider some of the following suggestions as you plan your schedule for the next semester. First, it's important to remember that you can't always take every course offered in your major or every course that looks interesting during any one semester. You will benefit in the long run if you balance your schedule between courses in your major subject and courses that fulfill your general education requirements. By taking one or two of your required general education courses each semester, you will gradually fulfill your requirements while getting to sample a number of subject areas that you may find interesting. Balance these courses with one or two of the courses in your major or related to your major each semester. Some students make the mistake of scheduling all general requirements (often called core courses) during the first few semesters just to get them out of the way. Without a few courses related to their major, students often lose interest and lose motivation. Other students try to schedule only courses in their major and then find themselves completing core classes during their junior and senior years, when they should really be concentrating on their major or on fulfilling a minor.

You also should try to balance your classes by mixing heavy reading courses with courses that emphasize more writing, problem solving, or lab work. Taking four or five courses that all involve reading five- to six-hundred-page texts can put a strain on your time and affect your motivation. Scheduling an English course or a math course along with several reading courses can provide you with a welcome change of pace when you are completing your assignments and preparing for exams.

Taking a lighter load during the first year of college also will help you adjust to college more easily. Most colleges require students to take at least twelve credits to be considered full-time students. In many programs, however, students are required to take fifteen to eighteen credits during their first semester. This is too heavy a load for a new college student. Until you have completed one semester of college, you won't really understand how much more demanding college courses are. You may want to talk about your credit load with your advisor or some of the other students who attend your school. It's probably not too late to reduce your load. Many schools allow students to drop a class or two without penalty early in the semester. Check out the withdrawal policies at your college before you reduce your load.

Another way to balance your schedule is to plan your schedule according to time frames. Many students try to lump all of their classes together into two or three days of the week. This can lead to long, exhausting days of class and the feeling that the other days are free for work or relaxation. If you do schedule all of your classes on Mondays, Wednesdays, and Fridays, for example, you will need your Tuesdays and Thursdays to complete your assignments. If you spread your classes out throughout the day, you allow yourself time to complete work between classes and ensure that you will have an hour or two for a final review before exams.

Students who schedule one class right after the other often find themselves taking two exams on the same day with little or no time to review in between.

GETTING YOUR MONEY'S WORTH

A college education is your key to the future, but it is also one of the most expensive investments you or your parents will ever make. A college education can cost anywhere from twenty thousand to one hundred thousand dollars, give or take a few thousand. If you break down your tuition costs, you may find that you are paying between several hundred to several thousand dollars for each course you take. Divide that number by the number of class sessions that you have in each course. You may be astounded by the actual cost of each of your classes. What's the point of all of this math? Well, it's to help you realize that every time you miss a class, you are wasting money. Some students are excited when a professor cancels a class or doesn't show up. But students who are paying the bill or attending college on loans — which they'll have to repay — often feel angry because they believe that they are not getting their money's worth. In the same way, each time you cut a class, sleep through one, or show up unprepared, you aren't getting your money's worth either. To get your money's worth and maximize your success, go to class and stay up-to-date with your assignments.

GETTING ALONG WITH YOUR ROOMMATE

One of the most difficult adjustments for many college students is learning to live with a complete stranger. Getting along with your roommate is an important step in making the adjustment to college life. More and more colleges try to ensure a good match between roommates. They ask students to complete long surveys in order to match students on the basis of lifestyles and academic preferences. Some colleges even allow students to select their roommates during their orientation sessions. These and other similar methods do help make the process less random, but sometimes roommate problems still occur. At the beginning of the semester, talk to your roommate about your expectations and ask your roommate to describe his or hers, too. If either of you is uncomfortable about any of the living arrangements, talk about it immediately. Be willing to compromise and expect your roommate to do the same. If you set clear ground rules early in the semester, you can avoid a great deal of trouble later on. Each of you will have to give a little in order to make things work out. If you do have problems, go to your resident assistant or resident director. Getting friends involved in the conflict only makes matters worse. Unfortunately, if problems with roommates get out of hand, they can affect your academic performance as well as your personal life.

TAKING CARE OF YOURSELF

Although you probably have made some plans for when to study or when to do your laundry, you also need to take care of your physical health. It's important to eat well-balanced meals so that you will maintain your physical health and your energy level. Skipping meals and living on junk food is okay every so often, but a steady diet of junk food takes its toll over the course of the semester. Try to set up a regular exercise routine as well. The demands of college-level work will require you to spend more time sitting and reading or studying than high school ever did. Many students tend to gain weight during the first year of college—it's not the starchy food that causes the weight gain as much as the lack of physical exercise for many students. Not getting enough sleep is another common problem. Some college students study late at night and still have to get up early for class. Others try to squeeze work, school, and a personal life into their schedule. To make time for all these demands, they sacrifice sleep time. Although you can get by with four or five hours of sleep every so often, you can't do it for weeks at a time. Not only will fatigue interfere with your ability to concentrate and work at your optimum level, but also it may lead to exhaustion and lower your resistance to infection.

If you feel sick, go to your college health services office. If you wait too long, you may become so ill that you have to miss class or even drop out of school. Since you don't have anyone to tell you to see a doctor or take your medication, you need to take on that responsibility yourself. If you have a medical problem, be sure that the health services officer knows about it and has the proper medication available in case of an emergency. Also, you should notify your resident director and your professors of your condition. If you do have to miss classes due to illness or hospitalization, ask the dean's office or health services office to notify your professors. Often, formal notification is necessary so that you can make up missed assignments or exams when you return to school.

MAINTAINING FAMILY TIES

Even though you are learning to be more independent, you still should maintain close ties with your family. Many students change during their first year in college. They mature, become more independent, and gain new insights in personal and academic areas. In fact, some parents marvel or moan that Susie or Johnny isn't the same child that they sent off to school just a few months earlier. Sometimes these changes are good ones, while other times they aren't. One of the hardest adjustments that students must face is going home for a visit or term break and finding that their families expect them to be "dependent" again. After setting their own rules and taking charge of their lives, they suddenly are being told what to do and when to do it. The resulting conflict often leads to distance and bad feelings within the family. This experience can be avoided, however, by maintaining ties to your family throughout the semester. Calling home, writing letters, or spending a little time with your family each month can help them adjust to the new you more gradually. Talk about what's happening in your life and share both the good and the bad times.

WHAT IF YOU HAVE A PROBLEM?

Some students are reluctant to ask for help; they think that they should be able to solve all of their problems on their own. Although you are working at being independent, sometimes you still may need some help. If you have a personal or an academic problem, there are a number of resources on your college campus that are available to you. In most cases, you should probably begin dealing with your problem by talking about it with someone you trust. You may want to discuss the problem with your parents, your roommate, or a friend. If you need to take some type of action in order to resolve the difficulty, you may need to talk to someone with some authority on campus. If you have a personal problem related to your dormitory, the first step in dealing with it would be to talk to a resident director. If your problem is related to some other aspect of college life, set up an appointment with the Dean of Students or go to the counseling center. Most colleges have professionally trained counselors who can help you with personal problems. Ask a friend to go with you or ask your resident director to make the appointment for you if you are unsure of what to do or say. Go to your financial aid office for help when you need to apply for scholarships, loans, or grants. The financial aid staff are well trained and well practiced in helping students find funding for college.

If you're having a problem in one of your classes, set up an appointment to discuss it with your TA (teaching assistant) or professor. If you feel uncomfortable going to your professor, talk to your advisor. If your professor or advisor can't help you personally, he or she will know where you can get the help you need. Get a tutor if you are having difficulty understanding the course material or doing the homework assignments. Most colleges provide some type of tutoring services—find out where tutoring in your subject area is available and go sign up. Go to your college learning center if you are having difficulty with test preparation, note taking, reading your text, and so on. If you have a more complex problem, you may need to speak to the department chair or to the academic dean.

WHY ARE YOU IN COLLEGE?

As you are making your adjustment to college, maintain a positive attitude toward your progress. Think about why you are in college and what you plan to accomplish during your college career. Take some time to visit the career services office on your campus and explore the job opportunities available in your major field of study. Talk to other students and to your professors about the options that are available to you. Having a clear set of goals can be very motivating and help you over some of the hurdles that you will have to face. If you haven't chosen a major yet, that's okay, too. Use your first year or two of college to explore various courses and majors. Make an appointment to discuss your interests with the department chairperson or with someone in the counseling or career services office. Colleges offer courses of study that you never even heard of in high school—one of them may be the right one for you. If you are thinking about changing your major, that's okay, too. Most college students do change their major at least once; many change their major several times. The important thing to remember is that career goals help motivate you to set and achieve your academic goals, which help motivate you to set and achieve your study goals. Why are you in college? Think about it.

ACTIVITIES

1. List up to ten new responsibilities that you have or will have as a college student.
2. Make a list that includes the office numbers and phone extensions of your professors, advisor, academic dean, and any other important contact person on your campus.
3. Set up a study buddy in each of your classes. A study buddy is someone with whom you can share class notes, check homework assignments, and review for exams. Be sure to write down your classmate's name and phone number.
4. List at least three places that you can go if you have a problem. Jot down the names of the contact people, office numbers, and phone extensions.
5. Write a paragraph or two describing why you are in college.

POSTTEST

Where Are You Now?

Now that you have completed Chapter 1, take a few minutes to answer *yes* or *no* to the following questions. Compare your answers with those in the pretest.

	YES	NO
1. Do you know how to set up a budget and stick to it?	_____	_____
2. Do you know where to go on your campus to get financial aid, a tutor, and information on clubs and organizations?	_____	_____
3. If you miss class, do you expect your professor to go over the material with you at a later date?	_____	_____
4. Do you know who your advisor is?	_____	_____
5. Do you plan to take a lighter course load during your first semester in college?	_____	_____
6. Do you attend class regularly and stay up-to-date with your assignments?	_____	_____
7. Do you cut back on your sleep in order to get your assignments done for the following day?	_____	_____
8. Do you maintain regular contact with your family?	_____	_____
9. Have you really thought about why you are in college?	_____	_____
10. Do you expect college to be the same as high school?	_____	_____

Give yourself one point for each *yes* answer to all questions except 3, 7, and 10, and one point for each *no* answer to questions 3, 7, and 10. Now total up your points. Compare your score on this posttest with the score that you had on the pretest. Did you improve? In which areas? Do you still need to improve more?

CHAPTER 2

Setting Goals

> "Goal setting has helped me in a number of ways. I have found that setting goals for myself creates a sense of excitement. I know that if I set my mind to accomplish something, I can. This has been especially helpful in planning long-term goals. I have a sense of knowing that I will accomplish those goals no matter what obstacles may come into view."
>
> Maria Mardis

WHAT ARE GOALS?

Goals are the ends toward which we direct our efforts. In other words, goals are things we want to achieve, things we aim for as we pursue a certain course of action. You have been setting goals since you were very young, although you probably weren't aware of it. Did you ever climb up on the kitchen counter to get a cookie out of the cupboard? Your goal was to get that cookie, and you worked out a plan to get it even though it was out of reach. You need to take the same approach in college. You must decide what you want and then figure out how to get it.

Goals are important in college because they help motivate you to do your work, attend classes, and study for exams. Even though you already may have set some goals for the semester, chances are you thought little about whether those goals

PRETEST

Where Are You Now?

Take a few minutes to answer *yes* or *no* to the following questions.

	YES	NO
1. Have you decided what grade point average (GPA) you want to achieve this semester?	______	______
2. Have you decided what grade you want to achieve in each of your courses this semester?	______	______
3. Have you written down the grade that you want in each of your courses this semester?	______	______
4. Are the goals that you set for your courses attainable?	______	______
5. Do you use words like *try* and *hope* when you describe your goals?	______	______
6. Do you set goals for yourself each week?	______	______
7. Do you set daily study goals?	______	______
8. Do you tend to achieve the goals that you set?	______	______
9. Do you tend to give up if you don't achieve your goals?	______	______
10. Do you revise your goals during the semester?	______	______

Give yourself one point for each *yes* answer to all questions except 5 and 9, and one point for each *no* answer to questions 5 and 9. Now total up your points. A low score indicates that you need some help in setting goals. A high score indicates that you are using effective goal-setting strategies.

were realistic. You can improve your academic performance in college by learning to set goals that motivate you to do well and that increase your chance for success.

CHARACTERISTICS OF GOALS

In order to be both useful and realistic, the goals you set must have some important characteristics. Your goals should be self-chosen, moderately challenging, attainable, measurable, specific, and positive.

1. *Goals should be self-chosen.* Goals that are set by your parents, teachers, or friends may not always work for you. You need to determine or choose your own goals; *you* need to decide what you want to accomplish. If you set your own goals, you will have a better chance of achieving them.

2. *Goals should be moderately challenging.* You probably were told to set high or even exceptionally high goals for yourself in college; you may have been told to "shoot for the stars" or "go for straight A's." In fact, this may not be the best advice. If your goal is to achieve all A's during your first semester in college, you may be disappointed. As soon as you "lose your A" in one of your classes, you may feel that you failed to achieve your goal, and you may be tempted to give up.

   One of the ways to set moderately challenging goals is to consider what you have done in the past. Of course, everyone is different, but high school grades are fairly good predictors of college success. Why were you successful in some classes yet unsuccessful in others? Of course, if you didn't work very hard in high school, you can do better in college if you choose to apply yourself—study skills can make a big difference. Even so, you should set goals that are moderately challenging—goals that will require you to achieve more than you did before, but will not place undue pressure on you. Goals can always be revised if you discover you can achieve more than you originally set out to accomplish.

3. *Goals should be attainable.* Think about whether your goals are realistic. It would be unrealistic to set a goal of a B or better in Calculus if your math background is very weak and your high school grades in math were never higher than a C. In order to set attainable or realistic goals, you must evaluate your chances of achieving each goal.

4. *Goals should be measurable.* A goal is measurable if you can determine whether or not you reached it. It would be difficult to determine whether you achieved your goal if you just wanted to "do well in a course." How can you measure that? What does "well" really mean? It undoubtedly means different

PEANUTS reprinted by permission of UFS, Inc.

things to different people. It would be much easier to measure your success if you had aimed for an A or a B or a C. At the end of the semester, you should be able to look at your final grade in a course and at the grade you set as your goal and evaluate your efforts.

Goals for specific study sessions need to be measurable, too. Studying chemistry is not a measurable goal. "I will read pages 12 to 22 in my chemistry text and work all of the sample problems" is a good example of a measurable goal statement. At the end of your study session, you will be able to determine if you did what you planned to do.

5. *Goals should be specific.* If you formulate vague or unclear goals, you will be less likely to accomplish them. Getting a B+ in College Algebra is a specific goal; getting a "good grade" in College Algebra is not. Study goals should be specific, too. The goal, "I'll do my homework at 7:00," is rather vague. It's important to think of your homework as a series of individual assignments. You need to write separate goals for each of these assignments. A more specific goal statement is, "I'll do problems 1 to 20 in my chemistry text (page 54) at 7:00 on Tuesday."

6. *Goals should be positive.* Negative goal statements tend to make you feel that you can't really be successful. "I don't want to get any lower than a C in any of my classes," "I won't go to dinner until I get this calculus work done," and "I'm not going to fail this test" are all examples of negative goal statements. You will always do better if you are working *toward* something—when you have a positive attitude.

   You also should avoid using words like *try, think, hope,* and *should* when you describe your goals. What's wrong with including those kinds of words? You're right if you said that they offer "a way out." If you state your goal this way: "I'm going to *try* to write my sociology essay tonight," and later push your paper away unfinished, you may say to yourself, "Well, I did *try.*" More positive goals that emphasize success are the ones that will help you get your work done.

LONG- AND SHORT-TERM GOALS

Most students have long-term goals in mind when they enter college. Even if you don't know exactly what major you want to pursue, you have probably thought about getting a degree and getting a job. You may even know what field interests you most, whether it be education, engineering, nursing, or politics. Long-term goals are helpful to your success in college because they give you direction. However, when the going gets rough, reaching long-term goals can seem awfully far in the future. That's where short-term goals can help. Long-term goals are the objectives we set for ourselves for the end of the year, for four or five years from now, or even for a lifetime. Short-term goals, on the other hand, can be set for an hour from now, for the end of the day, the week, the month, or the semester. Short-term goals include things like completing a reading assignment, writing an essay, getting a B in a course, or making the Dean's List for the semester. Think of your short-term goals as steps toward achieving the long-term goals you have set for yourself. By accomplishing daily, weekly, and semester goals, you move closer to your long-range academic, career, and personal goals.

ACADEMIC AND PERSONAL GOALS

In college it's important to balance your academic and personal goals. Your academic goals relate to your course work. They include things like going to class, completing assignments, and preparing for exams. In order to achieve your academic goals, you need to learn to set study goals, too. Study goals can be defined as the objectives you want to achieve during a particular study session. They may include reading your sociology assignment, reviewing your class notes, conducting research for a term paper, or preparing for an exam. Your academic goals should be your highest priority in college. Personal goals, like making new friends, participating in clubs or sporting events, losing weight, or even doing your laundry are important, too. However, if you allow yourself to focus on your personal goals, you may find that you have little time left for study. By learning how to balance your goals, you can have time for both your academic and your personal life.

WRITING EFFECTIVE GOAL STATEMENTS

By putting your goals in writing, you increase the chances that you will actually accomplish them. However, another factor that affects your success is how you formulate your goal statements. You can just write down the first thing that comes to mind, or you can take a few extra minutes and explore each of your goals by using the Five-Step Approach to goal setting.

USE THE FIVE-STEP APPROACH

Writing effective goal statements isn't as easy as it sounds. You need to consider what you want to accomplish, any obstacles that could prevent you from achieving your goal, and the resources available to you. You then need to formulate your goal statement and polish it. Because each of your courses has different requirements, you must consider each course separately. If you are taking five courses, you must go through this process five times. Use the Five-Step Approach to set goals for

Figure 2.1 Example of the Five-Step Approach to Setting Goals

COURSE: AMERICAN HISTORY

STEP 1: Tentative Goal Statement

I want to get an A in my history course.

STEP 2: List of Obstacles	STEP 3: List of Resources
1. Attendance policy (only three cuts before grade is lowered)	1. I'll go to all classes. I'll ask someone to stop by to make sure I'm up on time.
2. Essay tests (I never could write when I had a time limit on me)	2. I'll go to the Learning Center for help. I'll ask my professor for a sample test so I know what to expect.
3. Quizzes on reading assignments (I sometimes put my reading off)	3. I'll do my reading assignments right after each class. I'll set up a study group to review the readings before each class.
4. Homework policy (I can't turn in my assignment if i miss the class when it is due)	4. I won't have to worry about this one since I don't plan to cut classes. I won't cut after I put hours into doing the work.
5.	5.
6.	6.

STEP 4: Revised Goal Statement

I think that I can still get an A if I keep up with my reading and go to all of my classes.

STEP 5: Polished Goal Statement

I will earn an A in American History this semester.

each of your courses this semester. Look at the sample in Figure 2.1 if you need some additional ideas.

STEP 1: WRITE DOWN WHAT YOU WANT TO ACCOMPLISH

This initial description can be thought of as a *tentative* goal statement. The easiest way to begin your tentative goal statement is with the words, "I want to." Think about what you want to accomplish.

STEP 2: WRITE DOWN ANY OBSTACLES

Think about whether there are any course requirements, assignments, tests, or other factors that could jeopardize your success. Make a list of the difficulties you may encounter. Some students, for example, panic when they find out that their exams are going to be essay tests. You might consider this an obstacle if you know that you ordinarily don't do well on essay tests. Others may be concerned about attendance policies or oral presentations.

STEP 3: WRITE DOWN ANY RESOURCES AVAILABLE TO YOU

First consider your *general* resources. You have successfully completed twelve years of school, so you have acquired some of the skills that can help you become a successful student. You have also acquired a background in quite a few subject areas. In addition, you probably earned some A's and B's, so you know that you can be successful in your academic pursuits. All of these things are general resources that will help you achieve your goals. Next, consider each of the obstacles you listed individually. Think about how you might use your resources to overcome each obstacle. Write down *specific* resources you could use in order to achieve each goal. Specific resources include your friends and family, the faculty and staff members at your college, and you yourself. For instance, if you have difficulty with essay tests, you could go to your professor or to your college learning center to get some help before the exam.

STEP 4: REVIEW AND REVISE YOUR TENTATIVE GOAL STATEMENT

Now that you have thought about any difficulties you might have, and have figured out whether they can be resolved, you are ready to write your final goal statement. In some cases you may find that you don't change your tentative goal statement at all; in other cases you may do a lot of revising.

STEP 5: POLISH YOUR GOAL STATEMENT

Check to be sure that your final statement is well written and takes into consideration the six characteristics of effective goals.[1]

STRATEGIES FOR SETTING YOUR GOALS FOR THE NEW SEMESTER

The most important time to set your goals and start using specific strategies for achieving your goals is during the first three weeks of the semester. If you make academics your first priority and get off to a good start in each of your classes, you

---

[1]Based on some ideas from Pauk, Walter, *How to Study in College*, 4th ed. (Boston: Houghton Mifflin, 1989).

will find you'll continue to do well during the remainder of the semester. Breaking down your goals, revising them periodically, and learning to calculate your GPA can all help you set your academic goals and write effective goal statements.

BREAK DOWN YOUR GOALS

In order to achieve your long- and short-term goals, you need to break them down into several smaller goals. These are the actual *tasks* that you have to complete in order to reach your goals. To lose ten pounds, you may need to diet, exercise, and reward yourself for each two-pound loss. What steps have you used when searching for a job? These same techniques can be applied to your academic goals.

Not every course has the same requirements, so it's important to break down your goals for each course separately. You can begin by referring to your syllabus and to the course grading or requirements sheet. Any assignment or activity that generates points toward your grade should be included on your list.

REVISE YOUR GOALS PERIODICALLY

It's important to rethink your goals at some point during the semester. Some students tend to "play it safe" and set unrealistically low goals for themselves at the beginning of the semester. It may seem like a good idea to set safe goals; that way you always are successful at what you set out to do. However, "safe goals" can also hold you back, because they keep you from achieving all that you might be able to achieve. Some students have the opposite tendency; they set goals that may be completely unattainable. By doing this, they are setting themselves up for failure and disappointment.

Remember, goals should be moderately challenging; they should be just a little out of reach so that you can work toward them. How can you find just the right level of challenge? You can't, at first. Once you gain some experience in college, however, you'll become much better at knowing what you can achieve. Until then, you need to revise your goals as you gather more information about your skills and your study behavior. Of course, you could change your goals, raise them or lower them, at almost any time during the semester. However, the best time to review your "grade" goals is after the first exam. If you decided to work for a B in Algebra but got a high A on the first exam, you should revise your goal upward. Your first exam demonstrated that you are capable of doing "A" work and consequently capable of getting an A in Algebra.

Many students continue to improve in courses after the first exam, so you need to review your goals again after the second, third, or even fourth exam. In general, you should sit down and really think about where you are and where you want to be after the first round of exams, after midterms, and about two weeks before final exams.

LEARN TO CALCULATE YOUR GPA

Learning how to calculate your Grade Point Average (GPA) will help you set better goals for the new semester. You should decide on a specific grade that you want to achieve for each of your courses. You may want to decide on the overall GPA that you want for the semester and then work backwards in order to set your individual course goals. For example, let's say you decided to aim for a 2.75 for the semester. You could achieve that average in a number of ways. You could have one A (4.0), one B (3.0), and two C's (2.0) and still get a 2.75. You could also earn three B's and one C and still earn a 2.75 for the semester.

In order to calculate your GPA, you need to calculate the *grade points* that you earn in each of your courses. Grade points are determined by multiplying the grade's numerical value by the number of credits assigned to the course. An A in a one-credit class is worth 4 grade points, while a C in a four-credit course is worth 8 grade points. It appears here that the C is worth more, but it is not, because you have to divide your total grade points by your total credits in order to determine your GPA. (If your college does not use the same numerical values for grades, adjust the table accordingly.) Consider the following example:

John's Grades

Course	Grade	Numerical Value	Credits	Grade Points
Sociology	B	3.0	3	9.0
English	C	2.0	3	6.0
Algebra	A	4.0	3	12.0
Chemistry	B	3.0	4	12.0
Phys. Ed.	A	4.0	1	4.0
			14	43.0 = 3.07 GPA

In order to determine his GPA, John listed each of his courses, the grades he earned, and their numerical value. He then listed the credit value for each course and multiplied that by the numerical value to determine the grade points for each course. After calculating the grade points for each course, he added up his total credits and his total grade points. The final step involved dividing the total grade points (43) by the total credits (14). John earned a 3.07 for the semester. If John had used this method at the beginning of the semester to predict his grades, he would have had the opportunity to decide if a 3.07 was a satisfactory goal for the semester. If he decided that he wanted to earn a higher GPA, he could have gone back and recalculated his GPA by changing one or more of the grades in order to reach his goal. If John's goal had been a GPA of 3.25, he might have decided that he had to earn a B, instead of a C, in English. This would have improved his grade point total to 46 points, while his credit total would stay the same at 14. His new GPA would be a 3.285.

STRATEGIES FOR ACHIEVING YOUR GOALS FOR THE NEW SEMESTER

Setting priorities, planning for early success, and planning rewards can all help you achieve the academic goals you have set for yourself. It is important to start using these strategies right from the start of the semester.

SET PRIORITIES FOR THE FIRST THREE WEEKS

If you make academic goals your priority for the first three weeks, you will practically ensure your success for the semester. Many students think that the first few weeks of a new semester are a breeze; typically, there are no exams, and often there are few papers, projects, or presentations. What you do during those first few weeks, though, often affects your performance during the rest of the semester. If you start doing your reading and other assignments right from the beginning, getting your work done will become a habit. In the same way, attending classes and meeting with study groups and tutors will also become part of your daily routine. By working especially hard at the beginning of the semester, you learn to make your academic goals your priority.

PLAN FOR EARLY SUCCESS

Another way to get off to the right start is to plan for early success. Getting an A or a B on the first quiz or first homework assignment should be one of your short-term goals for the semester. Once you get an A on one of your quizzes or assignments, you won't want to lose it. That first A lets you know you can do it. You know that by attending all of your classes and by doing your assignments, you can be successful. A success in one class also motivates you to keep working hard in all of your classes.

If you try to breeze through the first few weeks of the semester, you may end up with a D or F on your first assignment or quiz, and that low grade can have a negative effect on your future performance. Some students begin to doubt their ability to succeed in a particular course or in college in general. Even though they really may not have applied themselves, the doubts still are there. Some students respond well to a low grade early in the semester; it shakes them up and they "start to hit the books." Others, though, just get depressed about their performance and eventually give up. It's much better to avoid those early low grades by striving hard for early success. The chart in Figure 2.2 includes ten tips that should help you get off to the right start this semester.

PLAN REWARDS

When you think about achieving your goals, a fifteen-week semester can seem a long time to wait. Unfortunately, there aren't a lot of "warm fuzzies" or immediate rewards in college. You may not get a grade on an assignment until the fourth or even the seventh week of the semester. You also may find that you miss that pat on the back or verbal recognition that you got in high school. It can be hard to stay motivated when no one is "telling you" that all that hard work is paying off, so you need to begin to reward yourself. Establish a method for rewarding yourself for knowing the answers to the questions that the professor asks in class, for being able to explain the solution to a problem, or even for being up-to-date on your reading assignments. If no one else is there to give you that pat on the back, you may need to give it to yourself.

ACTIVITIES

1. Write a paragraph or two in which you describe your life five years from now. Include as many details as you can.
2. Make a list of ten goals that you would like to accomplish this semester.
3. Make a list of ten goals that you want to accomplish for tomorrow.
4. Now go back to your lists from Activities 2 and 3 and label each goal as an academic (A) or personal (P) goal. Do you have an overabundance of personal goals? Were your first three goals in each list academic or personal goals? If they were academic goals, you have your priorities in order. If not, how would you change your lists so that your academic goals have top priority?

Figure 2.2 Ten Tips to Get off to the Right Start This Semester

1. **Go to All Classes and Take Notes.** Your goal is to write down as much information as you can. Four weeks from now, you will remember little of what you heard today. Edit your notes within twenty-four hours to organize and expand the information.

2. **Keep Up with Your Reading Assignments.** Break down long reading assignments into more manageable units of about seven to ten pages. Read the ten pages and then switch to another subject. Take a short break and go back and read ten more pages. Remember to carefully highlight your text or take notes as you read.

3. **Reward Yourself for Getting Your Work Done.** If you want to watch a TV show or movie, plan to do your work first so that the movie or TV show can serve as a reward for accomplishing your goals. You'll enjoy it more when you know you are ready for class.

4. **Learn to Say No.** Think about what you must accomplish each day. When your friends stop by to gab or go out, tell them to come back later after you have completed your work, or tell them you'll meet them later.

5. **Evaluate Your Study Environment.** Does the place you've chosen provide quiet and motivation? If not, find another place to study.

6. **Set Goals for Each Course.** Decide what grade you can get in each course. Then make a plan for how you will go about achieving that grade.

7. **Study for Exams by Writing and Reciting Out Loud.** You won't learn the information just by reading it over and over.

8. **Learn to Predict Exam Questions.** This is important for all exams, but it is critical for *essay* exams. After you predict five to ten possible questions, write out the answers before the exam and then memorize the main points.

9. **When Taking Exams, Relax and Be Sure to Read the Directions.** Answer the easiest questions first, skipping the ones that you don't know immediately. Then go back and complete the ones that you skipped.

10. **Go to Your College Learning Center When You Need Help.** Don't wait until it is too late. Stop in to talk about any classes in which you are having difficulty. Gathering suggestions on how to study or signing up for tutoring can improve your grades dramatically.

5. Look at the list of short-term goals that you wrote in Activity 2. Choose one academic and one personal goal and list all of the steps that you would have to go through in order to achieve each of those goals.
6. List the grades that you want to achieve in each of your courses this semester. Then calculate what your GPA for the semester would be.

POSTTEST

Where Are You Now?

Now that you have completed Chapter 2, take a few minutes to answer *yes* or *no* to the following questions. Compare your answers with those in the pretest.

	YES	NO
1. Have you decided what grade point average (GPA) you want to achieve this semester?	_____	_____
2. Have you decided what grade you want to achieve in each of your courses this semester?	_____	_____
3. Have you written down the grade that you want in each of your courses this semester?	_____	_____
4. Are the goals that you set for your courses attainable?	_____	_____
5. Do you use words like *try* and *hope* when you describe your goals?	_____	_____
6. Do you set goals for yourself each week?	_____	_____
7. Do you set daily study goals?	_____	_____
8. Do you tend to achieve the goals that you set?	_____	_____
9. Do you tend to give up if you don't achieve your goals?	_____	_____
10. Do you revise your goals during the semester?	_____	_____

Give yourself one point for each *yes* answer to all questions except 5 and 9, and one point for each *no* answer to questions 5 and 9. Now total up your points. Compare your score on this posttest with the score that you had on the pretest. Did you improve? In which areas? Do you still need to improve more?

CHAPTER 3

Time Management

"Before I studied this material, I had trouble managing my time. It seemed like there was never enough time to get everything done. By making a Fixed Commitment Calendar, I realized how much time I actually do have. The assignment calendars also helped. Now I know exactly what has to be done in a given week, and I can plan effectively."

Natalie Morrison

WHAT IS TIME MANAGEMENT?

Time management refers to the way you regulate or schedule your time. You can make more efficient use of your study time and complete your work in less time by using good time management skills. The key to successful time management is allowing enough time to complete your work while still finding time to take advantage of the other opportunities for growth and development that occur in college. Attending concerts, meeting with friends, and going to conferences or rallies are an important part of the college experience. However, these activities can be more fully enjoyed when you know that you have your course work done. Learning good time management techniques can help you accomplish the goals that you set for yourself in Chapter 2.

PRETEST

Where Are You Now?

Take a few minutes to answer *yes* or *no* to the following questions.

	YES	NO
1. Have you estimated how many hours you need to study this semester?	_____	_____
2. Do you tend to complete your assignments on time?	_____	_____
3. Have you estimated how long it takes you to read one chapter in each of your textbooks?	_____	_____
4. Do you begin working on long-term assignments early in the semester?	_____	_____
5. Do you make lists of things to do in your head rather than on paper?	_____	_____
6. Do you find that you go out even when you know you should be studying?	_____	_____
7. Do you schedule time to study for exams?	_____	_____
8. Are you working at a job more than twenty hours a week?	_____	_____
9. Do you know exactly what you are going to work on when you sit down to study?	_____	_____
10. Do you do the assignments from your favorite class first?	_____	_____

Give yourself one point for each *yes* answer to all questions except 5, 6, 8, and 10, and one point for each *no* answer to questions 5, 6, 8, and 10. Now total up your points. A low score indicates that you need some help in time management. A high score indicates that you are already using good time management techniques.

WHY IS TIME MANAGEMENT IMPORTANT?

Time management is one of the most important skills for beginning college students. Being able to accomplish your goals depends, in part, on your ability to make the most efficient use of the time that you have available for study. In high school, your study time was fairly well defined or structured. Your parents and/or your teachers may have been careful to "make sure" that you completed your work. In college, though, you won't find that kind of structure or monitoring.

Another big difference between high school and college is the amount of time that you're in class. In high school you were in class from early in the morning until mid to late afternoon. In college, your class schedule is much more variable. You may be in class only during the morning hours or only during the afternoon hours. You may find that all of your classes are on Mondays, Wednesdays, and Fridays, or all on Tuesdays and Thursdays. Unlike high school students who are in class for almost thirty-five hours a week, most college students are in class for only twelve to fifteen hours a week. To a college freshman, this seems like a breeze. However, in college *most of your work must be completed outside of class.* And, even though you may not want to admit it, you can't get all that work done in just a few hours every evening. In order to achieve your goals, you also need to make use of your available daytime hours for study.

Learning to schedule your time is a complicated task for several reasons. First, you have many hours of time that need to be scheduled. Instead of sixty hours of structured class and study time, you may have only about fifteen structured hours. You are the one who is responsible for structuring the remaining hours. If you are in class on Mondays, Wednesdays, and Fridays, you cannot consider Tuesdays and Thursdays to be free days. You need to use these days for out-of-class study time. In the same way, if you are enrolled only in morning classes, you should schedule afternoon study hours. Also, you'll need to adjust your schedule as your workload changes during the semester. You may find that your plan to sleep until noon each day must be revised as exams, projects, and paper deadlines approach.

Good time management skills can actually save you time. A few minutes each week spent on planning can make a real difference in how your study time is organized and spent. Once you learn good time management skills, you may be surprised to find that you can do all the things you want to do. You may find out that for the first time in your life, you are in control of your life. The first rule of good time management is: Don't let time manage you; you must learn, instead, to manage your time.

ANALYZE YOUR USE OF TIME

You can establish a good time plan once you know how you actually spend your time. Identifying how much time you have available for study and how much time you need for study can help you decide whether or not you need to make any changes in your current time plan.

HOW DO YOU MANAGE YOUR TIME NOW?

The first step in learning better time management is to evaluate how you actually use your time now. Jotting down what you actually do during each hour of the day for several days or even a week may reveal some trouble spots for you. Did you accomplish all of your goals?

Learning to manage your time effectively also depends on how well you can adhere to a schedule. One frequently used technique for evaluating your ability to manage your time involves taking a before-and-after look at how you use your time. Comparing what you *plan* to do on a given day with what you *actually* do will help you see how carefully you are able to stick to a time schedule. What you do during each hour of the day is not important here. Instead, the key is how well you stick to your plan.

IDENTIFY TIME AVAILABLE FOR STUDY

Identifying how much time you have available for study is the next step in setting up a good time plan. This step involves both looking at how much of your time is committed to other activities and also how much time you, as an individual, need in order to complete your work.

In order to establish how much of your time is committed to other activities, you should complete a Fixed Commitment Calendar.[1] What are fixed commitments? If you said classes, work hours, or even mealtimes, you were right. Start by photocopying or replicating the blank Fixed Commitment Calendar at the end of this chapter (Figure 3.5). When completing your calendar, the first thing you should mark off are your classes. (You can write down exactly what you are doing during each hour of the week, or you can simply cross out time blocks that are committed to fixed [regularly scheduled] activities.) You also should mark off hours when you are asleep (normal sleep hours, not naps), mealtimes (setting regular times for

---

[1]Adapted from Time Analysis Worksheet in Wood, Nancy V., *Reading and Study Skills*, 3rd ed. (New York: Holt, Rinehart & Winston, 1986), pp. 18–20.

meals helps you stay on a schedule), and work hours. If your work hours vary, don't cross them off yet; we'll talk more about study and work later in this section. If you're involved in clubs, organizations, or sports, you may need to cross off additional hours for regularly scheduled meetings (same time each week) or practices and games. If you know that you will be socializing on most Friday and Saturday evenings, you should cross off those times even though your plans are not definite. If you plan to sleep in Saturday or Sunday mornings, cross off those hours as well.

After you have crossed off all of the regularly committed hours, you should begin to see some patterns in your uncommitted time. You may have some very short blocks of time between classes, some two- or three-hour blocks in the morning or afternoon, and some longer blocks in the evening and on weekends. Think of these time blocks as time available for study rather than free time. You also may notice that you have a lot of time to study on certain days, but very little on others. All of this information will be useful as you begin to schedule your study time.

After determining your available study time, trace around the perimeter of each time block (see the sample in Figure 3.1). Use a brightly colored marker to outline each block. Being able to see at a glance the hours when you have time to study can be very helpful during the process of scheduling.

Some students, unfortunately, have work schedules that change each week. If your work schedule varies, this calendar is even more important for you. Start by marking down all of your other fixed commitments. Then, before you put your work hours down, make a photocopy of your partially completed calendar for each week of the semester. As you get your work schedule each week, take one of these photocopies and cross off your work hours for the week. This method will save you a lot of time, because you won't have to start from scratch each week.

As a final step in preparing your Fixed Commitment Calendar, count the number of hours available for study. If you're not working, you may find that you have fifty to seventy hours available for study. If you are working, however, this number may be substantially smaller, depending upon the number of hours that you work each week. When you have completed your calendar, post it where you can see it easily—for example, above your desk.

IDENTIFY TIME NEEDED FOR STUDY

Knowing how much time you have available for study is useless until you identify how much time you need for study. Formulas, such as those that allot one hour of outside study time for every hour in class or two hours of outside work for every

Figure 3.1 Sample Fixed Commitment Calendar

	Monday	Tuesday	Wednesday	Thursday	Friday	Saturday	Sunday
8:00	Sleep	Sleep	Sleep	Sleep	Sleep	Sleep	Sleep
9:00	Class	lift weights	class	lift weights	class	Sleep	Sleep
10:00	lift weights	lift weights		lift weights	lift weights	Sleep	Sleep
11:00	class	class	class	class	class	eat	eat
12:00		Class		class		work	Watch football
1:00	eat	class	eat	class	eat	work	watch football
2:00						work	Watch football
3:00						work	watch football
4:00	practice	practice	practice	practice	practice	work	Watch football
5:00	practice	practice	practice	practice	practice		Work
6:00	eat	eat	eat	eat	eat	eat	work
7:00							work
8:00					out	out	work
9:00					out	out	work
10:00					out	out	
11:00	TV	TV	TV	TV	out	out	
12:00	Sleep	Sleep	Sleep	Sleep	out	out	Sleep
1:00	Sleep	Sleep	sleep	Sleep	out	out	Sleep
2:00	sleep	sleep	sleep	Sleep	Sleep	Sleep	Sleep

Hours Available for Study 35 Hours Needed for Study 32

hour in class, are designed to simplify your job of identifying how much time you need for study. Many educators believe most students need an average of two hours of study time for each hour that they are in class. So, a student taking fifteen credits would need thirty hours of study time per week. Many students find that this simple formula just doesn't work for them, however. In order to get a more accurate figure, you really need to consider the number of credits that you have, the difficulty of the courses that you are taking, the goals you have set, and how quickly or slowly you work.

Consider Your Credit Load

If you have fifteen credits, you should figure a minimum of two hours of study time for every hour in class. Remember that this is a minimum and probably will change when you consider the other factors—the goals you have set, how quickly or slowly you work, and the difficulty of your courses. You may need to increase your study hours, for example, if you are taking very difficult classes. If you're taking a course that is especially demanding, you should allow three or four hours of outside work for every hour that you are in class. You may also want to increase your study time if you want to get A's in one or more of your courses.

Add Weekly Study Time for Long-Term Assignments

You need to allow time to study for exams, prepare term papers, and complete semester projects. Some students expect the regular assignment load to disappear when test or paper deadlines roll around. Unfortunately, this doesn't happen. If you do not adjust your study schedule for these long-range assignments, you may find that you have to "steal" time from your regular work in order to prepare for them. As a result, you may fall behind in everything else.

Monitor Your Current Study Time

By keeping track of how many hours you actually spend doing your assignments and studying during a typical week, you can evaluate the accuracy of your estimate of study time needed. You can also repeat this experiment during a week that is not so typical. Choose a week in which you have one or more exams and a paper or project due. Did you get everything done, or did you fall behind in your work?

Learning to estimate the time needed for smaller, individual assignments can be extremely helpful as well. Time yourself the next time you read one of your textbooks. Finding out how long it takes to read ten pages in each of your texts will help you plan more accurately. You can also time yourself as you complete math and writing assignments or as you review your notes. Knowing approximately how long it takes to do the routine work will allow you to plan more accurately.

ESTABLISH A NEW TIME PLAN

If you find that you need more time to complete your work than you actually have, you need to modify your time plan. Basically you have two options. One is to make more time for study, and the other is to reduce the amount of time that you need for study.

One possibility you can consider for reducing the amount of time you need for study is to reduce your credit load. Some students try to take too many credits during one semester. If this is your first semester in college, you should take twelve to fourteen credits only. Earning good grades the first semester is much more important than earning a lot of credits. You have plenty of time to make up a few credits later in your college career. It's much easier for a junior or senior to carry a seventeen- or eighteen-credit load than it is for a freshman to carry even fifteen credits. Give yourself time to adjust to college and being on your own. If you're working full-time, you may have to take a lighter load as well. After all, what's the point of working so hard to attend school if you can't find enough hours to do your best?

If you absolutely can't reduce your credit load, then you need to reduce some of your fixed commitments and make more time for study. In many cases that means reducing work hours. If you are attending school full-time, you should not work more than twenty hours a week. Certainly some people can go to school full-time and work full-time, but many of them report that they don't have time for *anything* else (even meals or sleep).

Another huge time consumer is extracurricular activities. Although it is important for students to be involved in college experiences outside of the classroom, some students go too far. Do you know anyone who seems to be involved in everything? If you're always running off to some meeting, practice, or activity and don't have enough time to study, you need to rethink your level of involvement in extracurricular activities. You don't have to eliminate all activities; instead, be selective and choose one or two that you really enjoy. Let the others go for another semester. Remember, your academic goals must come first.

ORGANIZE YOUR STUDY TIME

Once you have set up a time plan that allows you enough time to complete all of your work, you need to learn how to organize your time so that it can be used efficiently. By learning to plan and schedule your study time, you can begin to take control of your time.

CREATE A SEMESTER CALENDAR

One of the best ways to organize your study time is to create monthly assignment calendars. These calendars, like the ones you use at home to list important dates like birthdays and holidays, help you organize your time. Seeing what you have to do for each day of the semester is the first step in planning your study time.

The easiest way to prepare a monthly assignment calendar is to use a blank block calendar like the calendars used in Figures 3.2 and 3.3. First, write in the name of the month, and number the days of the month. Next, pull out your course syllabi. You need to write all of your assignments on your calendar. (You may find, for example, that you have reading assignments, math exercises, and an English paper all due on the same day.) If some of your professors don't give you a day-to-day syllabus, you will need to add new assignments to your calendar as you learn of them. You may find it helpful to put the assignments for each separate course in a different color or to list them all in black ink and then use colored markers to differentiate each subject. By color coding your assignments, you can quickly identify the work that you have to do each day. By the way, it also is important to make exams stand out on your calendar. The best way to do this is to write them in large capital letters and put a box around them.

After you have completed your calendars for each month of the semester, post them where you can see them easily — for example, on your bulletin board — and make sure that you are able to see two months at any one time. There is nothing more frustrating than turning the page on your calendar too late and realizing that you missed an important event. This is true for assignments and exams, too. Look at the sample calendars in Figures 3.2 and 3.3. The last week of September looks like a pretty easy week — after the sociology exam on Monday. There is a little reading to do, but the work load definitely seems to be on the light side. If this were your calendar, you might think that you could take it easy for a week. Now look at the first week of October. You have an exam in History and Algebra, two papers due for English, and two chapters of reading. If you had waited until the beginning of October to turn the page of your calendar, it would have been too late to prepare for your exams and complete your papers.

PREPARE WEEKLY TASK SHEETS

After you have completed your semester calendar, you should begin to think about identifying your study tasks and planning when to do them. Each assignment that you put on your calendar represents a study task that must be completed. One way to plan your study time is to prepare weekly task sheets. It's a good idea to set aside one hour a week to use for planning. Many students find that Sunday after-

Figure 3.2 Sample Monthly Assignment Calendar for September

MONTH September

Sunday	Monday	Tuesday	Wednesday	Thursday	Friday	Saturday
2	3	H - Ch 1 4	A - 1.1 & 1.2 5 E - 1-35 Journal	H - Ch 2 6	A - 1.3 & 1.4 7 E - 38-52 Journal S-Ch 1 (2-24)	8
9	A - 1.5 & 1.6 10 E - experience essay–draft	H - Ch 3 11	A - 2.1 & 2.2 12 S-Ch.2 (26-48)	13	A - 2.3 & 2.4 14 E - experience essay	15
16	A - 2.5 & 2.6 17 E - 53-64 S-Ch 3 (52-74)	H - Ch 4 18	A - 3.1 & 3.2 19 E - Observation Essay–draft	20	A - 3.3 & 3.4 21 E - Observation Essay due	22
23	A - 3.5 & 3.6 24 S–Exam I	H - Ch 5 25	A - 4.1 & 4.2 26 S - Ch 4 (75-103)	27	A - 4.3 & 4.4 28 E - 65-81	29
30						

A = College Algebra H = Western Civilization
E = English Composition S = Sociology

Figure 3.3 Sample Monthly Assignment Calendar for October

MONTH October

Sunday	Monday	Tuesday	Wednesday	Thursday	Friday	Saturday
	A - 4.5 & 4.6 1 E - Exposition Essay - draft	H - Exam I 2	A - Exam I 3 E - Revision S - Ch 5 (105-130)	H - Ch 6 4	A - 5.1 & 5.2 5 E - Exposition Essay due	6
7	A - 5.3 & 5.4 8 E - 82 -111 S - Ch 7 (162-189)	H - Ch 7 9	A - 5.5 & 5.6 10 E - Revision due	11	A - 6.1 & 6.2 12	13
14	A - 6.3 & 6.4 15 E - Portfolio due	H - Ch 8 16	A - 6.5 & 6.6 17 S - Ch 8 (191-240)	18	A - 7.1 & 7.2 19 E - 112-125	20
21	A - 7.3 & 7.4 22 E - definition essay - draft S - Exam II	H - Ch 9 23	A - 7.5 & 7.6 24 E - 127-140	H - Ch 10 25	A - Exam II 26 E - Definition essay due S - Ch 11 (278-310)	27
28	A - 8.1&8.2 29 E - Argument Essay due	H - Exam II 30	A - 8.3 & 8.4 31 E - 141-162			

A = College Algebra H = Western Civilization
E = English Composition S = Sociology

noon is an ideal time to begin to plan. Of course, you couldn't wait until Sunday to plan for the assignments that are due Monday and Tuesday. You must always look ahead at least several days when you make out your plan.

Students use a variety of plans for deciding which tasks to do during any given week. By referring to your semester assignment calendar, you can decide which tasks should be completed during the next week. Remember to look ahead for exams or long-range assignments and to include these tasks in your plan. You can list your assignments for the week in the order that they are due or by the course; either way is fine. The important thing is to learn to plan ahead.

USE DAILY "TO DO" LISTS

After you decide what you need to do for the week, you need to begin to plan what you are going to do each day. Making a list of the tasks that you want to complete each day is just another form of setting goals. Break down some of the tasks from your weekly task list. You might decide to read your history assignment over the next two days or work on writing your English essay for one hour every day during the week.

Putting your personal goals on the list is important, too. First, this further reinforces your commitment to put all of your plans in writing. In addition, writing your personal goals on your "To Do" list will help you stay more organized. The more organized you are in completing your personal goals, the more time you will have to complete your academic goals.

Making out "To Do" lists can become habit forming, so by all means get started immediately. Don't worry if you don't accomplish everything on your list; few people do everything they set out to do every day. Just move the one or two tasks that were left uncompleted to the top of the list for the next day. Remember, though: It is important that you plan realistically. A pattern of planning too much to do and

FRANK AND ERNEST reprinted by permission of NEA, Inc.

then moving half of your tasks to the next day can leave you feeling overwhelmed and can lead to procrastination.

You may find that breaking down your tasks into manageable units will help you accomplish your goals. Which would you rather read, a fifty-page chapter or a ten-page chapter? Most people would agree that a ten-page chapter sounds much more appealing. If you have long reading assignments, break them down on your "To Do" list. You may actually want to turn that fifty-page chapter into five separate tasks. It may make your list a little longer, but it also will allow you to shorten it more rapidly. Once you complete the first ten-page chunk of reading, you will feel a sense of accomplishment. You also will notice that it wasn't that bad at all, and you'll be motivated to read the next ten pages. Be sure to cross off each task as you complete it.

You also should consider prioritizing some of your tasks. You can use numbers, a star, or another symbol to indicate that certain tasks need to be done first. Look at the "To Do" lists in Figure 3.4. In the first example, the student mixed study goals and personal goals together. As you might expect, the personal goals were completed, and the study goals were left undone. When all of your goals are mixed together, you can sometimes forget that your academic goals should come first. For that reason, always separate your academic and personal goals. Put your academic goals at the top of the page and your personal goals at the bottom. By putting your study goals first, you are reinforcing your commitment to academics. It's also a good idea to add priority numbers for each of your tasks. By setting priorities, Robin was able to complete all of her study tasks (see Figure 3.4) before beginning her personal goals.

"To Do" lists can be made on any piece of paper. You can do them on three-by-five-inch index cards, in a small assignment notebook, on a pad of paper, or in a section of your loose-leaf binder. It's a good idea to do your "To Do" list on the same kind of paper or in the same notebook each day. Then you will recognize what it is and know exactly where it is. If you study in more than one place, you should carry your "To Do" list with you. If you find that you have lists all over the place, you probably should keep your lists in a notebook. Not only will your lists be in one place, but also you will be able to refer to old lists to check for any unfinished tasks.

ASSIGN TASKS TO AVAILABLE STUDY TIME

After you have determined what assignments you have to do, you need to think about when you are going to do them. Many students don't give much thought to whether to do certain assignments first or last, the time of day that they choose to do assignments, or even how long they should work at the same task. All of these

Figure 3.4

JEAN'S SAMPLE "TO DO" LIST

Day Wednesday

Study goals:

- [1 ✓] Go to Student aid office
- [2 ✓] Do laundry
- [7] Final draft Engl paper
- [6 ✓] Go copy Fr tape Ch 3
- [3 ✓] Get card for Grandma B-day
- [11] Make to do list 4 tomorrow
- [5] Study Ch 2 Fr
- [8 ✓] Read Art pp 53-63
- [9] Do Alg Ch 2-5
- [4 ✓] Dentist Appt. 2:30
- [10 ✓] Meet Tom 5:30

Personal goals:

ROBIN'S SAMPLE "TO DO" LIST

Day THURSDAY

Study goals:

- [2 ✓] MAKE COPY OF SPEECH OUTLINE
- [3 ✓] PRACTICE SPEECH
- [4 ✓] READ PP. 135-145 IN BLACK LIT
- [1 ✓] READ ESSAY 2 IN POL SCI
- [8 ✓] DO FEB. CALENDAR
- [6 ✓] READ PP. 146-156 IN BLACK LIT
- [5 ✓] READ 10 PPS. OF CH. 1 POL SCI
- [7 ✓] READ PP. 163-173 IN SS
- [9 ✓] DO THINGS TO DO FOR TOMORROW

Personal goals:

- [10 ✓] WRITE LETTER HOME
- [11 ✓] CHECK MAIL
- [12 ✓] GO TO BASKETBALL GAME
- [13] CLEAN ROOM

factors affect how efficiently you use your study time and how effectively you complete your assignments.

USE GOOD TIME MANAGEMENT STRATEGIES

Organizing your work and scheduling your time can make a huge difference in how much time it takes to do your work. However, just planning to read twenty pages at 2:00 P.M. is no guarantee that you will get it done. Schedules are designed to organize your use of time, but they are not designed to make you do the work. *You* have to do that. One thing that can make a difference in whether or not you accomplish your goals is your level of motivation. You can keep your level of motivation high by using some specific techniques.

STUDY IN ONE-HOUR TIME BLOCKS

One effective strategy for keeping yourself motivated is to study in sixty-minute time blocks. As you schedule your study tasks, break down tasks so that they can be accomplished in a one-hour block of time. Then plan to read, do problems, write, or study for fifty minutes. If you find that you can't concentrate on your work for the entire fifty minutes, take a three- to five-minute break when you begin to feel bored or tired.

TAKE BREAKS

After each study block of fifty minutes, you should plan a ten-minute break. Be realistic about the kind of activity that you plan for a study break. Taking a ten-minute nap just will not work, and going out to play a quick game of basketball inevitably will lead to a longer game of basketball. What can you do in ten minutes? You can grab a snack, write a short letter, work on a crossword puzzle, play a hand or two of solitaire (a good concentration builder), or make a phone call. (Resist the temptation to call a good friend to chat—you won't be able to hang up in ten minutes.) You can even shoot baskets—but do it in your room. (The next time your parents ask if there's anything you need, tell them that a Nerf basketball set would be a great study tool.) Shooting baskets is a good activity for a study break because it gets you moving around. Doing aerobics or just stretching are also great activities for a break between study periods.

SWITCH SUBJECTS

Another good strategy for retaining your motivation to study is to switch subjects. By alternating between reading psychology and working algebra problems, for example, you can get more done without becoming bored and tired. If you have a long time block available for study (for instance, from 6:00 to 11:00), you should switch subjects every hour. Occasionally, you will find that you are really progressing on an assignment and, after a ten-minute break, want to continue working on it. In such cases, you should do so. However, most students find that after an hour they are only too willing to work on something else for a while.

TACKLE DIFFICULT ASSIGNMENTS FIRST

Think about the courses that you are taking this semester. Is there one class that you really like? Is there one course that you hate or dislike? Do you have a class that is really easy? One that is really hard? Which assignment do you tend to do first? When asked these questions, most students respond that they do the assignments for the subject they like the most first. Is that what you said, too? This is a very common response because we all tend to do things that we like first. However, this isn't the best strategy when it comes to getting all of your work done. Do the assignments for the course you dislike first and get them out of the way. You will find that leaving the assignments that you enjoy the most until late in the day has several benefits. For one thing, you will probably find that you can easily complete the assignments for your favorite classes late in the day, even when you are feeling tired.

Also, if you do the assignments that you like the most first, you have nothing to look forward to. You may also find that if you leave the more difficult tasks for the end of the day, you worry about them as you work on other tasks. A difficult assignment can feel like a heavy weight hanging over your head. Doing your least favorite or most difficult assignments first and your easiest or favorite assignments last will help you stay motivated throughout the day.

PLAN REWARDS

You can think of your ten-minute study break as a reward for having completed one block of study tasks. These short breaks, however, aren't always enough of a reward to keep you motivated. It's a good idea to get into the habit of rewarding yourself for completing difficult tasks or for completing all of your work on a particular day. Rewards come in many different kinds of packages. Essentially, they are whatever you can plan to do that will help keep you working when you want to stop. Students use many kinds of rewards to stay motivated. Ordering a pizza after finishing a tough assignment works for some students. Others work hard to complete their studying in time to watch a favorite television show. If you know that you want to watch Monday night football, plan your work on Sunday and Monday so that you can be finished in time; then you will be able to sit back and watch the game without feeling guilty. Going to a party or watching your favorite "soap" each day also can be used as rewards for completing one or two specific study goals. By completing some of your study tasks *before* you go out or watch television, you can eliminate the guilt feelings that often accompany these activities.

WORK AHEAD

To be in control of your time, learn to work ahead on your assignments. You will find college much less stressful if you get out of the habit of doing Tuesday's assignments on Monday. Get into the habit of doing the work due for Tuesday on Sunday or even on Friday. Always being a little ahead of the game will give you a feeling of security. If something comes up (and something always does, at just the wrong time), you will still be prepared for class the next morning. It's a terrible feeling to walk into class unprepared. It is incredible, too, how professors always seem to call on students the one time that they didn't do the reading.

You also should work ahead on long-range assignments. Schedule one to two hours each week to work on a term paper or project. By starting early in the semester, you can easily complete your term paper and still keep up with your regular assignments. To plan ahead for a long-range project, first make out a list of all of the steps you need to go through in order to complete the project. For a term paper, some of the steps would be: select a topic, develop a bibliography, find books and journal articles, read and take notes, develop an outline, do more research if necessary, write the rough draft, and so on.

After you have developed a list of tasks for your paper or project, decide when you will work on each task. Get started immediately by assigning each task to one or two weeks of the semester. You may need several weeks to do your research and several more to do the reading. Actually scheduling time in the library on your "To Do" lists will get you moving on your paper. Putting up a time line across the top of your bulletin board or on the wall over your desk also may motivate you to work on completing your project. Write each of your planned tasks on the time line, and then write deadlines for every one. Check off each task as you complete it. By working ahead, you can eliminate the time crunches that often occur at the end of the semester. You can more easily adjust your schedule for exams, for time off, and for personal plans.

RE-EVALUATE YOUR TIME PLAN

After you have used your time plan for a while, you may find that it is not working well for you. You may need more time for long-range assignments, or you may discover you have more time available for study than you thought. It is important to take a look at how you are using your time several times during the semester.

A good time to re-evaluate your time plan is after the fourth week of the semester; that's when the first round of exams usually occurs. One good way to determine if you are putting in enough time studying is to consider the grades you received on your first set of exams. If your grades are in line with the goals you set, your time plan is probably working effectively for you. You also can judge whether you are using your time efficiently by looking back at some of your calendars and "To Do" lists. Have you been accomplishing the study goals that you set each day? Are you moving many tasks to the next day? Are you leaving work undone? Did you have time to prepare adequately for your exams? By answering these questions, you can determine whether you need to change your time plan.

The second point at which you should evaluate your time plan is after midterm exams. By this time in the semester, you should be able to determine quite accurately which parts of your time plan work and which don't. This is the best time to make some changes that will help you improve your grades. Finally, you also should rethink your time plan about two weeks before final exams. We'll talk more about this in Chapter 14.

LEARN TO COPE WITH PROCRASTINATION

Procrastination is a common behavior pattern for many students. It's often the result of not wanting to start a task that seems difficult or time-consuming. Unfortunately, procrastination can become a habit. The more you avoid the task, the more daunting it becomes; the more you tend to dwell on the negative aspects of the task, the more it's blown all out of proportion. After a while you may feel that you can't ever complete the task because you don't have the time to finish it.

CAUSES OF PROCRASTINATION

According to Albert Ellis and William Knaus, the three main causes of procrastination are "self-downing," low frustration tolerance, and hostility.[2] Students often put themselves down when they don't complete their tasks successfully or on time. If you put yourself down often enough, you may begin to believe that you're not a very capable person, and that feeling often leads to procrastination. One reason students begin to feel incapable of completing their tasks is that the goals they have set for themselves in the past have been unrealistic. For example, they tell themselves they should spend the *entire* weekend studying, or that they must get an A

---

[2]Ellis, Albert, and Knaus, William J., *Overcoming Procrastination* (New York: Signet, 1977), p. 16.

in every course. It's very difficult to live up to these goals, and fear of not living up to them causes the student to avoid the tasks required to reach them.

Low frustration tolerance is another cause of procrastination. Some students experience a great deal of frustration when they attempt to complete certain assignments or projects. Writing a twenty-page term paper for your political science class, for example, may be extremely difficult for you. Every time you decide to go to the library to work on it, you may think about how much time it's going to take to research, write, and type that paper. You may also believe that even if you do put in all that work, it still won't be a good paper. The task may appear to be too difficult or require too much of your time, and just thinking about it may become a very unpleasant experience. Your low tolerance for frustration may lead you to put off this difficult task and do something else instead. Before you know it, you've fallen into the procrastination trap.

Ellis and Knaus's third cause of procrastination is hostility toward others. You may put off doing that term paper because of your anger toward your professor. Comments like, "He just expects too much of our class" or "She didn't even assign us that paper until two weeks before the end of the semester" or "That assignment is so unfair" are indicative of angry feelings toward your instructors. If you're angry at one of your instructors for giving you a difficult assignment, because you received a poor test grade, or for criticizing or embarrassing you in class, you may find it unpleasant to work on the assignment for that class. Your angry feelings can, in fact, increase your feelings of frustration about the task. Together, these feelings lead to procrastination.

OTHER REASONS STUDENTS PROCRASTINATE

Some students put off studying for exams until it's almost too late. They may be procrastinating for another reason—to protect themselves from feelings of inadequacy. By not studying adequately, you can protect your ego, because you can blame your failure on your lack of preparation rather than on your lack of ability. For example, you might say, "Well, if I had studied, I would have gotten a B, but I just didn't have time." In this way you tell yourself that you *could* have done a good job if you had chosen to.

Procrastination also can be the result of poor time management. Not scheduling time early in the semester for long-range assignments leaves some students in a time crunch when they realize that a paper or project deadline is approaching. Instead of having six to eight weeks to prepare a term paper, procrastinators may find themselves with one week or less to complete it. Of course, this often leads to panic and poor performance.

Procrastination can become a habit, a way of life, for some students. Procrastination leads to more procrastination. Once you start to put work off, things pile up. As your work load grows, getting it all done becomes even more difficult. Fortunately, most students don't habitually procrastinate on all of their tasks. Especially difficult assignments, however, can lead to procrastination on the part of even the most motivated student. At times, students procrastinate because they just don't know how to get started. Many college freshmen have difficulty writing their first (or second) essay for Freshman Composition. Although they aren't afraid of failure, they just can't figure out how to begin. This is also a common problem for students who are required to do projects and papers on subjects in which they lack expertise or with which they have little familiarity.

STRATEGIES FOR OVERCOMING PROCRASTINATION

A number of strategies and techniques can help you overcome procrastination. Setting realistic goals is the first step in stopping procrastination. If you set reasonable expectations for yourself, you are more likely to accomplish your goals and less likely to have negative feelings about your capabilities.

Use Good Time Management Strategies

Estimating how much time it will take to complete your daily tasks can help you avoid overscheduling. If you plan only what you can accomplish in the time you have available for study, you won't have a long list of tasks to carry over to the next day. Keeping up with your work from the very first day of the semester will help you avoid getting behind. Putting your tasks into writing also will help you get them done. When you think of something that you have to do, do it immediately if you can. If you can't, write it down. Your written note is a commitment to complete the task; simply telling yourself that you'll do it later can easily lead to procrastination. Setting priorities also is important. You can't always get everything done every day. However, if you complete your most important tasks first, you won't feel as though you have failed or let yourself down.

Plan Ahead for Long-Range Tasks

By setting up a schedule for completing a term paper or final project, and sticking to your plan, you can keep from getting caught in a time crunch at the end of the semester. Start on big projects early in the semester when you don't have as much to do. (The best time to start any long-range assignment is on the day on which it is assigned.) Getting started early will give you the time you need to do the task well.

Break Down Large Tasks

It's always easier to get yourself motivated to do a small task. Remember how much easier it was to read ten pages of sociology than the fifty pages that were assigned? This strategy is especially effective for time-consuming or difficult tasks. Instead of trying to complete a twenty-page paper all at once, decide that you will find five sources on your topic this week. Next week, you can skim your sources and decide on a thesis for your paper. Once your thesis is determined, you can take notes for your paper and then plan your main points. After you have an outline of what you want to include in your paper, you will be ready to write your first draft. At that point, you may decide to do some additional research to locate specific information for a couple of sections of your paper. Doing each of these smaller tasks will result in a final draft that is well done and ready on time.

Recognize That Not All Assignments Are Easy

You will have to do some assignments that you don't like or enjoy. Some of them will be difficult or even time-consuming. If you can accept the fact that not all of your tasks will be pleasant experiences, that in itself will help you approach them more willingly. It's easy to do things you like; working on the task often provides its own feeling of satisfaction. Doing things you don't like, however, may require some outside compensation. Using some of the reward systems that were described earlier may help you overcome your tendency to procrastinate on certain tasks. Remember, plan to do something that you really like as a reward for completing something you don't like to do.

Work for Five Minutes

When you decide to work on your term paper or your English assignment, don't think about why you should or shouldn't do it—just start it. Do anything. Take out paper and write anything. Tell yourself that you are going to read only the first page or even the first paragraph. Make a deal with yourself to do the easiest part of the assignment or only a small part of it. Once you start the assignment, you are likely to continue. Remember, getting started is half the battle. A number of time management experts suggest that you work on a task for five to ten minutes. At the end of that time, you can decide if you want to work for another ten minutes. This strategy has proved to be very successful for many students.

Identify Escapist Techniques

Being aware of the ways that you talk yourself out of doing your work will help you eliminate them. Keep track of what you do to avoid doing your work and then avoid those avenues of escape in the future.

ACTIVITIES

1. Complete the Fixed Commitment Calendar included in Figure 3.5. Write in all of your regularly scheduled commitments for class, work, and other obligations. Then box in the time blocks that are available for study.
2. Calculate the number of hours that you will need for study this semester and write them on your Fixed Commitment Calendar. Remember that this number will change each semester depending upon your schedule of classes and your goals. Now compare the time that you have available for study to the time that you need. Do you have enough time to complete all of your work? Do you have any additional time left to complete personal goals and for relaxation?
3. Draw or purchase a blank calendar and write in the months and dates for the entire semester. Then use your syllabi to list all of your assignments on the calendar. Don't forget to write exams in capital letters and to box them in so that they really stand out.
4. Choose one of your long-range assignments for the semester and list the steps you will have to accomplish in order to complete the project. Then set up a schedule for when you will complete each step. Write the week number or numbers next to each step, or develop a time line for your project. Be sure to include deadlines for the completion of each major part of the project.
5. Create a chart using the following headings, then jot down all of the escapist techniques that you use in a one-week period to keep from doing your work. What can you do to keep from repeating these avoidance patterns?

Date	Assignment or Study Task	What did I do to escape?	Why did I want to escape?	What strategies can I use to keep from trying to escape my work?

Figure 3.5 Blank Fixed Commitment Calendar

	Monday	Tuesday	Wednesday	Thursday	Friday	Saturday	Sunday
8:00							
9:00							
10:00							
11:00							
12:00							
1:00							
2:00							
3:00							
4:00							
5:00							
6:00							
7:00							
8:00							
9:00							
10:00							
11:00							
12:00							
1:00							
2:00							

Hours Available for Study__________ Hours Needed for Study__________

POSTTEST

Where Are You Now?

Now that you have completed Chapter 3, take a few minutes to answer *yes* or *no* to the following questions. Compare your answers with those in the pretest.

	YES	NO
1. Have you estimated how many hours you need to study this semester?	____	____
2. Do you tend to complete your assignments on time?	____	____
3. Have you estimated how long it takes you to read one chapter in each of your textbooks?	____	____
4. Do you begin working on long-term assignments early in the semester?	____	____
5. Do you make lists of things to do in your head rather than on paper?	____	____
6. Do you find that you go out even when you know you should be studying?	____	____
7. Do you [illegible] to study for exams?	____	____
8. Are you working at a job more than twenty hours a week?	____	____
9. Do you know exactly what you are going to work on when you sit down to study?	____	____
10. Do you do the assignments from your favorite class first?	____	____

Give yourself one point for each *yes* answer to all questions except 5, 6, 8, and 10, and one point for each *no* answer to questions 5, 6, 8, and 10. Now total up your points. Compare your score on this posttest with the score that you had on the pretest. Did you improve? In which areas? Do you still need to improve more?

CHAPTER 4

Improving Concentration

"I really thought that I was concentrating, but now that I look back, I realize that I was being distracted all the time. By finding a personal place at home, I have found that my concentration is getting better. Now, I can read two or three chapters in one of my textbooks without thinking about anything else."

James Frankhauser

CONCENTRATION AND PERFORMANCE

If you follow a study plan but find that you still don't accomplish your goals, you may have a problem with concentration. Some students believe that if they say they are going to study and proceed with the intention of completing certain tasks, they will be able to accomplish what they set out to do. However, that isn't always what happens. If they are constantly thinking about other things or are distracted by outside noises or other people, they may in fact accomplish very little.

WHAT IS CONCENTRATION?

Concentration is focusing your attention on what you are doing. Concentration is important in just about anything you do, but in this chapter we will focus on improving concentration during reading, listening, and studying. It's hard to de-

PRETEST

Where Are You Now?

Take a few minutes to answer *yes* or *no* to the following questions.

	YES	NO
1. Do you have trouble getting back into your work after you've been interrupted?	______	______
2. Do you read and study in a noisy, cluttered room?	______	______
3. Do you find that even though you schedule study time, you don't actually accomplish very much?	______	______
4. Do you use any strategies to help increase your ability to concentrate?	______	______
5. Can you concentrate on your work even if the subject doesn't interest you?	______	______
6. Do you generally read or study with the TV or stereo on?	______	______
7. Do you tend to think about personal plans or problems when you are reading and studying?	______	______
8. Do you find that when you finish reading your textbook assignment, you don't really remember what you read?	______	______
9. Do you get totally engrossed in the material when you read and study?	______	______
10. Do you daydream a lot when you are listening to lectures?	______	______

Give yourself one point for each *yes* answer to questions 4, 5, and 9, and one point for each *no* answer to questions 1, 2, 3, 6, 7, 8, and 10. Now total up your points. A low score indicates that you need some help improving concentration. A high score indicates that you are already using many good concentration strategies.

scribe what concentration is, but it's easy to explain what it isn't. Consider the following examples. If you are reading a chapter in your sociology text, you are concentrating on it only as long as you are thinking of nothing else. As soon as you think about how many pages you have left to read, what time you are going to eat dinner, or what the professor will discuss in class, you are experiencing a lack of concentration. If you think about the fact that you *should* be concentrating on your assignment, that means you have in fact lost your concentration. Let's look at another example. If, during a lecture class, you become interested in the conversation going on in the row behind you, you have lost your concentration. You may even find that you have missed several new points that your professor just introduced.

Being distracted interferes with your ability to attend to or focus on the task at hand. In each of the above examples, you were actually concentrating on something. The problem is that you were concentrating on something other than the lecture or the reading material—you were concentrating on the distractions.

Difficulty with concentration is a common problem for college students. Every semester, I ask students to look over the syllabus for my course in college study skills and mark the three topics that they think will help them the most. Improving concentration is always one of the most common choices.

THREE LEVELS OF CONCENTRATION

Set a timer or ask someone to time you as you read for about twenty minutes. Each time you think of something else or even look up from your reading, put a check mark in the margin of your book. How long did you read? How many check marks did you have? What types of distractions did you experience? As you were reading your text assignment, you may have found that you were not always concentrating at the same level. At some points during the twenty-minute period, you may have noticed that you were more focused on the material than at other times. Look at the check marks you made in your book. Were more of them located in the early pages of the assignment? Why does this happen?

In order to understand why students are less distracted toward the end of a twenty-minute reading period, let's take a better look at how concentration works. Anne Bradley has divided concentration into three levels: light, moderate, and deep.[1] Look at the diagram in Figure 4.1.

---

[1]Adapted from Bradley, Anne, *Take Note of College Study Skills* (Glenview, IL: Scott, Foresman, 1983), pp.41–42.

Figure 4.1 The Concentration Cycle

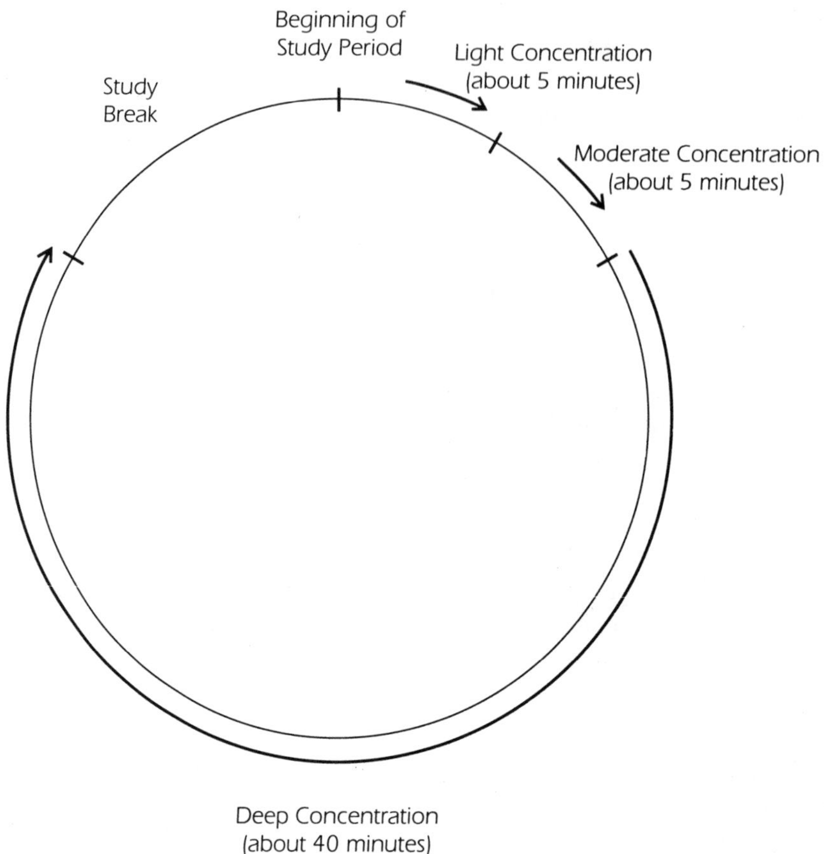

LIGHT CONCENTRATION

When you first sit down to read or study, you are in a state of light concentration. This stage of concentration continues for about the first five minutes of study. At this point, you're just getting settled into your reading, listening, or study. Students in light concentration can be seen wiggling around in their chairs, twisting their hair, or pulling out study supplies. When you are in light concentration, you are easily distracted. You may hear people talking down the hall, notice other students walking into the room, be annoyed by any noise occurring around you, or find yourself thinking about other things.

MODERATE CONCENTRATION

During the next five minutes or so, you move into moderate concentration. At this point you begin to pay attention to the material that you are reading, hearing, or studying. You may find that you are actually getting interested in the lecture or text material. In this stage you will probably find that you are not as easily distracted. Although you may lose your concentration if someone talks directly to you, you may not notice the voices of people talking down the hall, or even someone coughing in the same room.

DEEP CONCENTRATION

Once you move into deep concentration, you aren't thinking about anything except what you are hearing or reading. At this point, you are totally engrossed in the material. Have you ever jumped when someone came up behind you and touched your arm? Because you were in deep concentration, you may not have even noticed that person enter the room or call your name. When you are in deep concentration, you are not aware of the clock ticking, the door opening, or other things that you normally would find rather distracting. It is at this stage in the concentration cycle that you are working most effectively.

Think of a time that you were totally engrossed in what you were doing. It doesn't have to be a study activity, although that would be especially relevant. What were you doing? What did you do to achieve that level of concentration? What strategies did you use?

THE CONCENTRATION CYCLE

You may be thinking that it sounds fairly easy to reach a high level of concentration—that after an initial ten minutes or so, you can expect to remain at a level of deep concentration. Unfortunately, this is not the way it really works for many students. Instead, they move in and out of the three stages of concentration.

Look at the diagram in Figure 4.2A. This represents the ideal study session. In this situation, you would be able to work in deep concentration for forty minutes. You can learn the most during this type of study session, because when you are in deep concentration, you are working at your highest level of comprehension and learning.

Unfortunately, some students never get into deep concentration. They move back and forth between light and moderate concentration because they are distracted constantly (see Figure 4.2B). Every time that you are distracted, you move back to level one, light concentration. If your roommate asks if she can borrow your navy sweater and you respond, you have just experienced a distraction. If you stop to

Figure 4.2 Study Sessions and Levels of Concentration

A. The Ideal Study Session: Good Concentration

5 min.	5 min.	40 minutes	10 minutes
B LC	MC	Deep Concentration	Study Break

B. A Common Study Session: Poor Concentration

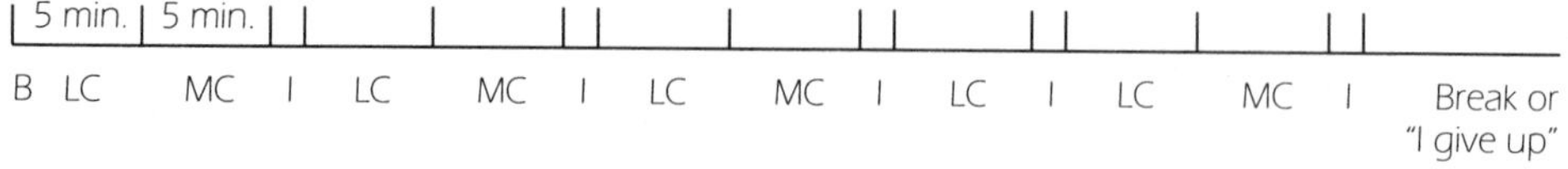

LC: Light concentration
MC: Moderate concentration
I: Interruption
B: Beginning of study session

check how many more pages you still have to read, you have been distracted. If you look up when someone walks past you in the library, you have been distracted. Each time you are interrupted as you are listening to a lecture, working on a homework assignment, or studying for a test, you move out of deep concentration.

You may find it doesn't take you quite as long to get interested in the material on your second or third try. However, you will still have to move through these "warming up" stages again before you can reach a state of deep concentration. If you tend to study in places where you are interrupted a lot, your study session may more closely resemble the concentration cycle in Figure 4.2B. Without strategies that will improve your ability to concentrate, you may have difficulty concentrating on a lecture, or you may spend a lot of time reading or studying yet accomplish very little.

You may also find that your ability to concentrate varies from text to text (what you study), place to place (where you study), and from time to time (when you study). You may have to use more strategies or different strategies in order to increase your ability to concentrate when you are studying subjects that are of little interest to you and when you work in noisy study areas or at certain times during the day.

CAUSES OF POOR CONCENTRATION

The two main causes of poor concentration are external and internal distractions. External distractions include things like noise, an uncomfortable study area, and, of course, other people. If you try to study in a noisy place, you may find that you are constantly distracted and interrupted. Dorm rooms and the kitchen table at home are not always good places to do your work. The phone rings, people stop by, and TV's and stereos are on all the time.

Although you can walk away from noisy study areas, you can't escape internal distractions; they go with you wherever you go. Internal distractions are things that you think about or worry about. Common internal distractions include anxiety caused by a certain course, the feeling that study won't help, worry over personal problems, indecision about what to do next, and so on. Many students even worry about the fact that they can't concentrate, and that worry interferes further with their ability to concentrate on their work.

In the remaining portion of this chapter, you will learn about some of the causes of poor concentration and a number of strategies that you can use to overcome them. Although students experience concentration problems while working on all kinds of academic tasks, the most common problems tend to occur during lecture classes, when reading text assignments, and while studying for quizzes and tests.

CONCENTRATION PROBLEMS DURING LECTURE CLASS

Many students experience problems with concentration when they are trying to listen and learn in class. Do you ever have trouble concentrating on the lecture your professor is presenting? What gets in your way? One of the more common problems is distractions caused by other students. It's hard to concentrate on what your professor is saying when the person sitting next to you is constantly talking to you or to someone near you. Even a conversation two or three rows behind you can interfere with your ability to stay focused on the lecture. Noises outside of the lecture room also can be distracting and can interfere with your ability to stay focused.

The way the professor presents the lecture can also affect how well some students are able to concentrate. If the professor mumbles or speaks in a quiet or monotone voice, many students have difficulty staying focused on the lecture. They do better if the professor speaks in a loud voice or tends to vary the tone of the presentation. Lectures that are disorganized may also lead to concentration problems. If a lecture becomes difficult to follow, some students just give up. A number of students also have concentration problems if the professor repeats information over and over again. They become bored and stop listening.

Internal distractions are another cause of difficulty during lecture classes. Worrying about personal problems or thinking about what you have to do after the class are common internal distractions. Feeling hungry or tired is another common internal distractor.

Finally, some students have concentration problems during lecture classes because of their attitude toward the class or the material. Many students have more trouble concentrating when they place a low value on the material or the course. Moreover, they experience more difficulty paying attention to the lecture when the topic is uninteresting or difficult to understand. In situations like this, some students begin to daydream or even doze off.

CONCENTRATION PROBLEMS WHEN YOU READ A TEXTBOOK

Many students have difficulty concentrating when they read textbook assignments. Unlike lecture classes, where the professor may help keep you focused by varying her tone of voice or by asking questions, you alone are responsible for concentrating on your reading assignments. Do you have trouble concentrating when you read some or all of your text assignments? If you think that you're the only student with this problem, you're wrong. Many students have difficulty concentrating on reading assignments. In fact, many students indicate that they have more trouble concentrating when they read than at any other time.

External distractions such as a cluttered or uncomfortable study environment, noise, and other people are common causes of poor concentration when reading. How many times this week were you interrupted as you tried to read your text assignment? Many students need complete silence in order to concentrate on reading assignments. If you live in a dormitory, finding a quiet study place can be quite a problem. Some students elect to live at home to avoid these types of distractions. However, many find that living with a family can be just as noisy as living in a dorm.

The time of day that you tackle your reading assignments also can affect your ability to concentrate. If you try to do your reading late at night, you may experience more difficulty staying focused, because you are tired. Concentration requires effort, and it is harder to make that effort when you are tired. Have you noticed that it is more difficult to concentrate on the road when you are driving late at night and feel tired? For the same reason, many students have more difficulty maintaining their concentration when they try to read for long periods of time without a break.

Although most students indicate that their problems with concentration stem from external distractions or from internal distractions such as their lack of interest in the material or the low value they place on the course, other internal distractions can also be a factor. Personal problems, concerns about grades or progress in the course, and fear of not knowing the answer or how to do the problems in class can all interfere with a student's ability to focus on the material. Many students find that when they have difficulty concentrating (for any of the above reasons), they tend to think about other things. Sometimes they worry about both academic and personal problems. At other times, they tend to use escapist techniques and daydream about something that they would rather be doing — something that would be a lot more interesting or a lot more fun than reading a textbook.

CONCENTRATION PROBLEMS WHEN YOU STUDY FOR EXAMS

Some students have a lot of trouble concentrating when they are preparing for exams. Aside from the typical external distractions, they often experience special problems. Some students may not be as motivated to focus on the task of test preparation early in the semester because they don't put as much value on the first exam. It is more difficult to concentrate when you are studying for a test on which you place little value. Other students get distracted when they study because the material is difficult or uninteresting. Some students have concentration problems because studying is not a specific assignment, as is reading pages 186 to 201, for example. Anytime your goals are vague or you are not sure what to do, it is more difficult to stay focused.

Another problem that leads to poor concentration when preparing for exams is passive study techniques. Most students still study for college exams by simply reading over the text and lecture material, which can be quite boring. Procrastination can also lead to poor concentration. When you leave your test preparation to the last minute, you may feel overwhelmed by too much to learn in too little time. In situations like this, students generally try to cram for the exam, which often results in passive study and increased worry about the results.

STRATEGIES FOR IMPROVING CONCENTRATION

By now you probably realize that problems with concentration are fairly common for college students. Although it may make you feel better to know you aren't the only person in the world who can't concentrate, it doesn't help you correct the problem. Many students indicate that they have few, if any, strategies for improving their concentration; they have a problem concentrating, but they don't know how to correct it. Fortunately, there are a number of strategies you can use to help improve your ability to concentrate when you listen to a lecture, read a text assignment, or study for a test. Even though you've already learned about some of them in the chapters on goal setting and time management, there are many others that may be new to you. You can improve your ability to concentrate by creating a good learning environment, by dealing promptly with internal distractions, by using active learning strategies, and by monitoring your concentration.

CREATING A POSITIVE LEARNING ENVIRONMENT

You can dramatically improve your ability to concentrate by creating a positive learning environment. The first step is to control external distractions, and the best way to control external distractions is simply to eliminate them.

In lecture classes, you can avoid most external distractions by moving to the front of the room. Fortunately, most students who chat during class tend to sit in the back. However, you still occasionally may find yourself sitting near some noisy students. If the students sitting nearby keep you from concentrating on the lecture, get up and move! You also can be distracted by things going on around you. If you find yourself looking out the window or watching what goes on in the hall, find a seat where you can't see the window or the door. Make the professor the center of your line of vision and sit near the front of the room.

Although it's fairly easy to find a new seat during lecture classes, it's not as easy to find a new place to study when you can't concentrate. If you live in a dormitory, or even if you live at home, you're surrounded by noise. You may find it fairly easy to control the noise level inside your room, but unless you are living in a dorm where quiet hours are enforced, you won't have much luck controlling the noise level outside of your room. Some students stay in their rooms even when they can't concentrate, almost out of stubbornness. "It's my room and I should be able to work there" is a commonly heard statement. But if you have tried unsuccessfully to eliminate the distractions in your room and you still can't concentrate on your work, you have only one other option. You need to find somewhere else to study. It may not seem fair that you have to gather up all your materials and go somewhere else, but if you can't change your study environment, you have to find a new one. If you force yourself to continue working in a noisy room, you probably won't be able to accomplish very much and you may become even more frustrated.

Finding a good place to read and study may require some experimentation. Try working in different places at different times of the day to see which study area works best for you. The library, study rooms, and empty classrooms are usually good study areas, but you may find that some locations are better than others at different times of the day. Once you find a good place to work, establish a regular routine. Studying in the same place at the same time each day helps you get down to work. It may even help to use special objects that you associate with study. By sitting in a special chair, wearing your "study" slippers, or even using a special pen or clipboard, you'll help yourself get into a study mode, and this will help you improve your concentration.

Sometimes, you may be able to study in your room. Plan your schedule so that you will be working in your room when your roommate or family members are out doing other things. If you do plan to study in your room, you can improve your study environment by following some of these suggestions:

1. Put your desk against a wall so that you face the wall when you study.
2. Put all pictures, mementos, and decorations on the other side of the room so that they don't distract you from your work.
3. Don't use your desk for anything other than studying. When you sit down, you will automatically think about studying.
4. Study in a comfortable (but not too comfortable) chair. You will work best in a semi-tense position.
5. Never study lying in bed. If you get too comfortable, you'll have trouble concentrating and may even fall asleep.
6. If you're always interrupted by phone calls, take the phone off the hook or get an answering machine to screen your calls.
7. Put a sign on your door with a message such as "Do not disturb — killer exam tomorrow" or "Physics now, party later — stop back at midnight."
8. Turn off the television, stereo, and radio. Use light, familiar music in the background *only* if it serves to block out other noise. Save that new tape or CD you bought, and keep it as a reward for completing your work.

DEALING WITH INTERNAL DISTRACTIONS

Once you set up a quiet study environment, you should see a big difference in your ability to concentrate. However, just eliminating external distractions doesn't guarantee that you'll be able to focus on your work. Many students find that once they eliminate the external noises around them, they notice the internal "noises" even more.

Although you can't really eliminate internal distractions, you can take steps to keep them from interfering with your work. If, as you're studying, you think of something that you want or need to do, or if you come up with an idea for another assignment, jot it down and then continue with your work. If you don't write it down, you'll probably continue thinking about it or even begin to worry that you may forget it. In either case, you will be concentrating more on the internal distraction than on your assignment. In the same way, if you feel hungry or thirsty, get something to eat or drink and then return to your work.

Developing a positive attitude about study and setting daily study goals will help you overcome more serious internal distractions. It's easy to concentrate on your reading or studying when you find the material interesting, relevant, and important to you. When you aren't all that interested in one of your courses, you need to find ways to make the material more interesting and more relevant. By setting goals and developing a more positive attitude toward all of your work, you can learn to concentrate better. Also, the more specific you make your study goals, the better chance you will have of completing them. If you know exactly what you plan to accomplish when you sit down to read or study, it will be easier to stay focused. When you don't plan ahead, you'll find you spend a lot of your study time thinking about what you should do instead of actually doing it.

Worrying about academic problems is a common internal distraction. Instead of worrying—do something! Go see your professor and share your concerns about the course. Get a tutor or have a talk with yourself about what you need to do to meet your goals. Remind yourself that getting down to work and doing your best is the first step in the right direction. Then, if you still don't understand the material or can't do the problems, ask for help. Remember, it's easier to block out internal distractions when you have confidence in yourself as a student. You will gain this confidence by learning that you can be successful in college, not by worrying about it.

Personal worries and concerns are another common internal distraction. Many students allow an argument with a boyfriend or girlfriend, or problems with family to interfere with their concentration for hours or even days. Make a decision to do something about your problem as soon as you complete your work. Call a friend and talk honestly about your troubles, or schedule an appointment at your campus counseling center. You may even be able to deal with the problem quickly, before you begin to work. Some students find that writing about whatever is bothering them in a journal or talking it out with friends helps them experience a feeling of closure about the problem. They then can concentrate on their work and don't keep thinking about what happened.

USING ACTIVE LEARNING STRATEGIES

One of the best ways to keep external and internal distractions from interfering with your concentration is to become more involved in the lecture, the text, or your test preparation. You can generate this high level of involvement by using active learning strategies. Many students allow internal and external distractions to interrupt their study because they use passive learning strategies that just don't work.

Taking notes during lecture classes helps you focus on what the professor is saying. If you know that you are going to have to write something down, you'll be more motivated to pay attention. Many students are bored and begin to daydream or look out the window during lecture classes because they don't have anything to do. The class seems to drag on and on and they begin looking for other things to pass the time. Does that ever happen to you? If you limit yourself to the role of the passive observer, you can expect to be distracted in all but the most exciting classes. Although it would be great if all classes were that interesting, not all of them are. However, some students find that lecture classes become more interesting and actually go much faster when they take notes. This is because the students have reached a state of deep concentration.

Many students have trouble concentrating during lecture classes simply because they are not actively involved in what's going on in the class. Asking questions, predicting main points, and generating recall columns are all ways of becoming more involved during lecture classes. (You'll learn about these strategies in the next chapter.) Becoming a more active participant in class is one of the keys to eliminating internal and external distractions and increasing concentration.

Becoming an active reader will significantly improve your ability to concentrate when you read your textbook assignments. Reading with your eyes but not your brain leads to daydreaming and other concentration problems. Have you ever read a paragraph or even an entire page of text and then realized that you had no idea what you had just read? Even though your eyes did "look at the words," your mind was somewhere else. Previewing, highlighting, outlining, and taking notes are all active strategies that can improve your concentration. We'll talk more about them in Chapters 6, 7, and 8.

How can you maintain your concentration as you prepare for exams? You need to increase your involvement with the material. When you prepare for an exam, dig through the material, looking for important information. Taking notes, developing study sheets, and creating graphic displays will help you become totally engrossed in the material. Reciting the key information out loud and doing some self-testing are just two of many rehearsal strategies that also can help you learn. We'll talk more about them in Chapters 9 and 10. For now, however, remember that the more actively involved you are in studying the material, the easier it will be to maintain your concentration.

You can also increase your concentration by using motivational strategies. Taking breaks, switching subjects, and planning rewards are helpful in increasing your motivation, and they also can help increase your concentration. It's much harder to stay focused on your work when you become tired or bored. When you just can't concentrate anymore, stop and take a break. Then switch to a different subject to eliminate feelings of boredom and frustration. Setting deadlines and limiting the amount of time that you allow for each of your study tasks also can motivate you to use your time more effectively. Deadlines make you feel rushed, so you actually force yourself to concentrate better (unless you've left yourself *too* little time—in that case, your anxiety will only increase).

MONITORING YOUR CONCENTRATION

Monitoring how often you lose your concentration can be very helpful in learning how to improve your concentration. Put a check mark, dash, or write the time in the margin of your book every time that you are distracted. At the end of your study session, count the number of interruptions. Write the number in your book and make a commitment to reduce that number the next time you read. In a few weeks, you may find that your ability to concentrate improves dramatically.

When you notice that you're daydreaming or thinking about other things, try to figure out what actually triggered your loss in concentration. If you can pinpoint the cause of your distraction, you're only one step away from the solution. Hold yourself accountable for your lapses in concentration—find a way to overcome them. Remember, you can improve your ability to concentrate, but it is you who must take the responsibility for doing so.

ACTIVITIES

1. Draw a time line to evaluate your last fifty-minute study session. Plot the interruptions that you experienced and how much time you spent in each of the three levels of concentration on the diagram. What did you discover about your ability to concentrate?
2. Make a list of the problems or difficulties that you experience in at least two of your lecture classes. Did you notice any differences in your lists or your ability to concentrate in each class?
3. Pick a chapter in one of your textbooks that you haven't read yet. Jot down the time and then read as you normally do. Every time that you think of something else or look up or start to daydream, note the time in the margin of your text.

At the end of your study session, count the number of interruptions that you noted. Also, calculate the longest uninterrupted time period that you had. Try this same experiment with a textbook for a class that you like a lot, or in a different study area, or at another time of day. Did you notice any difference?

4. Make a list of the problems or difficulties that you experience the next time you prepare for an exam. If you have several exams in the next few weeks, evaluate your preparation for one class that you are very interested in or place high value on, and one that you don't. Did you notice any differences in your lists or your ability to concentrate as you prepared for each of the exams?

5. Create a chart to monitor your concentration using the following headings. Record up to ten of the concentration problems that you encounter over a one-week period. Include one or more strategies that you did use or should have used to improve your concentration.

Date	Assignment or Study Task	Concentration Problem	Cause	Strategy

POSTTEST

Where Are You Now?

Now that you have completed Chapter 4, take a few minutes to answer *yes* or *no* to the following questions. Compare your answers with those in the pretest.

	YES	NO
1. Do you have trouble getting back into your work after you've been interrupted?	_____	_____
2. Do you read and study in a noisy, cluttered room?	_____	_____
3. Do you find that even though you schedule study time, you don't actually accomplish very much?	_____	_____
4. Do you use any strategies to help increase your ability to concentrate?	_____	_____
5. Can you concentrate on your work even if the subject doesn't interest you?	_____	_____
6. Do you generally read or study with the TV or stereo on?	_____	_____
7. Do you tend to think about personal plans or problems when you are reading and studying?	_____	_____
8. Do you find that when you finish reading your textbook assignment, you don't really remember what you read?	_____	_____
9. Do you get totally engrossed in the material when you read and study?	_____	_____
10. Do you daydream a lot when you are listening to lectures?	_____	_____

Give yourself one point for each *yes* answer to questions 4, 5, and 9, and one point for each *no* answer to questions 1, 2, 3, 6, 7, 8, and 10. Now total up your points. Compare your score on this posttest with the score that you had on the pretest. Did you improve? In which areas? Do you still need to improve more?

CHAPTER 5

Taking Lecture Notes

"The new strategies for taking lecture notes really do work. They make the class time move faster, and at the end when I leave, I really feel like I learned something instead of just spending fifty minutes deciding what to pack for spring break. Good lecture notes come in handy when it comes time to study for tests, too. Paying attention in class is so much easier when I take notes."

Nicole Modechi

WHAT IS NOTE TAKING?

Taking notes during college lectures is a difficult task for most entering college students. Many received little or no real practice in note taking when they were in high school. There, note taking involved copying the information off the chalkboard as the teacher talked and wrote. In college, however, most professors don't do the job of note taking for their students. Instead, students must listen, select the appropriate information, and then write it down with few if any clues from the professor. Developing good note-taking skills takes both time and practice. However, learning and practicing effective strategies for how to take lecture notes will help you become a more successful student.

PRETEST

Where Are You Now?

Take a few minutes to answer *yes* or *no* to the following questions.

	YES	NO
1. Do you review and edit your notes within twenty-four hours after each of your classes?	______	______
2. Do you try to write down exactly what your professor says in class?	______	______
3. Do you separate the main points from supporting information in your notes?	______	______
4. Are you able to read and understand your notes when you study for your exam?	______	______
5. Do your notes include Roman numerals, capital and small letters, and numbers?	______	______
6. Do you tend to write down only important or key words when you take notes?	______	______
7. Do you review your notes by reciting them out loud?	______	______
8. Do you tend to miss a lot of information when you take notes?	______	______
9. Do you rely on a tape recorder instead of taking notes in some of your classes?	______	______
10. Do you read your textbook assignment before you go to your lecture class?	______	______

Give yourself one point for each *yes* answer to questions 1, 3, 4, 7, and 10, and one point for each *no* answer to questions 2, 5, 6, 8, and 9. Now total up your points. A low score indicates that you need some help in note taking. A high score indicates that you are already using many good note-taking strategies.

WHY TAKE LECTURE NOTES?

Other than attending class every day, taking good lecture notes is probably the single most important activity for college students. Taking notes in class promotes active listening and provides you with an accurate record of the information that was presented.

Taking notes in class promotes active listening by helping you to concentrate on the lecture and feel involved in the class. In order to write down what your instructor is saying, you need to be actively involved in the lecture—listening, thinking, and writing. Have you ever sat in class and realized that you had no idea what the professor just said? For many students, this is a common experience. Even though everyone gets distracted once in a while, it becomes a real problem if you daydream so much that you miss what your professor is saying. By taking notes, you can improve your ability to concentrate, because you're focusing your attention on what is being said; you are listening for the next point that will be made so that you can write it down.

Some students find sitting in lecture classes very boring; they prefer classes where they are more actively involved in the learning experience. Taking notes, however, is a very active process. You can generate a high level of involvement in your own learning by taking notes. Note taking involves more than just writing down what the instructor is saying. It includes thinking about what has been said, determining what is important, recognizing how different points relate to others, anticipating what will be said next, putting the information into your own words, and organizing the information in your notes. The process of taking good lecture notes can help you become both an active listener and an active participant in your classes.

The most important reason for taking notes is to get an accurate record of the information that was presented in class. Taking notes can actually help you learn and remember the information. Even if you learn some of the information during the lecture class, there is no guarantee that you will remember it by the time you take your exam. In college, exams are given after four, seven, or even fifteen weeks; you won't remember all of the lecture material by the time you take a test. If you don't leave a lecture class with a good set of notes, an accurate record of information, you will not have the opportunity to review that material again before the exam. You can't just rely on your memory of the lecture; you need your notes, too!

HOW SHOULD YOU TAKE NOTES?

Learning to take notes effectively and efficiently takes time. You can improve your note-taking skills rapidly, however, if you learn to use some basic strategies. There is no one correct way to take notes, but some methods or systems work better than others. In this section, you will learn a number of basic strategies to help improve your note taking, as well as several options for form and format. Instead of just selecting one method to use, you may find it beneficial to try all of the techniques and then decide which ones work best for you.

PREPARE BEFORE TAKING NOTES

Reading the assigned or relevant textbook chapter before going to class has several advantages. First of all, it gives you some background for the lecture. You will be able to understand more of the lecture and recognize many of the main ideas as they are presented. As a result, you should be able to take better lecture notes during class. If you find that listening to the lecture helps you understand the textbook better, *skim* the chapter before the lecture and then read it more carefully afterward. Skimming involves reading the introduction, the headings, the first sentence of each paragraph, and the conclusion in order to get some idea of what the main ideas are and how they are organized.

Once you walk into the lecture classroom, get ready to take notes. If you sit near the front, you'll be able to see and hear better. Also, you'll probably find that other interested and motivated students also tend to sit in the first few rows of the class. By avoiding the back of the room, you will avoid those students who tend to chat and walk in late. While you're waiting for class to begin, review the notes that you took during the last class meeting. Many professors pick up where they left off in the last lecture. Your review will remind you of the main topics and the general organization of the lecture and will prepare you for the next point that will be made.

GENERAL FORMATTING TIPS

Below are some general formatting tips that will help you set up your notes more effectively. Most successful students have already adopted many of these strategies. Keep track of how many of them you are already using.

1. Use an 8½-by-11-inch notebook for each of your classes. Using smaller notebooks can lead to taking fewer notes and to being too selective in what you write down.

2. Take notes on one side of the page if you want to add information on the facing page or reorganize your notes for study. (If you like this idea, you should write on the right-hand page and leave the left-hand page [the facing page] blank.) However, if you are accustomed to using both sides of the page and you leave some room in your notes for additional information, you could continue to write on both sides. The choice is yours.
3. Always date your notes. If you are using loose-leaf paper, put the date on every page of notes. You also should put the topic of the lecture at the top of the first page of notes. By including the topic, you are helping to organize your mind for listening and your notes for study.
4. Take notes with a pen or fine-point marker; pencil tends to smear. Avoid light-colored inks, which are difficult to read.
5. Draw a line down the page about one inch to the right of the margin line. By leaving a two-inch margin on the left side of the page, you will be able to add recall words or questions that will help you study. Leave space between main points in case you want to add something later.
6. Write your notes in phrase form rather than in sentence form. It's almost impossible to write word for word what your professor is saying. While you are busy writing one sentence, you may miss other important points. Instead, condense the professor's words into meaningful phrases that can be noted more quickly. It takes a little practice to learn to translate what the professor has just said into phrases to write down, but you'll get the hang of it in no time.

NOTE-TAKING SYSTEMS

Dozens of systems have been developed to help students become effective note takers. Some of them are quite complex and provide explicit details on every step of the process. Unfortunately, a number of these systems involve so many steps and so much work that many students resort to their old methods or just don't take notes at all. Other systems are rather simple and provide only a few basic guidelines. For the new college student, they may not provide enough structure about how actually to get the information on paper.

It's important that you find the right note-taking system for you. It would help a great deal if every college professor lectured in the same way, but they don't. Some lecturers present very well-organized lectures that lend themselves to an outline system of note taking. Others, however, seem to move rapidly and abruptly from point to point. You may need to use several styles of taking notes in order to adapt to the style of the lecturer. Two of the most common methods for organizing your notes are the outline method and the paragraph method.

The Outline Method

Many students use the outline method to take notes in lecture classes. One of the reasons this style is so popular is that it's familiar to many students. Is this the style that you're using now? You probably learned formal outlining in high school and feel comfortable putting information into outline form. Another reason many students use outlines is because their professors provide them with some form of outline at the beginning of the lecture. This outline may only be four or five points long, or it may be a handout containing a full outline of the lecture. Even the four- or five-point outline written on the board, though, can set the pattern that you use for taking notes. Outlines work, however, only when the lecturer is well organized and proceeds in an orderly manner from main points to supporting points.

You can effectively use an outline style of note taking as long as you are careful not to fall into several traps. Some students are actually distracted by the "rules" of formal outlining and spend too much time thinking about how they should label or designate the next point in their notes. They are thinking about whether they should write a "B" or a "2" in their notes, instead of concentrating on the content of the lecture.

Too often, students equate outlining with just writing down key words. One-word outlines contain too little of the content of the lecture to provide an accurate record of information. Sometimes students don't realize how little information they have in their notes until they look at another student's notes. Look at the sample notes in Figure 5.1, which were taken by two students in the same economics class. Gary simply wrote down key words. His notes look well organized and effective until you compare them to the notes taken by Bryan, who was in the same class. Bryan's notes contain much more information about the topics presented in the lecture. When it's time to prepare for exams, students with "one-word notes" simply don't have enough information from which to study. Which set of notes would you rather have before the exam?

If you do plan to outline as you take notes, use an informal outlining style. You may want to use Roman numerals or capital letters to indicate the main divisions of the lecture, especially if they have already been presented on the board or in a handout. However, after designating the main points, just use indentation to show that the next points are subordinate. (Instead of aligning the next point with the sentence above, move it in a little from the left-hand side.) If the lecturer numbers points as he or she is speaking, by all means, include the numbers. But don't try to make your professor's lecture or your notes adhere to a formal outline style. Outlines that stress content and de-emphasize labels can be very helpful in organizing your notes. Bryan's notes (Figure 5.1) are a good example of informal outlining.

Figure 5.1 Sample Outline Forms

1) All people act "selfishly"
buying product (outputs)
selling factor (inputs)
2) "many" buyers & sellers
Product Markets: sellers
Monopoly: 1 seller
substitutes - for successful market

Gary's notes

Starting pts. for an economic system
A. All people act selfishly (economically)
Two Broad Types of Markets
Product Market (output) Market Activity Selfish
Factor Market (Input)
1. Product Market
Sellers → firms (bus organ) such as Corporations
→ Maximize profits
Consumers → buyers
- maximize utility
- as prices increase, less is bought
2. Factor Market
Sellers - laborers, workers
- Maximize wages, minimize effort
buyers - firms (bus organ)
- Maximize profits
B. All markets structural - great #'s of buyers & Sellers
Market is competitive - no single buyer or seller
influences the outcome

Bryan's notes

The Paragraph or Block Method

The paragraph- or block-style of note taking is another very simple system to learn. After noting the topic of the lecture and the date, write the first main topic in heading form (for example, "Depth Perception") or question form ("What About Depth Perception?") starting at the left-hand margin of your notebook. Indent a few spaces and then begin to write your notes in paragraph or block form. Listen for what the lecturer has to say about the topic and write down as many of the details as you can. Remember, you don't have to write complete sentences just because your notes are shaped like a paragraph; you still want to concentrate on using meaningful *phrases*. If you want to emphasize certain points, you can use numbered or unnumbered lists along with the block-style phrases. An example of the paragraph-style format is shown in Figure 5.2.

In this example, the details are written continuously across the line and separated only by dashes. As you can see, all of the details that relate to "Social Structure" are noted in a block under that heading. (If another main topic were mentioned, you would simply write it next to the margin line and then indent again to jot down any details about that topic.) Because the professor indicated that there were four classes of laborers, the student numbered them as they were described.

The paragraph method allows you to take notes efficiently and effectively because you have to concentrate on only two things: (1) getting down the main points (topics), and (2) getting down any details about them. You don't have to spend a lot of time trying to figure out where to place or how to label each new piece of information.

The Mapping Method

Some material lends itself to the mapping technique. Using this method, notes are recorded in a chart or in a graphic format. An example of mapping is shown in Figure 5.3. The placement of the material shows how each point is connected to the others. Although mapping can't be used for all lecture information, it is useful in some instances. A more complete discussion of mapping can be found in Chapter 8.

WHAT SHOULD YOU WRITE DOWN?

Although there are some general rules that will help you figure out what to include in your notes, there is no simple answer to this question. Some students are so afraid that they will miss even one point during the lecture that they try to write

Figure 5.2 Paragraph or Block Form

Social Structure

Each developed a social structure – not all people alike in activities – Skills determine social structure – called specialization of labor – 4 parts - 4 classes - 4 layers

1. bottom - farmers (peasant farmers) relatively poor - did not own the land they farmed - tenant farmers - hard labor - low level skill

2. Craftsmen - next level up - carpenters, stonemasons, pottery makers - usually req. apprenticeship - takes practice - lived in cities

3. Nobility - land owners - hired peasants to farm land - nobility had leisure time - used it in skilled professions of gov & fighting Governors, tax collectors, warriors (defense)

4. Priests - Knew how to write (req. great deal of learning) - great deal of apprenticeship. Writing was privilege of very small group

Languages difficult - Pass on skills to heirs. Looked to the future - communicated w gods - What did gods want for society - Dealt w communication w gods

Topography

Tigris & Euphrates Valley more open - encourages migration in & out of valley - Conjunction of Asia, Africa, & Europe ∴ many tribes & ethnic groups - Nile Valley - one group - surrounded in every direction by deserts - formed natural barrier

T & E - floods erratically - very destructively - Nile Valley - floods more predictable - pattern - Egyptians more content to stay where they were - river would flood yearly to maintain fertile land

Figure 5.3 Mapping

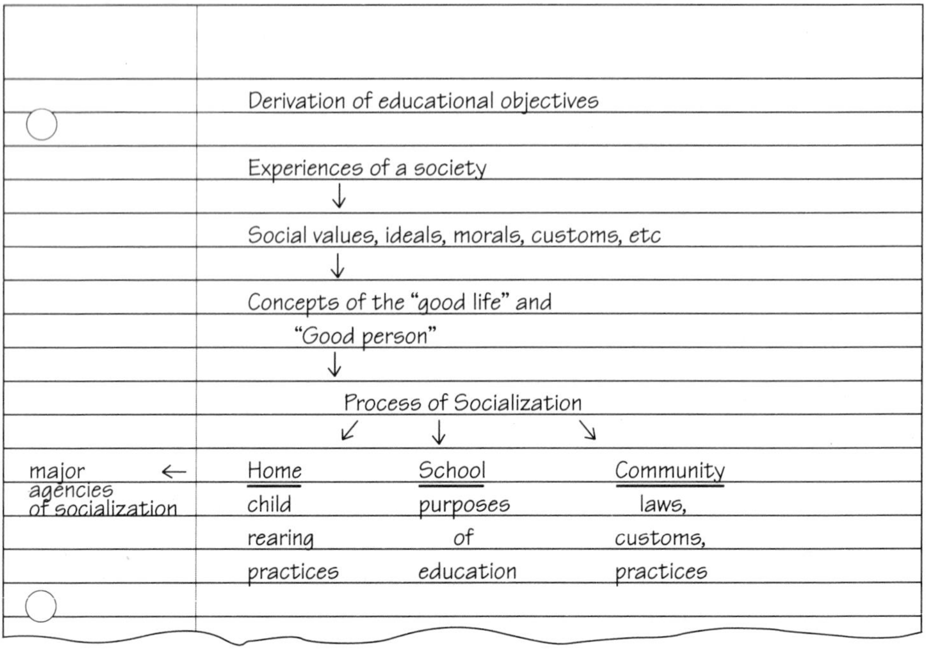

Derivation of educational objectives

Experiences of a society
↓
Social values, ideals, morals, customs, etc
↓
Concepts of the "good life" and "Good person"
↓
Process of Socialization
↙ ↓ ↘

major agencies of socialization ←	Home	School	Community
	child rearing practices	purposes of education	laws, customs, practices

down every word the professor says. This is both impractical and ineffective. You can't write as fast as your professor can talk. On the other hand, noting only a few points is not an effective solution either. A good general rule is to treat a lecture class like a lab class. You should be an active participant during the entire period. The best thing to do is to take as many notes as you can in a well-organized format. As soon as you pick out the heading, listen carefully for any information that explains or expands upon it, and add that information to your notes. Have you ever caught yourself thinking, "I wonder if I should write that down?" Anytime you do think about whether or not to write something down, *go ahead and write it down.* You may even find that your hand hurts at the end of the period; that's fine. Remember: When in doubt, write it out.

MAIN POINTS

Always note all main points that are made during a lecture. You may find that sometimes you have no trouble at all identifying the main points, and other times you have a lot of trouble. Main points appear to be obvious during some lectures because the lecturer states them in an easily recognizable manner. Introductions such as: "The next thing we're going to talk about is . . . ," "Another reason is . . . ," "What about vision?" and "First of all, . . ." make main points easy to pick out. Listen during your next lecture and see how your professor introduces each main topic. If your professor puts an outline on the board, you may want to copy it into your notebook at that point. However, as each main topic comes up during the actual lecture, write it down again in your notes. In this way, you organize the information in your notes and remind yourself of the overall content of the next section of the lecture.

TIPS ON WHAT ELSE TO INCLUDE IN YOUR NOTES

Until you develop more sophisticated note-taking skills, you may want to rely on some of the following tips for what to include in your notes.

1. Include details, facts, or explanations that expand or explain the main points that are mentioned.
2. Include definitions, word for word, especially if your professor repeats them several times.
3. Include enumerations or lists of things that are discussed.
4. Include examples. You don't need to note all of the details for each example, but you do need to know to which general topic each example relates.
5. Include anything that is written on the chalkboard or on a transparency (on an overhead projector).
6. Include anything that is repeated or spelled out.
7. Include drawings, charts, or problems that are written on the board.

WHAT TO DO IF YOU MISS INFORMATION

No matter how carefully you listen or how quickly you write, you still may not be able to get down all of the important information. For example, you may be trying to remember the rest of one definition and realize that the professor has moved to the next point. What do you do? If you're like most students, you probably sit there trying to remember what you were going to write until you finally realize that you have missed even more of the lecture. If you try getting the information from the person sitting next to you, both of you may miss the next point in the lecture.

There are several more effective strategies for retrieving missed information. When you do miss something during the lecture, just skip a line or two and continue taking notes. If you are writing down an important definition or statement and you suddenly can't remember a key word that you planned to write, draw a line to indicate that a key word is missing. Another thing to do is to ask the professor to repeat the statement. However, this is an effective strategy only if used once in a while. Most professors are willing to answer questions or repeat lecture information occasionally, but not fifteen or twenty times per lecture.

You also can fill in missed information after class. As soon as class is over, check with the person sitting next to you. You can easily locate the place where you missed a word or even an entire section of the lecture by searching for the blank lines or spaces that you left; it then will take just a minute or so to fill in what you missed. If you can't get the information from a classmate, ask the professor after class. Again, you can point directly to the place in your notes where the gap occurred, and the professor probably will be able to help you fill in the missing information very quickly. Finally, if neither of these strategies works, you may be able to find the missing information in your textbook.

HOW TO IMPROVE YOUR NOTE-TAKING SKILLS

There are a number of ways that you can practice taking notes and learn to improve some of the specific skills necessary for effective note taking. You may need to learn new techniques for some areas but not for others. Keep track of how many of these strategies you already use.

LEARN TO LISTEN AND WRITE

One of the necessary skills for taking notes is learning to listen and write at the same time. One of the most difficult things to learn may be how to truly listen when others are speaking. Practice this skill anywhere. Force yourself to *concentrate* on what the other person is saying. Listen carefully and think about what is being said. Think about what you would write down if you were taking notes.

Another technique that may require some practice is learning to pick out the main points and then jot down the details. An excellent way to practice this skill is to take notes on the evening news. The news provides an excellent vehicle for note-taking practice because it is set up like a group of short lectures. The newscaster typically begins with the headline or topic of the piece and then follows that with related details, facts, and examples. Each section is short, so you'll get lots of practice picking out the main points and then noting the details.

FRANK AND ERNEST reprinted by permission of NEA, Inc.

LEARN TO ABBREVIATE

Learning to use some abbreviations when you take notes can help you keep up with your professor. Don't get carried away with abbreviations, though. You want your notes to be readable and understandable when you are ready to review for your exam. Avoid using shorthand or shorthand methods that require you to transcribe or rewrite your notes after the lecture.

Do you use any abbreviations now? Check back through some of your notes and make a list of the abbreviations that you are already using. If you aren't already using some standard abbreviations when you take notes, refer to Figure 5.4 and choose about five to try this week. After you feel comfortable using these five abbreviations, you may want to add more. Remember, if you find yourself thinking about how to abbreviate a word instead of about the content of the lecture, you may be trying to learn too many new things at once.

HOW NOT TO TAKE NOTES

Sometimes students think they are using effective note-taking strategies when they really aren't. Recopying notes, using tape recorders, and taking notes on outlines, handouts, or textbook pages are not effective or efficient strategies.

1. Avoid rewriting your notes just to make them look neater. Recopying notes without elaborating on them or reorganizing them is usually a very passive activity.
2. Avoid taking notes on outlines that are provided by your professor. You generally don't have enough room on the outline sheet to note all of the important information. Instead, use the outline as a guide. Write the headings from the outline in your notes and then jot down as many of the details as you can.

Figure 5.4 Commonly Used Abbreviations

hour	hr	inch	"
year	yr	ft	'
therefore	∴	months	mo
equals	=	information	info
not equal	≠	water	H_2O
with	w	square	sq
without	w/o	company	co
example	ex	number	#
dollar	$	amount	amt
question	q	government	gov't
parallel	||	century	C
perpendicular	⊥	similar to	≈
chapter	ch	first	1st
second	2nd	plus (more)	+
more than	>	less than	<
period	pd	versus	vs
and	&	page	p
north	N	south	S
east	E	west	W
volume	vol	word	wd

3. Don't rely on handouts. Although some professors provide students with handouts of their notes, you should still take your own notes as you listen to the lecture.

4. Don't try to take notes in your textbook unless the lecturer follows the text faithfully. However, if your professor is discussing a play, poem, or even a novel and is constantly referring to specific lines and pages, you may want to follow along in your text and make notes in the margin. If you don't have enough room to record all of the pertinent information, indicate the line and page in your notebook and make the notes there instead.

5. Don't use tape recorders in class. Although tape recorders do make an accurate record of the information, students who tape lectures spend more than twice as much time taking notes as the student who takes notes during the

lecture, because they wait until after the class to play the tape and take notes. Instead of spending three hours in class each week, these students spend six hours or more. If you are just learning to take notes, you may want to use a tape recorder for a few weeks (no more) to help you fill in missing information or make corrections in your notes. If you decide to use this crutch (and it is a crutch), you must remember that you should take the best notes you can, and use the recording only to help you edit your notes.

EDIT YOUR NOTES AFTER THE LECTURE

Taking good lecture notes is only the first step in the note-taking process. After you leave the classroom, you need to edit your notes to correct errors, clarify meaning, make additions, and improve organization. Editing is a fairly easy process once you know how to do it. Early in the semester you may spend a lot of time making corrections or additions to your notes. You may need to reorganize your notes or rewrite them to make them readable. You'll soon benefit from these editing experiences, however, and your ability to take good notes will improve. You'll probably find that by the second half of the semester, you won't need to spend nearly as much time editing and can instead devote this time to more active review of your notes.

Edit your lecture notes within twenty-four hours after the lecture. If you wait much longer, you won't remember the lecture well enough to make any necessary additions or corrections in your notes. Look back at your Fixed Commitment Calendar, and set aside a certain time each day to edit your lecture notes. In as little as half an hour, you can turn "so so" notes into excellent notes.

FILL IN THE GAPS

The first thing you should do is read through your notes and fill in any missing information that you can recall from memory. As you read through your notes, the lecture will "come back" to you. You may be able to add a few words to further clarify a point, fill in additional details, or even add information that you didn't have time to record during the lecture.

You also can refer to your textbook to help fill in gaps in your notes. If you still feel your notes are incomplete, you may need to use a friend's notes to expand on the ones you took in class. If you taped the lecture, listen to the recording and fill in the information you weren't able to write down during the lecture.

CHECK FOR ACCURACY

As you go through your notes, you also need to check for accuracy. If you notice some incorrect information in your notes, or if you are unsure of the accuracy of some points, check with the professor or a friend, or use your textbook to verify whether the information is correct. If you find that some of your information is incorrect, change it. Some students lose points on exams because they have incorrect information in their notes. Even though they study for the exam, they still get questions wrong because they have been rehearsing inaccurate information.

CLARIFY MEANING

You may find that some of your notes are cryptic or hard to understand. In order to make your notes more readable and understandable, you may need to expand some abbreviations, finish some words, or correct spelling errors. If you use a lot of abbreviations or shortcuts in note taking, you should try to clarify some of them while you still know what words they represent. For example, if you wrote "priv" in your notes, you may want to add on "ileged" after class, because "priv" is not a common abbreviation and you may become confused as to what you meant when you review your notes at a later time. It's not necessary, however, to go back and add on the tail ends of all words that you shortened or abbreviated. For example, the abbreviations "w" or "w/" are commonly used to stand for "with," so there would be no need to write out the word.

REWRITE TO IMPROVE ORGANIZATION

You may need to rewrite your notes in order to improve the organization of the information. If you took notes on a lecture that was poorly organized, your notes may be disorganized, too. Even though they provide an accurate record of the information, you may find it difficult to study from them. By reorganizing the information in your notes, you can clarify the relationship between the main points and supporting details. You may need to add headings or make the headings that you have in your notes stand out. You can do that by writing the headings next to the margin and then indenting the subordinate points. You also may need to reorganize your notes in order to group related information together. If your professor tends to jump from point to point during the lecture, you may find that information on the same topic is scattered over several pages in your notes. As you rewrite your notes, group these points together under the appropriate heading. Reorganizing and editing your notes will make your notes more useful when you are ready to study for the exam.

Compare Nikki's original life science notes (Figure 5.5) to her revised notes (Figure 5.6). All of the information in script was added after the lecture. What changes

Figure 5.5 Nikki's Original Notes for Life Science

1/22

③ Decomposers
- do not have digestive tracts

Scavengers
- let something else kill organism
- bacteria that break down dead tissue

Waste Feeders
- feed on dung, feces, undigested food
- type of scavenger
- have digestive systems
- eat food

detritus - miscellaneous organic material passing by

Filter Feeders - pass water thru comb-like feeders
take things floating in water
may use

Cycling of materials vs Flow of Energy
Carbon, Oxygen,

do you see that improved the overall organization of the information? What other changes did Nikki make as she edited her notes?

Another way to organize your notes is by using concept maps, diagrams, charts, and matrixes to show the relationships between main points and supporting details. You may find that you can restructure some or all of the information from the lecture into a visual display that is easy to picture and recall for exams. Creating maps, diagrams, and charts is an active editing process. You will learn more about these strategies in later chapters, but if you think this is something you would like to try now, refer to Chapter 8 for some tips.

ADD RECALL WORDS

Adding recall words or questions in the margin also helps to increase the value of your notes. As you review your notes, try to condense each point into a key word or short phrase that will help you recall the information. The process of making up these recall words will force you to identify the most important aspect of each statement and condense the information down to its essence. The recall cues serve as prompts to your memory. Recall words have been added in the margin for the first half of the notes in Figure 5.7.

Figure 5.6 Nikki's Revised Notes for Life Science

	1/22
What are decomposers?	③ Decomposers – heterotrophs – get nourishment from other organisms – do not have digestive tracts
What are scavengers?	④ Scavengers – let something else kill organism – bacteria that break down dead tissue
What are waste feeders?	⑤ Waste feeders – feed on dung, feces, undigested food – type of scavenger – have digestive systems – eat food Ex: Egyptian scarab beetles
What is detritus?	detritus – miscellaneous organic material passing by – mixture of decaying organisms + dung w/ partially digested food Land – mixes w/soil – earthworms/soil insects eat – May float or settle on bottom
How do filter feeders eat?	⑥ Filter feeders – pass water thru comb-like feeders – take things floating in water – may use mouth parts, gills, special limbs
	Four types of consumers are decomposers/scavengers, waste feeders, and filter feeders. Detritus is a mixture of decaying organisms + dung along with partially digested food.

Figure 5.7 Sample Recall Words and Questions

	Piaget - Intellectual Development
	Development of Perception
1960s	Knowledge of infants limited - 60s no visual or hearing ability -
	difficult to test - infants do have percep abilities at birth - even
	prenatally can hear
	Vision
acuity at birth	visual acuity poor 20/600 at birth - see 20 ft what we see
	600 ft away
1 mo	1 mo 20/150 = someone w glasses
12 mo	12 mo 20/20
	abilities improve as does abil to use them newborns - only
focus	fixed focus 9" - same distance as mom to baby's eyes when
	fed - eye muscles weak- lack coordination = normal
abilities	Abilities at birth
sight	1. can see - follow bright light
What are their	2. have preferences - exper infant in seat - 2 panels - objects on each
preferences?	peep - experimenter watch infant's pupils - see obj in eye - now use TV
How did they	board camera to computer - Prefer complex pattern to simple -bk/w
test them?	checkerboard over red board - most preferred at 2 mo - simple
What is most	human face in born pref for human face - smile first
preferred?	
	Depth perception
Who first exper	Born w it? 1st to look at it - Gibson 50s studied in young animals
on depth percep?	ex: 18 mo old & wife Eleanor visit to Grand Canyon
What is the	Exper - Visual Cliff - plexiglass table - red/wh cloth - drape it under
Visual Cliff Exper?	table so half looks solid - looks like half drops off
	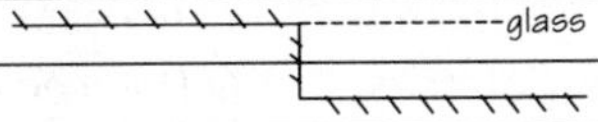 glass
When do infants	Infant will crawl on solid side not along clear (open) side - By time
devel depth percep?	they crawl or creep they perceive depth. Unsure if born w it.

ADD QUESTIONS IN THE MARGIN

You may prefer to add questions in the margin (rather than just recall words) when you edit your notes. Some students find that generating actual questions about the material helps them focus on the important information. They also find that they are able to review their notes more easily, because they can read the questions and then try to answer them. In some cases, questions can help you focus on specific aspects of the material better than cue words. Questions have been added to the recall column for the second half of the notes in Figure 5.7. You may also have noticed that Nikki's notes (Figure 5.6) also contain recall questions in the margin. Try using both recall words and questions with your own notes. Then you can decide which method works best for you.

REVIEW YOUR NOTES AFTER THE LECTURE

Reviewing your notes is the third step in the note-taking process. Even though editing your notes provides you with a review of the lecture material, daily, weekly, and pre-exam reviews are all important for helping you master the information in your notes and prepare for exams. After you edit your notes and complete the recall column, you are ready to review. You can't learn all of the information in your notes just by editing or reading over them. You also need to study the information in your notes using more active methods. How you review your notes often determines how much of the information you learn.

WHEN AND WHY SHOULD YOU REVIEW?

You need to review your lecture notes on a regular basis in order to retain the information in your memory. Even though you may have an accurate record of the information presented, you still need to learn it. The best time to review and edit your notes is immediately after the lecture, when the material is still fresh in your mind. You also can review your notes when you are waiting for your next class to begin. You also may want to set aside an hour or two each weekend to review the notes that you took in all of your classes during the week. If you have been reviewing daily, you will need only to test your memory (using the recall column) during your weekly review. Reviewing your notes frequently during the semester will keep you actively involved in the learning process and will reduce the amount of time you need to study before exams.

HOW SHOULD YOU REVIEW YOUR NOTES?

The best way to review your notes is to recite the information — to say it out loud. Just reading over your notes is a very passive activity. You may not really concentrate on the information at all. Reciting also helps because you may learn more by *hearing* information than just by seeing it. Use the recall columns that you created or the headings in your notes to test your memory of the information. This self-testing will let you know whether you really do know the information in your notes.

USE THE RECALL COLUMN

When you think that you know the information in your notes, use the recall cues to test your memory of the important points and supporting details. Put your hand or a piece of paper over your notes so that you can see only the recall words or questions. Then, recite the points that you made in your notes. If you can't say them out loud, you don't really know the material. Use this technique in order to review the information in your notes on a regular basis. You should perform this kind of active review immediately following the lecture, at the end of the week, and again before the exam.

USE HEADINGS

You also can review your notes by using the headings or topics to prompt your memory. After you review your notes by reciting them aloud, cover the information under each heading and try to recall all of the points relating to that topic. Try to explain or recite aloud all of the details you can remember about each of the main topics in your notes. Then check your notes to see if you missed anything. If you study in a place where you can't recite out loud, you can accomplish the same thing by mumbling quietly to yourself or by writing out the information from memory. Repeat this process until you know all of the information in your notes.

ACTIVITIES

1. A good set of notes should stand up to the test of time. Try the following exercise several times during the semester. Be sure to test the notes from each of your classes.

   Go back to the notes that you took yesterday in one of your classes and read them. Do they make sense to you? Do you feel as though you are sitting in the lecture and hearing your professor talk about the topic? Now go back to the notes that you took at the beginning of the semester. Do they still make sense? Do you feel as though you are sitting in the lecture and hearing your professor talk about the topic?

2. After the first exam, reread your lecture notes, looking for information that appeared on the exam. Did you find the answers to most of the questions that were on the exam? Did you find that the answers to many of the test questions were missing?

3. Take notes in one of your classes using the strategies presented in this chapter. Compare a set of notes that you took earlier in the semester to this new set of notes. What improvements or differences do you notice in the two sets of notes?

4. Choose a set of lecture notes that you took within the last twenty-four hours. Edit them, making any necessary changes or corrections. Also, write down any additional information that you remember. If you know that you are missing specific information, refer to your text or to someone else's notes in order to complete your notes. Finally, add recall words or questions in the margin and then review your notes. Write a short paragraph describing the changes that you made, the types of recall cues that you used, and the method of review that you found most effective.

POSTTEST

Where Are You Now?

Now that you have completed Chapter 5, take a few minutes to answer *yes* or *no* to the following questions. Compare your answers with those in the pretest.

	YES	NO
1. Do you review and edit your notes within twenty-four hours after each of your classes?	______	______
2. Do you tend to write down exactly what your professor says in class?	______	______
3. Do you separate the main points from supporting information in your notes?	______	______
4. Are you able to read and understand your notes when you study for your exam?	______	______
5. Do your notes include Roman numerals, capital and small letters, and numbers?	______	______
6. Do you tend to write down only important or key words when you take notes?	______	______
7. Do you review your notes by reciting them out loud?	______	______
8. Do you tend to miss a lot of information when you take notes?	______	______
9. Do you rely on a tape recorder instead of taking notes in some of your classes?	______	______
10. Do you read your textbook assignment before you go to your lecture class?	______	______

Give yourself one point for each *yes* answer to questions 1, 3, 4, 7, and 10, and one point for each *no* answer to questions 2, 5, 6, 8, and 9. Now total up your points. Compare your score on this posttest with the score that you had on the pretest. Did you improve? In which areas? Do you still need to improve more?

CHAPTER 6

Reading Your Textbook

"Although it takes more time than some of the other methods, the S-RUN method helped me with my sociology reading. With this method, I actually finished the reading instead of closing the book after reading only a few paragraphs. Along with underlining and taking notes in my own words, I created a recall column next to my notes. Taking notes helped me pay more attention to what I had read, and it (note taking) also helped me grasp the material better."

Michelle Podraza

YOU NEED A NEW APPROACH IN COLLEGE

Reading college textbooks is a different kind of reading from that that you did in high school. College textbooks are more "idea-dense" than most high school texts; that is, they contain many more facts and ideas per page. Not only is there much more information to learn, but also you may have much less time in which to read and learn it. You probably spent an entire school year covering only a part of your high school textbook; in college you may find that you are responsible for completing an entire text in only ten to fifteen weeks. In addition, college textbooks are written at a higher reading level than high school texts. They don't just seem

PRETEST

Where Are You Now?

Take a few minutes to answer *yes* or *no* to the following questions.

	YES	NO
1. Do you highlight or mark your textbook as you read?	______	______
2. Do you use a reading/study system when you read text material?	______	______
3. Do you preview a chapter before you begin to read it?	______	______
4. Do you usually try to read an entire chapter once you start?	______	______
5. Do you take notes as you read your textbook?	______	______
6. Do you tend to read your text chapters again before the exam?	______	______
7. Do you generally pause at the end of each paragraph or page to think about what you have read?	______	______
8. Do you use different strategies to read more difficult text assignments?	______	______
9. Do you often forget what you have read when you complete a reading assignment?	______	______
10. Do you "talk to" (interact with) the author of the text as you are reading your assignment?	______	______

Give yourself one point for each *yes* answer to questions 1, 2, 3, 5, 7, 8, and 10, and one point for each *no* answer to questions 4, 6, and 9. Now total up your points. A low score indicates that you need some help in text reading. A high score indicates that you are already using many good text reading strategies.

harder—they are. This may be one of the reasons many college students find that even though they read their textbooks, they don't understand what they read. By using a combination of time management techniques and comprehension-building strategies, you can improve your ability to read and understand your textbooks.

GENERAL STRATEGIES FOR READING COLLEGE TEXTS

You can use a number of general strategies to improve your ability to read and comprehend college textbooks. If you are already using some of them, you know that they do help. If some of the strategies are new to you, experiment to see if they are effective, too.

BUY YOUR TEXTBOOK EARLY

You can get a head start on your reading for the next semester if you buy your textbooks before you leave campus for semester break. Even if you purchase only one or two of your texts, you can read the first two or three chapters during semester break. While other students are madly trying to get all of their reading done during the first week or two of the new semester, you will be able to devote time to some of your other classes. Reading ahead also will give you additional time to study for quizzes and nail down some A's and B's during those first few weeks.

GET ACQUAINTED WITH YOUR TEXTBOOK

As soon as you buy your textbooks, take a good look at them. You can learn a lot about your course and your textbook just by thumbing through the text. A quick look at the table of contents will give you a good idea of the topics you will be discussing in the course. By looking at the headings in each chapter, you will get a general idea of how each chapter is organized. By reading the preface or the "notes to the student," you may learn a little about how the author designed the text or how some topics relate to others. The end of your text also includes important study aids. Check to see if there is an index, glossary, or answer key. Often, students don't know that the answers to chapter exercises or review tests are in the back of the text until the class is almost over.

You also should look through one of the chapters to see how the information is presented. Look to see how the main points are identified. Are they in bold print? Does the author provide an outline or introduction for each chapter? Look to see if there are any study aids in the text; they are designed to help you comprehend the material. Check to see if the chapter includes lists of key vocabulary words that you should master, questions or problems, or even a sample test to check your understanding of key concepts. These study aids will help you monitor your comprehension of the text material and your mastery of the main and supporting points.

READ TEN PAGES AT A TIME

Take a look at the chapters in some of your textbooks. You may be surprised by how long they are. Fifty-page chapters are standard for many texts. Reading fifty pages at one time may not seem like a difficult task. Keep in mind, however, that one page of a college textbook may contain as many words as three pages of a novel. Have you ever sat and read 150 pages of a novel at one time? Not only are there more words on the page, but also the text may be difficult to read and understand. If you find that your attention begins to wander or you just aren't grasping the information anymore, you should stop reading and continue later. Some students find it takes them much longer to read the second half of the chapter than the first, because as they get tired or lose interest, their reading rate begins to drop. Time yourself as you read one of your chapters. Note the time at the end of each ten-page section. Did you read the earlier sections more quickly?

Using good time management strategies can help you improve your textbook reading. Reading a chapter in chunks of ten pages or even five pages at one sitting may help you maintain a faster reading speed and still have excellent comprehension. You also may find that when you are working on only ten pages of text at one time, you feel more motivated to highlight, outline, or take notes as you read.

MONITOR YOUR COMPREHENSION

As you read your textbook, you should be aware not only of what you are reading but also of whether or not you understand what you are reading. You should pause frequently to reflect on what is being said. Too many students read their textbooks in a mechanical way. Their eyes see the words, but their minds are a million miles away. Comprehension monitoring will help you keep your mind on what you are reading. Comprehension monitoring refers to your own evaluation of whether or not you comprehend (understand) what you read. You can monitor your comprehension of the text material by stopping every so often (at the end of a paragraph, section, or page) and asking yourself what you just read and whether you understood it. The study systems that will be discussed in the next section of the chapter will help you monitor your comprehension and get more out of your reading.

USE A TEXT READING/STUDY SYSTEM

Dozens of reading/study systems have been developed to help students understand what they read. Because they are all very similar, we'll discuss only three of them in this chapter. After you learn how to use each system, try it out, and then choose the one that works best for you. You may find that you like some parts of one and other parts of another. Mix and match as you see fit. You also may find that one reading/study system works well with one of your texts, but a different one is more helpful for another text. Using the appropriate reading/study system will help you get more out of the time you spend reading your textbooks.

THE P2R SYSTEM

Many study skills instructors no longer teach students to use long, complicated reading/study systems. Even though these systems do work, too many of their students don't use them. Some students have trouble learning all of the various steps in the systems, and many others feel that they simply take too much time to use. You can get more out of the time you spend reading your textbook by using an easy, three-step approach. First, *preview* before you read. Next, *read actively* by marking the text or taking notes. Finally, *review* the important information after you have read it. If you would like an acronym for this system, why not call it the P2R system.

STEP 1: PREVIEW

You should always preview a chapter before you read it. Think of a time when you planned a trip to a place you had never visited before. Did you find out about weather conditions before you started out? Did you take a map or travel guide along with you? Reading a textbook without previewing the chapter first is like taking a trip to a place you have never been without getting directions or finding out anything about it beforehand. Your chances of getting to your destination are fair, but you're likely to get much less out of the trip than you otherwise might have. Previewing provides the guidance you need to read and understand your textbooks.

Previewing takes very little time and effort. Most students can preview a text chapter in two to five minutes. The first thing to do is read the title of the chapter. Then read the introduction, outline, or structured overview (a visual display of key information) at the beginning of the chapter. If your text does not begin with either an introduction, outline, or structured overview, read the first two paragraphs. As you turn the pages of the chapter, read the headings in bold print and glance at any pictures, tables, or graphs. Don't stop to read any of the text along the way. At the end of the chapter, read the summary or the last two paragraphs. If your text contains an extensive summary (a page or more in length), you may want to read only the first and last sentence of each of the paragraphs in the summary. If you're reading a journal article or other short selection, you may find it helpful to read the first sentence of each paragraph or every other paragraph.

Previewing the chapter gives you some background about unfamiliar topics. By reading the introduction, the headings, and the summary, you pick up some general information on what the chapter is about. You also gain a little understanding of how the information is organized and presented. Both of these kinds of information can help you understand the text material better. Previewing before reading may increase your comprehension of the textbook chapter by 10 to 20 percent.

STEP 2: READ ACTIVELY

Step 2 of the P2R system is read actively. This is also the time to mark your text as you read. In recent years there has been a great deal of discussion about the value of marking your textbook as you read. One view suggests that marking your textbook is a way to avoid learning the material as you read it. In some ways this is true. However, if you have already started college, you probably realize that you just don't have time to learn the material *well* the first time you read. Highlighting or note taking allows you to keep up with your class assignments and at the same time identify and mark that material that you will need to study further.

After previewing, read and mark the first ten-page chunk or even the entire chapter. One method of marking is to highlight the text with a highlighter pen. After you have read a paragraph of text, pause to think about what you have read. Go back and use a highlighter to mark any material that you think you will want to review again before the exam. By highlighting the text, you are actively involved in thinking about the material, and you are condensing what you will need to review at a later time. Chapter 7 includes much more information on how to highlight.

Another method of text marking is note taking. Taking notes on a text is a lot like taking notes on lectures. Although taking notes is rather time-consuming, it is the best method of "marking" your textbook. More information on how to take text notes is included in Chapter 8.

Many students are familiar with outlining text material. You probably did some outlining in junior or senior high school. If you find that outlining helps you read and understand your textbook, go ahead and use this strategy. Make each heading a main point in your outline, and be sure to include some details from the material under each heading. Watch out for one-word outlines, though—they don't provide enough information for later review. Outlining also will be described in more detail in Chapter 8.

The main reason for marking your text is to condense the text material so you never have to read the entire chapter again. Some students are responsible for more than two thousand pages of text material during a semester. It certainly is not unusual to have three hundred pages of text to review for just one exam. Think about how long it would take to reread all of this. And, remember, rereading the text does not ensure mastery of the material. You still have to *learn* the material for the exam. In addition, text marking (highlighting, note taking, or outlining) helps improve your ability to concentrate as you read and increases your comprehension.

STEP 3: REVIEW

After you complete a ten-page chunk of reading or a whole chapter, you need to review the important information. There are a number of ways that you can review the text material, but here are four of the most common ones. First, you may want to summarize the key points that the author made. Try to write three or four statements that you think summarize the key points made in the reading selection. Second, you can recite the information. Using the headings as a guide, cover the page of text and try to recite the key information under each heading. You also may want to recite from notes that you wrote in the book or from those that you took on paper. Third, you can do the test at the end of the chapter or do some of the activities in the study guide if one is available for your text. Finally, you can review your text chapter by predicting and answering questions that may appear on a quiz or test.

Don't try to use all of these strategies at the same time. Test them as you read assignments in several of your courses. Then choose the one that works best for you.

THE SQ3R READING/STUDY METHOD

SQ3R, developed by Francis Robinson in 1941, is one of the most widely taught reading/study systems. Many students learn how to use SQ3R in junior high school, in senior high school, or even in college. Have you ever been taught how to use SQ3R? Did you ever use it? SQ3R is an acronym for *S*urvey, *Q*uestion, *R*ead, *R*ecite, and *R*eview. By using these five steps when you read your college textbooks, you can overcome many of the difficulties you may encounter when dealing with hard-to-read and hard-to-understand material.

A number of the steps in the SQ3R system are similar to those in P2R. The main difference is that the steps are performed on each "headed" section rather than on ten-page chunks of text or on whole chapters. As you will see, this difference makes SQ3R a more time-consuming system. You may therefore want to save SQ3R for your most difficult textbooks. Although it does take a lot of time, many students have found that it is very effective. By using the five steps in the SQ3R system, you will become a second participant in the communication process that the author of the text has begun.[1]

STEP 1: SURVEY

Survey the chapter before you read it. Go through the chapter quickly, glance at the headings, and then read the final paragraph of the chapter in order to get a general idea of what the chapter is about and the main points that the author is making.

STEP 2: QUESTION

Before you begin to read the first section in your chapter, turn the heading of the first section into a question. Then read to answer the question that you generated. How would you change the heading "Ego Defense Mechanisms" into a question? Actually, you could generate a number of different questions. One of the most typical (though not necessarily the best) would be "What are Ego Defense Mechanisms?" Formulating questions forces you to think about what you are about to read; it makes you try to predict what the author's main point will be.

STEP 3: READ

Read the text material under the heading in order to find the answer to the question that you generated. Turning the heading into a question helps you focus your reading. Reading the section to locate the answer to your question helps you get actively involved in the text material. Read the following text selection to find the answer to the question "What are Ego Defense Mechanisms?" (or whatever question you formulated in Step 2). As you read the selection, check to see if you find the answer to your question.

Ego Defense Mechanisms

Defense mechanisms are *unconscious* ego processes that keep disturbing and unacceptable impulses from being directly expressed. In learning about defense mechanisms, it is helpful to examine them separately. Bear in mind, though, that people rarely defend themselves against anxiety with a single mechanism; typically, defense mechanisms operate in combination. Further, as will become apparent, there is considerable overlap in the way defense mechanisms protect the ego from overwhelming anxiety. Finally, anxiety is used here to designate the subjective discomfort people experience whenever

---

[1]The discussion of the five steps in the SQ3R system that follows was adapted from Robinson, F., *Effective Study*, 4th ed. (New York: Harper & Row, 1970), pp. 32–36.

they feel threatened. This includes many negative emotions, such as anger and rage, guilt and shame (moral anxiety), grief, jealousy, and envy.[2]

STEP 4: RECITE

At the end of the first headed section, recite the answer to the question that you formulated. Recite it in your own words, without looking at the text. If you find that you are unable to recall a part or all of the answer, glance over the section again. Then jot down a brief answer in outline form on a piece of paper. Don't make any notes until you have read the entire section.

STEP 5: REVIEW

After you have finished reading the entire chapter, look over the notes that you made to again familiarize yourself with the important information in the chapter. Check your memory by covering your notes and reciting the main points out loud. Then cover each main point in your notes and try to recite the subordinate points that you noted, until you have reviewed each headed section. This review should take only about five minutes.

ADVANTAGES OF SQ3R

One advantage of the SQ3R study system is that it sets the stage for a great deal of interaction with the text material. As you go through the five steps, you are surveying the chapter to gain information about the topics presented, formulating questions about the material, reading to find the answers, reciting important information aloud, and, finally, reviewing again what you have read. By focusing on each headed unit and going through all of the steps, you are breaking the task of reading an entire textbook chapter down into smaller units. If you have difficulty reading even ten pages of text at one time, you may find SQ3R to be very helpful. Most students who use the five steps in the SQ3R system do report a greater understanding of the text material than they had before.

One of the greatest advantages of using the SQ3R system is that it allows for a great deal of repetition of the important information in the chapter. As you will see later in this text, repetition is one of the key ingredients in learning. By going through all of the steps in the SQ3R system, you are repeating the key information in the chapter at least three or four times.

---

[2]Text material from Liebert, R., and Spiegler, M., *Personality: Strategies and Issues*, 6th ed. (Pacific Grove, CA: Brooks/Cole, 1990), p. 99. Used with permission.

Another advantage of SQ3R is that it has a built-in comprehension monitoring system. When you stop to recite the answer to a question that you formulated, you are testing your understanding of the material that you read. This step in the SQ3R process keeps you on track as you read. Knowing that you must be accountable for what you have read can prevent the passive reading that so often characterizes text reading.

DISADVANTAGES OF SQ3R

Unfortunately, there are a number of disadvantages associated with the use of the SQ3R reading/study system. Using all the steps in the SQ3R system can be very time-consuming when used with college textbooks. For example, I counted forty-seven headed sections in one chapter of a typical introductory psychology textbook. For most college students, the thought of going through the five-step process forty-seven times is enough to make them decide not to use SQ3R.

Another problem with SQ3R is that students too often formulate narrow questions or poor questions during the questioning step. In college texts, it is not unusual to find a number of main points discussed under one heading. If you simply ask "What is the . . ." type of question, you may be ignoring a great deal of important information. For example, the question, "What are Ego Defense Mechanisms?" would have led only to the review of the definition, "Defense mechanisms are *unconscious* ego processes that keep disturbing and unacceptable impulses from being directly expressed." A number of other important points would have been overlooked. When you are using the SQ3R system, you need to formulate additional questions as you read the section so that you don't limit your reading.

Why, then, should college students be taught to use SQ3R? First of all, SQ3R is an effective tool that can be used by many college students to aid comprehension of text material. Second, many of the disadvantages can be eliminated by modifying SQ3R to make it more appealing.

ADAPTING SQ3R

There are a number of ways that you can adapt or modify SQ3R to make it more effective and easy to use. First of all, you don't have to use SQ3R for all of your reading assignments. Many students use SQ3R or a variation of it only for reading their most difficult textbooks. You may not need to use SQ3R with your easy textbooks, but you may find that it helps improve your comprehension when you use it with your hard-to-understand texts.

Another change that you can make is to select the steps that you find helpful and omit the others. Some students do only the survey, read, and recite steps. They find that by eliminating the question and review steps, they reduce the time it takes to read the text material but still improve their comprehension of it. Others use only the question and read steps. You need to determine which, if any, of these steps are effective for you. Even though eliminating some of the steps may reduce the overall effectiveness of using SQ3R, doing some of the steps is still better than doing nothing.

Another modification that you may want to consider involves reciting. Rather than just reciting the answer to the question that you formulated from the heading, you may want to cover the section of text and try to recite all of the important information that it contained. Look back at the section entitled "Ego Defense Mechanisms." Which information would you recite from the selection? Perhaps you would choose some of the following: (1) Defense mechanisms are unconscious ego processes that keep disturbing and unacceptable impulses from being directly expressed; (2) Typically, defense mechanisms operate in combination; (3) Anxiety refers to the subjective discomfort people experience whenever they feel threatened; (4) Anxiety includes anger and rage, guilt and shame, grief, jealousy, and envy. It's not necessary to recite everything that's in the section; focus on the information that you think you will need to know or that you are having difficulty understanding. You don't have to recite word for word what's in the text; sometimes it helps you understand the material more if you try to put the information into your own words.

Again, if you have decided that SQ3R takes more time than you are willing to spend on it, underline or highlight the important information rather than writing it out. This will save you a great deal of time and may be just as helpful when you are ready to prepare for your exam. You may also decide to save the review step for later. You can review the important information at the end of each week or wait until before the exam. By modifying the way you use SQ3R, you can still make it an effective and an efficient study tool, especially for reading very difficult textbooks.

THE S-RUN READING SYSTEM

The SQ3R system has been adapted by many reading and study skills educators. Because of its simplicity, one variation that may be very useful for college students is the S-RUN (*S*urvey, *R*ead, *U*nderline, *N*otetaking) reading method designed by Nancy Bailey.[3] Bailey's students were reluctant to use SQ3R because it seemed like

---

[3]Bailey, N., "S-RUN: Beyond SQ3R," *Journal of Reading* 32 (1988): 170.

too much work. However, they used S-RUN with great success. Try it and see if it works for you, too.

First, survey the chapter by looking at the title, introduction, pictures, charts, graphs, headings, subheadings, italicized words, summaries, and the end-of-chapter questions. As in SQ3R, this survey provides a quick overview of the chapter. Before reading the first headed section, write the heading on a piece of notebook paper. Then read the section. Underline (or highlight) the key ideas that directly explain the section's heading. Finally, take notes after reading and underlining the section. Briefly summarize the underlined information under the previously written heading. Continue reading, underlining, and note taking for each remaining headed section.

You may have noticed that S-RUN is similar to the P2R method that was introduced earlier in the chapter. The main difference, however, is that the S-RUN system helps you focus on one headed section at a time. Therefore, like SQ3R, S-RUN should be used on more difficult text material.

ACTIVITIES

1. As you read your next text assignment, put a check mark in the margin every time you stop to think about what you have read and whether or not you understood it. After you complete the reading assignment, look at the placement of your check marks. Do they occur within paragraphs, mainly at the end of paragraphs, or at the end of the page?
2. Select a chapter in one of your textbooks and time yourself as you read the chapter. Then select another chapter. This time, preview the chapter and then read it. Which chapter took more total reading time? Did you notice any difference in your level of comprehension?
3. Use the SQ3R system to read the first five or ten pages of two of your text assignments. Choose one textbook that you find rather easy to read and another that you find the most difficult. Did you notice any difference between using SQ3R on the easy text and the difficult text?
4. As you read your text assignments during the next week, experiment with the various reading/study systems that were described in this chapter. Begin each assignment with the easiest system (P2R) and proceed to use more complex systems (SQ3R or S-RUN) if you find that you are not able to understand and/or remember the material. Which system did you find the most helpful?

POSTTEST

Where Are You Now?

Now that you have completed Chapter 6, take a few minutes to answer *yes* or *no* to the following questions. Compare your answers with those in the pretest.

	YES	NO
1. Do you highlight or mark your textbook as you read?	______	______
2. Do you use a reading/study system when you read text material?	______	______
3. Do you preview a chapter before you begin to read it?	______	______
4. Do you usually try to read an entire chapter once you start?	______	______
5. Do you take notes as you read your textbook?	______	______
6. Do you tend to read your text chapters again before the exam?	______	______
7. Do you generally pause at the end of each paragraph or page to think about what you have read?	______	______
8. Do you use different strategies to read more difficult text assignments?	______	______
9. Do you often forget what you have read when you complete a reading assignment?	______	______
10. Do you "talk to" (interact with) the author of the text as you are reading your assignment?	______	______

Give yourself one point for each *yes* answer to questions 1, 2, 3, 5, 7, 8, and 10, and one point for each *no* answer to questions 4, 6, and 9. Now total up your points. Compare your score on this posttest with the score that you had on the pretest. Did you improve? In which areas? Where do you still need to improve?

CHAPTER 7

Marking Your Textbook

"Text marking helps me the most when reading. It keeps me alert and involved in my reading. I have to pick out the main ideas in the text, so I pay attention more. I've also noticed that when I highlight, the reading isn't boring and doesn't take as long. Also, when I'm reviewing, I can spend my time focusing more on the main points instead of rereading the whole chapter."

Suzette Pavlo

IS IT WORTH YOUR TIME?

You probably know some students whose textbooks look as new at the end of a course as they did at the beginning. Have you ever wondered why? One explanation is that those students believe text marking is a waste of time. They may have heard that if you mark your text, you're just putting off learning the information. (Sometimes, though, this reasoning provides a convenient excuse not to mark.) Other students don't mark their texts because they want to sell them at the end of the semester; they think marked textbooks are less valuable at the resale table. Textbook buyers don't really care if books are marked. But you should! You may end up getting a lower grade in your class just on the chance of getting a few dollars more when you resell your book. Somehow that doesn't make much sense.

PRETEST

Where Are You Now?

Take a few minutes to answer *yes* or *no* to the following questions.

	YES	NO
1. Do you highlight or mark your textbook as you read?	______	______
2. Do you find that you often get to the end of a page and have no idea what you just read?	______	______
3. Do you begin to highlight or underline an important point before you finish the sentence?	______	______
4. Do you evaluate your text marking after an exam?	______	______
5. Does your marking make sense when you read it again before the exam?	______	______
6. Do you re-highlight or re-mark your text when you review for an exam?	______	______
7. Do you mark the headings and subheadings in your text?	______	______
8. Do you make notes in the margin when you read your text?	______	______
9. Do you tend to mark key words rather than phrases or entire sentences?	______	______
10. Do you ever reread the unmarked sections of your text before an exam?	______	______

Give yourself one point for each *yes* answer to questions 1, 4, 5, 6, 7, and 8, and one point for each *no* answer to questions 2, 3, 9, and 10. Now total up your points. A low score indicates that you need some help in text marking. A high score indicates that you are already using many good text marking strategies.

Some students who know text marking can be a valuable tool try to mark their books but give up because they don't quite know how to do it. In this chapter we'll discuss many strategies that can make text marking an easy and effective study technique.

WHY SHOULD YOU MARK YOUR TEXT?

Marking your textbook is a useful activity for several reasons. First, text marking promotes active reading. By now you probably have noticed that you're more actively involved in your lectures because you're taking lecture notes. By marking your textbooks as you read, you can achieve that same level of concentration and activity. Knowing that you should mark specific sections as you read helps keep you alert. It gives you a purpose for reading. Instead of daydreaming or thinking about something else you have to do, you're forced to concentrate on what you're reading. In order to mark your text effectively, you have to think about the content of the chapter. You constantly need to make decisions about what is important and what isn't. You may find that your reading takes on a whole new dimension when you mark your text. Text marking also provides you with feedback as to whether you did pay careful attention as you read a particular section of your text. If everything is marked, you know you really weren't making decisions about the importance of the material. If nothing is marked, you know you should check your understanding of the material to be sure your mind wasn't somewhere else when you read the section.

Text marking is also important because it condenses the text material for later review. Most students who don't mark their books don't go back and study the text before an exam. With four or more chapters to review for an exam, they don't even know where to start if their text is unmarked. They rely only on their lecture notes. Because most professors also test on text material, these students are at a decided disadvantage at exam time. By marking, you can reduce the amount of text material so that you can review the important text material as well as your lecture notes for the exam.

Text marking also improves your comprehension of the text material. Identifying and marking the main points and then looking for supporting details helps you understand the text. If you highlight or underline these same points after you've read the paragraph, you get a chance to read the information a second time. Have you noticed that your eyes follow your marker or pencil as you move it across the text? This second reading helps reinforce the key information. As you make notes or write questions in the margin, you further clarify the important information.

HOW SHOULD YOU MARK YOUR TEXT?

There are many methods for marking a textbook, but the two most common ones are underlining and highlighting. However, text marking involves more than just highlighting or underlining. The first step in effective marking is to read and think about the text material. Deciding what to mark and how to mark it are equally important. You can become an expert at text marking in a short time by just applying each of the following steps to your own text reading assignments.

READ, THINK, DECIDE, AND MARK

It's important to read an entire paragraph or headed section before you begin to mark your textbook. After you read a section, you need to decide what is important. Then you can begin to mark. Many students really don't know how to mark a textbook, so as soon as they read something that looks as though it might be important, they start to mark. If you mark part of a sentence before you even finish reading it, you're actually interfering with your comprehension of the material. Until you get the hang of marking, try to read at least to the end of the sentence before you begin to mark. Work up to two sentences, then to the end of the paragraph, and finally to the entire headed section.

MARK MEANINGFUL PHRASES

When you do identify information in your text that you think is important, you should try to mark meaningful phrases rather than just key words or entire sentences. Marking only the buzzwords really doesn't provide you with enough information from which to study. On the other hand, marking entire sentences doesn't force you to be selective about what is most important in the paragraph. Look for the main point, and then mark it along with any supporting details. Mark enough of the sentence so that one month later it will still make sense.

WHAT SHOULD YOU MARK?

Now that you know how to mark, the next step is figuring out what you should mark. As you read your text assignments, you may catch yourself thinking, "I wonder if I should mark this?" Until you become more experienced at marking, it's better to mark a little too much rather than not enough. Remember the rule of thumb from note taking: When in doubt, write it out. The same approach applies to text marking. You also may want to follow a general rule for text marking: If you think it might be on the test, mark it. Of course, after the first test, you'll be able to evaluate your marking and make a more accurate decision about what to mark in the next chapter.

There is no real set of rules for what you should mark. Some students mark only what the author puts in bold print or italics. This information is important and should be marked, but it is not the only important information on the page. Headings, main ideas, supporting details, definitions, examples, and statistics are also important, even though they are not always identified by bold print or italics.

MARK HEADINGS

As you read your textbook, mark the headings and subheadings. If you're highlighting, highlight them. If you're underlining, you may want to draw a box around the headings. Typically, when students review their marked textbooks, they read only what they have marked. It is incredible, but many students never even look at the headings or subheadings as they review. The headings contain the most important information in the text. They present the topics to which all of the other marking refers. You wouldn't think of reviewing your lecture notes without looking at the headings, would you?

MARK MAIN IDEAS

The second most important information to mark is the main idea statements. Main ideas are the general statements that the author makes about the topic. Where are these main idea statements usually found? If you think they are usually at the beginning of the paragraph, you're right. Main idea statements, or topic sentences, are generally found in the first or second sentence. Unfortunately, many students overlook these statements because they don't contain a specific fact or buzzword. You will find that it doesn't take much practice to learn to pick out the main idea statements in most of your textbooks.

FOCUS ON SUPPORTING MATERIAL

As you read and mark, you also should focus on definitions, examples, enumerations, facts and statistics, and signal words. Definitions are very important, and you will need to understand what the technical terms in the chapter mean both to comprehend the text material and to answer test questions. You can highlight definitions as you read, or you may want to copy them onto index cards so that you can begin to learn them. If you do, put the word on the front and the definition on the back, and then practice them out loud as you would with flash cards.

Examples are included in many textbooks because they help you understand abstract theories or concepts by bringing them down to a more concrete level. Examples are sometimes rather long and detailed or are set off in small print or in boxes, so students often view them as extraneous (outside or unrelated) information. However, examples can be critical to your understanding of the more abstract information in the text. You don't have to mark every word in the example; instead, mark just enough to see the connection between the example and the information to which it refers.

Lists or enumerations should always be marked. They may span several paragraphs or even several pages, but a main idea sentence will let you know what you should look for in a list. For example, the main idea sentence may state that there were three main adaptations that the vertebrates made. As you read, you should look for these adaptations so that you can mark all three.

Facts and statistics also are worth marking, because they typically support the main ideas that the author is making and often end up on tests. Finally, it's important to mark signal words like *however, on the other hand,* and *but.* These signal words or transitions indicate that the author has shifted direction from positive to negative points. Leaving them out can result in misinterpretations during later review.

DON'T OVERLOOK "EXTERNAL" TEXT MATERIAL

Don't overlook information that is presented outside the regular body of the text. Some textbooks are designed with all of the definitions of technical terms in the left-hand margin. This placement allows students to read and understand the definitions of difficult terminology before they read the text material that includes those terms. Because the definitions are set off from the body of the text, many students think they are unimportant. In the same way, some students ignore information that is contained in charts and graphs or written underneath photos or illustrations. This information, as well as information contained in footnotes and appendices (especially when assigned), is important in understanding the text material and may be on the test. Information in these "external" parts of the textbook must be marked just like any other text material.

HOW MUCH SHOULD YOU MARK?

Now that you have a good idea of what to mark, it's important to discuss how much you should mark. It may sound as though you'll need to mark everything on the page, but don't panic. Even when you mark all of the important information in a section, you'll still be able to condense the material. Learning to mark the right amount of text material is critical to effective marking. You should mark enough information so that you'll be able to review for an exam without ever reading any of the unmarked text again. On the other hand, you shouldn't mark so much that you're just wasting your time.

DON'T MARK TOO LITTLE

Sometimes students don't really understand how to mark a textbook, and they end up marking too little of the information. At the time, it may seem like marking only the important buzzwords in the text is effective marking. However, without marking any information about these words, the marking lacks meaning during later review. Look at the example below. Only the key words have been marked. Read only the underlined information. Does this marking make sense? Has this student marked all of the important information in the selection?

> During Paleozoic times, an early continent called **Gondwana** drifted southward from the tropics, across the south polar region, then northward. Other drifting land masses collided to form a tropical continent that is now called **Laurasia**. Then, near the end of the Paleozoic, Gondwana and Laurasia became massed together to form a single world continent, called **Pangea**, that extended from pole to pole. An immense world ocean covered the rest of the earth's surface; to the east of Pangea, it curved around to form the equivalent of a giant tropical bay, called the **Tethys Sea**. Pangea began to break up in the Mesozoic, and the drifting and collisions of the fragmented land masses continue today.[1]

DON'T MARK TOO SELECTIVELY

Another type of undermarking results from marking too selectively. Some students do mark meaningful phrases or sentences when they mark. They miss important information, however, by trying to pick out only one or two important points in each section of the text. These students may be trying to follow rules for how much to mark; they may have heard or read that you should mark only one main point in each paragraph or that you shouldn't mark more than 20 percent of the words on a page. These rules may have been intended as guides to help students learn to mark effectively (to reduce overmarking), but they should not be used as guidelines for how much or how little to mark. In the following example, the student marked only two pieces of information in the paragraph. Are these the only things you would have marked?

> During Paleozoic times, an early continent called **Gondwana** drifted southward from the tropics, across the south polar region, then northward. Other drifting land masses collided to form a tropical continent that is now called

[1]Text material from Starr, C., and Taggart, R., *Biology: The Unity and Diversity of Life*, 5th ed. (Belmont, CA: Wadsworth, 1989), p. 578. Used with permission.

Laurasia. Then, near the end of the Paleozoic, Gondwana and Laurasia became massed together to form a single world continent, called **Pangea**, that extended from pole to pole. An immense world ocean covered the rest of the earth's surface; to the east of Pangea, it curved around to form the equivalent of a giant tropical bay, called the **Tethys Sea**. Pangea began to break up in the Mesozoic, and the drifting and collisions of the fragmented land masses continue today.

DON'T MARK TOO MUCH

Overmarking can be just as detrimental as undermarking. Students who mark everything on a page are not forcing themselves to think about the content of the material. They haven't made any decisions about what is important and what isn't. Many times, overmarking is a signal that you're not reading actively. Marking too much also reduces your chances of reviewing the text material before the exam. If you have not condensed the text, you may be discouraged from reviewing it because there is just too much to reread.

WHAT SYSTEM SHOULD YOU USE?

There are at least as many systems or methods for marking your text as there are for taking notes. After you try some of them, decide which one works best for you. Choose a system that will help increase your understanding of the text as you read and also effectively condense the information for later review. This section describes three simple systems (or methods) for marking your text. You may want to try all three or develop one of your own. In addition, we'll consider several more complex systems. You may find that they are not as effective as they appear to be. If you're currently using one of these complex systems, you may want to re-evaluate its effectiveness.

HIGHLIGHTING

Highlighting the text as you read is probably the most efficient method of text marking. Because it takes so little extra time, more students are willing to do it. Highlighting does promote active reading, condense the information, and help improve your comprehension of the text material. It is a very practical method to use.

If you decide to use highlighting to mark your textbooks, use a very soft shade like yellow or pastel pink. Although fluorescent markers do make the text material stand out, they also cause eye strain when you go back to reread your marking. Also, be sure that as you mark the text material, you drag your highlighter across the printed words from left to right; in this way you'll be able to reread the sentence or phrase as you mark it. This second reading helps improve your comprehension and memory of the material. If you sweep backward across the line, you won't benefit from a second reading.

UNDERLINING

Underlining is similar to highlighting. Some students use a highlighter to underline important text material rather than dragging the highlighter across the words. Others use a pen or pencil. If you do decide to underline your text, don't use a ruler or straight edge to keep your lines straight—it will really slow you down.

PENCIL CODING

Some students don't like to mark up their texts. Are you one of them? If so, you can effectively mark the important information in your text and still have a "clean look" to the page. Instead of highlighting or underlining the information that you think is important, try pencil coding, a method that uses a combination of arrows and straight lines to designate important information. For instance, use a curved or horizontal arrow in the margin to indicate that something is marked in that line. Then use a caret (∧) within the line to indicate where the marking begins, and a vertical line (|) to mark where it ends. To mark from the beginning of a paragraph, draw a vertical arrow pointing down in the margin. Figure 7.1 shows a paragraph from a text selection on oceans that has been marked using the pencil coding method.

The first arrow in the margin indicates that the marking begins somewhere in that line, and the caret indicates that the marking begins with the word *Earth*. The straight line after *planet* (on the next line) shows the end of the marking. The second arrow and caret show that the next marking begins with the word *oceans*, and the straight line indicates that that marking ends after the word *surface*. What is marked by the third and fourth arrows? As you can see, the last arrow is a straight arrow that points down. That means that the marking begins at the beginning of the paragraph. The straight line indicates that it ends after the word *animals*.

Pencil coding does promote active reading, condense the text, and prepare your text for later review. On the other hand, pencil coding often leads to marking full sentences or even entire paragraphs. Also, unless your markings are fairly dark,

Figure 7.1 Example of Pencil Coding

Why Are the Oceans Important?

As landlubbers, we tend to think of Earth in terms of land, but Earth is largely a water planet. A more accurate name for the planet would be Ocean, because oceans cover more than 70 percent of its surface.

The oceans play key roles in the survival of virtually all life on Earth. Because of their size and currents, the oceans mix and dilute many human-produced wastes flowing or dumped into them to less harmful or even harmless levels, as long as they are not overloaded. Oceans also play a major role in regulating Earth's climate by distributing solar heat through ocean currents and by evaporation as part of the global hydrologic cycle. They also participate in other important biogeochemical cycles.

By serving as a gigantic reservoir for carbon dioxide, oceans help regulate the temperature of the troposphere through the greenhouse effect. Oceans provide habitats for about 250,000 species of marine plants and animals, which are food for many organisms, including human beings. They also serve as a source of iron, sand, gravel, phosphates, magnesium, oil, natural gas, and many other valuable resources.[2]

they may be overlooked when you review. Pencil coding probably is not as effective as highlighting or underlining; however, it certainly is better than not marking at all. If you don't like a "messy" book, give pencil coding a try.

MARGINAL NOTES

As you mark, you also may want to add some notes or questions in the margin of the text. These notes can be similar to the recall words or questions that you made when you edited your lecture notes, or they can summarize information presented in the selection. At times, you may even want to make notes to indicate that you agree or disagree with a point that the author has made. You could put a question mark in the margin to indicate that you don't understand something or would like to ask about it in class, or you could use a star to indicate that the professor hinted that something would be on the test. Making brief notes in the margin will help increase your level of interaction with the author as you read the text. Don't overdo

[2]Text material from Miller, G., *Living in the Environment*, 7th ed. (Belmont, CA: Wadsworth, 1989), p. 131. Used with permission.

Figure 7.2 Highlighted Text with Marginal Notes

Marginal notes	Text
	Why Are the Oceans Important?
Earth = "Ocean"	As landlubbers, we tend to think of Earth in terms of land, but Earth is largely a water planet. A more accurate name for the planet would be Ocean, because oceans cover more than 70 percent of its surface.
"O" → survival of all life 1. dilute waste 2. regulate climate	The oceans play key roles in the survival of virtually all life on Earth. Because of their size and currents, the oceans mix and dilute many human-produced wastes flowing or dumped into them to less harmful or even harmless levels, as long as they are not overloaded. Oceans also play a major role in regulating Earth's climate by distributing solar heat through ocean currents and by evaporation as part of the global hydrologic cycle. They also participate in other important biogeochemical cycles.
3. regulate temp 4. habitat ≈ 250,000 species 5. source nat. resources	By serving as a gigantic reservoir for carbon dioxide, oceans help regulate the temperature of the troposphere through the greenhouse effect. Oceans provide habitats for about 250,000 species of marine plants and animals, which are food for many organisms, including human beings. They also serve as a source of iron, sand, gravel, phosphates, magnesium, oil, natural gas, and many other valuable resources.

it, however. If you try to copy all of the important information in the margin, you're defeating the purpose of marking. The marginal notes in Figure 7.2 summarize the main points made in the selection. (You also could use recall words or questions in the margin.) Try adding a few marginal notes to some of the material you have marked recently. Do the notes make it easier for you to review the material?

AVOID COMPLEX MARKING SYSTEMS

Learning to mark your textbook is not that difficult. However, some students make text marking more complicated than it needs to be. They use complex marking systems that lead to ineffective and inefficient marking. Have you ever seen a beautifully marked textbook? If this question made you think of one with three or four different colors of highlighting, you know exactly what I mean. During a workshop several years ago, I asked students to mark a text selection. One student immediately pulled out five different colored markers and began to read and mark the selection. It took this student four times as long as everyone else in the room to mark the selection. At the end of the session, I asked the student about her marking system. She explained that she used one color for main ideas, one color for key words, another for definitions, a fourth shade for examples, and a fifth for supporting details.

Although this type of system does force you to think about how to mark the text material, it actually can interfere with comprehension. If you spend too much time thinking about whether something is a main idea, a supporting detail, a definition, an example, or a key word, you may not be thinking much about the content of the selection. Thinking about what color you should use also distracts you from concentrating on the material itself. Many students who use multicolored highlighting systems get caught up in the system at the expense of concentrating on the text material.

A number of other complex marking systems recommend using single lines, double lines, wavy lines, boxes, circles, curved brackets, square brackets, asterisks, numbers, and other similar marking symbols. These complex systems, like the multicolored ones, are very time-consuming and often lead to overmarking. Look at the example in Figure 7.3, which incorporates some of the above methods. Do you think the marking is more effective than the highlighted or pencil coded version? Which would you rather use? Using one or two of these symbols to designate specialized information can be very effective when marking text material.

Figure 7.3 Example of Complex Marking

Why Are the Oceans Important?

As landlubbers, we tend to think of Earth in terms of land, but Earth is largely a water planet. A more accurate name for the planet would be Ocean, because oceans cover more than 70 percent of its surface.

The oceans play key roles in the survival of virtually all life on Earth. Because of their size and currents, the oceans mix and dilute many human-produced wastes flowing or dumped into them to less harmful or even harmless levels, as long as they are not overloaded. Oceans also play a major role in regulating Earth's climate by ① distributing solar heat through ocean currents and ② by evaporation as part of the global hydrologic cycle. They also ③ participate in other important biogeochemical cycles.

① By serving as a gigantic reservoir for carbon dioxide, oceans help regulate the temperature of the troposphere through the greenhouse effect. ② Oceans provide habitats for about 250,000 species of marine plants and animals, which are food for many organisms, including human beings. ③ They also serve as a source of iron, sand, gravel, phosphates, magnesium, oil, natural gas, and many other valuable resources.

For example, if you find that using a different color or a box for headings helps you focus your reading or your study, use them. However, avoid any system that incorporates all of these marking methods.

HOW TO USE YOUR TEXT MARKING

Marking your textbook is a way of preparing your text for later review. You may think that if you read the material carefully and spend lots of time studying it, you shouldn't have to highlight, underline, or even take notes. For most students, however, this is not the case. Even if you were to spend hours reciting and reviewing the information in one chapter of your textbook, you probably wouldn't remember very much of that information by the time you had to take the exam. Although you will be able to remember "learned" material longer than material you read or hear only once, you still won't remember enough of it by test time. If you mark your text as you read it, you will have a vehicle for reviewing the material before your exam.

RE-MARK YOUR TEXT

One of the most common methods of reviewing for exams is to reread highlighted or underlined material. Unfortunately, most students do this in a rather passive manner. They quickly scan the lines of marked text, assuming that the information somehow will be absorbed into their memory. Think about the last time you studied for a test. How did you review the text material?

In order to conduct an effective review, you need to remain actively involved in your reading. This means you should re-mark your textbook as you review. By holding a marker (or pen or pencil) in your hand, you already are defining your reading activity. By planning to re-mark the text material, you're forcing yourself to read actively, to make decisions about the material that you marked before. As you reread the marked selections, you can determine whether or not the information is important. Remember, the first time you read the chapter, everything was new to you. At that time, many things may have seemed important. After having completed the chapter, worked through text questions or a study guide, and listened to the professor's lecture, you may be able to reduce the text material even more.

There are a number of ways to re-mark your text. If you used yellow highlighting when you first read the chapter, you could use a different color for re-marking. (If some of the information is already learned, you need not re-mark it.) You might also underline, checkmark, star, or even bracket the information that you want to review again. If you decide to reread your markings a third time, re-mark the text again. Each time you reread the text material, you should re-mark it in order to remain actively involved and to further condense what you need to review again.

TAKE NOTES ON YOUR MARKING

Taking notes as you review your markings is an excellent way—perhaps the best way—to remain actively involved in your reading. Not only does taking notes force you to decide whether or not the information is important, but also it requires you to condense the information and write it down. If you put the information in your own words, you also are using higher-level thinking skills to "translate" the text material. In addition, note taking allows you to organize the information so that it is more meaningful to you. You decide what to write down and how to arrange the information so that it makes sense to you. Finally, if you take notes, you can condense the critical information in a lengthy text chapter into a few sheets of notebook paper. In Chapter 8, you'll learn many new strategies and techniques for taking notes from text material.

EVALUATING YOUR TEXT MARKING

Each time you evaluate your marking, you should consider whether you have marked the material in a meaningful way, whether you have condensed the text material, and whether the method you used was efficient and effective. There are a number of ways to evaluate how well you mark your textbook. You can test your marking before an exam and again after the exam. Each evaluation will give you more information about how well you're marking your textbook.

The first way to test your marking is to see if it makes sense. Look back at a marked page in one of your textbooks. Read only the words that you marked. Does the information make sense? Now choose a page that you marked more than a week ago. Do the same test. Then try a page that you marked over a month ago. Do you still understand the information that you marked? Reread the entire page. Does your marking maintain the meaning of the selection?

Another way to test your marking is to compare your marked section of text to a classmate's marking. Talk about why each of you chose to include or leave out certain information. Read your classmate's marked page. Does it make more sense than yours? If it does, compare the marked information. You may find that by including a few additional words in your marking, you can dramatically improve its effectiveness.

You also can test your marking after an exam. That's often the time that students appreciate how much they condensed the material for review. Take your textbook with you when you go to take your exam. As soon as the exam is over, rush out into the hall, find a quiet corner, and sit down. Turn to any chapter that was heavily tested upon. Begin to reread that chapter. Read the unmarked as well as the marked areas of each page. Every time you come across something that was on the test, put a "T" in the margin of your book.

After you read through about a half of the chapter, stop and look at where the T's appear. How many of them are in highlighted or marked areas? How many are in unmarked areas? If all of the T's are in the marked areas, you did a good job of marking. You were able to recognize as important the same pieces of information that the professor thought were important. By marking those points, you identified them for later review. If, on the other hand, a number of your T's are in unmarked areas, you probably marked too little or too selectively as you read the chapter. Because those pieces of information were unmarked, you probably didn't review them before the test. Were you able to answer those questions correctly?

A final method of evaluating your marking is to talk to your professor or to someone at your campus learning center. Take your textbook with you and ask the person whether you're, in fact, picking out the important information in the selection. If you're just getting started marking a textbook, this additional feedback can let you know whether you're using effective strategies and techniques.

ACTIVITIES

1. Choose a selection from one of your textbooks that you read and marked at least a week ago. Re-mark the text material. Write a paragraph explaining what you did and what results you noticed.
2. Choose a selection from one of your textbooks that you read and marked at least a week ago. Take notes on the text material. How much were you able to reduce the material?
3. Choose several pages of one of your textbooks and evaluate your marking. Use a page you recently marked, one from at least a week ago, and one from more than a month ago. Write a short paragraph explaining how well you think you marked the material. Consider the issues discussed in this chapter as you frame your answer.
4. After your next exam, use the "T" method to evaluate your marking. Write a short paragraph explaining what you found. What do you plan to do differently next time?

POSTTEST

Where Are You Now?

Now that you have completed Chapter 7, take a few minutes to answer *yes* or *no* to the following questions. Compare your answers with those in the pretest.

	YES	NO
1. Do you highlight or mark your textbooks as you read?	______	______
2. Do you find that you often get to the end of a page and have no idea what you just read?	______	______
3. Do you begin to highlight or underline an important point before you finish the sentence?	______	______
4. Do you evaluate your text marking after an exam?	______	______
5. Does your marking make sense when you read it again before the exam?	______	______
6. Do you re-highlight or re-mark your text when you review for an exam?	______	______
7. Do you mark the headings and subheadings in your text?	______	______
8. Do you make notes in the margin when you read your text?	______	______
9. Do you tend to mark key words rather than phrases or entire sentences?	______	______
10. Do you ever reread the unmarked sections of your text before an exam?	______	______

Give yourself one point for each *yes* answer to questions 1, 4, 5, 6, 7, and 8, and one point for each *no* answer to questions 2, 3, 9, and 10. Now total up your points. Compare your score on this posttest with the score that you had on the pretest. Did you improve? In which areas? Where do you still need to improve?

CHAPTER 8

Taking Text Notes

"I now take text notes after I have completed reading the chapter. I don't wait until the night before the exam as I had done in the past. When I take text notes, I focus on the main points and ideas that are most important. I can relate my text notes to my lecture notes for comparison, which helps me learn the material better. I have found that taking text notes keeps me very active and involved with my reading."

Michelle Klimchock

NOTE TAKING: AN EFFECTIVE STUDY TOOL

Taking notes as you read is another way of "marking" your text. In fact, note taking is the best method for getting actively involved in text material. Knowing that you're going to have to write something down forces you to concentrate on what you're reading. In the process of making notes, you also are forced to distinguish between important and unimportant information in order to condense the material. In addition, note taking provides you with the opportunity to put the important information into your own words as you organize it for later review. This

PRETEST

Where Are You Now?

Take a few minutes to answer *yes* or *no* to the following questions.

	YES	NO
1. Do you take notes on your textbook after you have highlighted the chapter or section?	_____	_____
2. Do you take text notes when you read the chapter for the first time?	_____	_____
3. Do you read the whole paragraph before you begin to take notes?	_____	_____
4. Do you evaluate your text notes after an exam?	_____	_____
5. Do you usually copy information from the text using the same wording that the author used in the book?	_____	_____
6. Do you recite your text notes when you review for an exam?	_____	_____
7. Do you create maps when you take notes on your textbook material?	_____	_____
8. Are your text notes a good summary of the text material?	_____	_____
9. Do you tend to write down only key words when you take notes?	_____	_____
10. Do you use formal outlining to take notes on your text?	_____	_____

Give yourself one point for each *yes* answer to questions 1, 3, 4, 6, 7, and 8, and one point for each *no* answer to questions 2, 5, 9, and 10. Now total up your points. A low score indicates that you need some help in taking notes on text material. A high score indicates that you are already using many good note-taking strategies.

helps you understand the material better. Although note taking does take more time than highlighting, it can be an effective study tool when used at the right time.

WHY SHOULD YOU TAKE TEXT NOTES?

Taking notes on text material is the most effective method for becoming an active reader. Note taking keeps you actively involved in the text material. It also helps you condense the information that you will need to review before the exam. Finally, taking text notes allows you to determine a system of organization that is distinctly yours — a system that you design and that makes sense to you. This activity helps you clarify the meaning of the material and aids in your retention and retrieval of information.

NOTE TAKING PROMOTES ACTIVE READING

Taking notes keeps you alert as you read and provides you with a purpose for reading. Because you know that you have to write something down, you are forced to pay attention to and think about what you are reading. Note taking further increases your comprehension of the material by forcing you constantly to make decisions about the text information. (In order to take good text notes, you must determine what is important as you read.) In addition, taking notes provides you with feedback about how well you are concentrating on and understanding the material. If you aren't jotting down any information, it could be a signal that you were daydreaming as you "read" the page. If you find that you can't put the information into your own words, you may realize you really don't understand what you read. In many ways, taking notes is a comprehension monitoring system.

Although you also can read actively by highlighting or underlining the text, taking notes gets you actively involved in ways that text marking doesn't. First, you have to use higher-level skills to take notes, because you need to organize the material as you write. When you highlight or underline the textbook, you aren't operating outside of the author's organizational structure. In order to take effective notes, however, you may want to impose an organizational structure of your own. Remember, one important reason for taking text notes is to condense the material. As you take notes, you are thinking about what information to jot down under the main headings that you select and how best to summarize the text material. In order to write the information in your own words, you have to analyze what the author has said and relate it to what you already know. This interaction with the text increases your understanding of the concepts and ideas that are presented. Some note-taking strategies also force you to show the relationships within the material. If you use some of the mapping techniques for note taking, you also can represent the information in a visual display that demonstrates how the information is related. This may lead to improved memory of the material. Finally, the process of writing is itself an active learning strategy. Just by writing information from the text in your own words, rather than simply copying or highlighting the author's words, you increase your involvement with the text material and strengthen your memory of it.

NOTE TAKING CONDENSES THE MATERIAL

Another reason for taking notes on textbook material is to condense what you need to review before the exam. If you take notes on your text, you won't have to read the chapter again when you prepare for an exam. This is a real time saver. In fact, you not only will save time; you also will benefit from having the material organized in a way that makes sense to you. Your text notes, like your edited lecture notes, will be a well-organized representation of the material that you need to learn.

WHEN SHOULD YOU TAKE TEXT NOTES?

There are benefits to taking notes at different points in your reading and study of the textbook. You may want to take notes when you first read the chapter, after the lecture, at the end of the week, or before the exam.

WHEN YOU FIRST READ THE CHAPTER

Some students take notes as they read the chapter instead of highlighting or underlining. Although it is a more active method, note taking is very time-consuming. If you try to take notes the first time you read the chapter, you may find that you write down more information than you will need. After all, all of the information will be new to you, and everything may seem important. After reading the entire chapter and taking notes on the lecture, you'll find that you can be more selective in what you write down. If you already have covered a section of the chapter in the lecture and have all of the important information in your lecture notes, there is no need to write it all out again in your text notes. If you highlight the text when you first read it and then take notes afterward, you'll save time and have a better set of text notes. If you're using the S-RUN reading system, for example, you already may have discovered that taking notes after highlighting or underlining helps you condense the information even more.

AFTER THE LECTURE

Some students like to take their text notes right after the lecture. In this way, they are able to condense the information in the text and at the same time edit their lecture notes. If your professor's lectures follow the text fairly closely, you can fill in information that you may have missed during the lecture and at the same time note important points that were never touched on in class. It's not a good idea, though, to add all of the additional text information to your lecture notes. Instead, write your text notes in another notebook or on loose-leaf notebook paper so that you can lay your text notes and your lecture notes out side by side when you are studying.

AT THE END OF THE WEEK

You may find that taking text notes at the end of the week serves as a good way of reviewing the information that you read (and marked) and that you took notes on during the lecture. At the end of the week, the material probably will be more familiar to you because you have had a chance to read, listen, discuss, edit your lecture notes, and think about the information. At that point, you should be able to take more selective and more organized notes on the text material. Don't forget to follow along in your lecture notes as you take your text notes; this way, you'll avoid duplicating information.

WHEN YOU PREPARE FOR THE EXAM

Another good time to take your text notes is when you're preparing for your exam. Instead of just reading over the highlighted or underlined text material, take notes on it. As you know, just reading without some form of marking is a passive activity that often results in little actual learning. By the time you're ready to prepare for the exam, you already may have learned a lot of the information that you originally highlighted or underlined. Not only will you save time by waiting to take notes, but also you will benefit from the active review that requires you to determine what you still don't know. Writing down this information will help you learn it, as well as allow you to condense what you need to study for the exam. Of course, you still need to practice the information in your notes by reciting it.

HOW SHOULD YOU TAKE NOTES?

There are many different ways to take notes on text material. Some of the more useful methods include making written notes in the margin of the text, taking notes on index cards, outlining, mapping, and charting. Which method do you use? Although most of these techniques can be used with any text material, some seem to lend themselves more to specific types of material than to others. In this section, you'll learn when and how to use each of these note-taking techniques. Try them all as you do your own reading. Then decide which one works best for you.

WRITTEN NOTES

Taking written notes is probably the most common method that students use for taking notes from text material. You already may be making notes in the margin of your text as you read. These marginal notes help you focus your reading and can serve as recall cues for your highlighting. Some students prefer to take notes outside of the text (on a separate card or sheet of paper). In some cases, though, students really don't understand what taking text notes means. For some of them, text notes are simply disorganized lists of statements copied directly out of the book. In order to take good notes, you should follow the same general rules that you follow when you take lecture notes.

When you take notes, remember to use headings to organize your information. Indent slightly to show that other points are subordinate. (You also can number points or simply use a dash to indicate that you are listing information.) Leave room for a recall column so that you can use it to help prompt your memory when you review your notes. Write in meaningful phrases rather than copying entire sentences out of the book. Use your own words whenever you can. Refer to Chapter 5 to review some of the strategies for taking good lecture notes.

RECALL COLUMNS

Be sure to add a recall column as you take your text notes. By writing recall words or questions in the margin of your note page, you identify the most important points that you want to learn. In addition, you set up a great study sheet for later review. Nikki took notes on her life science text as a way of preparing for her exam (see Figure 8.1). She included recall questions and a summary statement on each page of notes.

Figure 8.1 Nikki's Notes

Chapter 7

Human Ecology

What has allowed us to live longer?	Ecology and Civilization – over last 2000 yrs. technological & medical advancements allowed us to live longer – support more offspring
How much has the pop increased?	– world pop. from 130M to 5B
	State of World
	2 Predictions about future
What are the 2 predictions about our future?	① Global 2000 – if present trends continue – world in 2000 will be crowded, polluted, less stable, vulnerable to disruption – people will be poorer
	② The Resourceful Earth: A Response to Global 2000 – Julian Simon & Herman Kahn – if present trends continue – world in 2000 will be less crowded & populated, more stable, & less vulnerable – world's pop. richer

Over the past 2000 years, technological and medical advancements have allowed us to live longer. Our world population has increased greatly. The Global 2000 and The Resourceful Earth have two opposing predictions about our future.

Figure 8.2 Sample Note Cards

Further Evolution

Major geologic events had an effect on land and sea life. During the Paleozoic Period the land masses Gondwana and Laurasia joined to form Pangea, a single world continent. All of the remaining surface of the Earth was covered by water - the Tethys Sea.

As the continents collided, the overall diversity of species declined and many habitats were lost. This resulted in a 96% reduction of marine species 240 million years ago. Climatic changes and changes in ocean currents affected all land & sea organisms.

Card A

NOTE CARDS

You also can take notes on index or note cards. As you will see in later chapters, note cards or index cards can be used for many study techniques. They are especially effective for taking notes, though, because they make it easy to organize information and they are so easy to carry around. You can use note cards to organize all of the important information on one particular heading or topic. Center the heading at the top of the card and then jot down any important supporting information that you want to review. You may want to write a summary of the text material or take notes in the same way you would if you were writing notes on notebook paper. Look at the sample note cards in Figure 8.2. Card A summarizes the main points that were made in the text. Card B presents more conventional notes in phrase form.

You also may want to use note cards to write down and study technical terminology. Words that are in bold print or italics in your text may be technical terms that are critical to your understanding of the course material. Write the term on the front of the card and write the definition on the back. Then carry the cards around and review them whenever you have a few minutes. (Don't limit yourself to techni-

Figure 8.2 (continued)

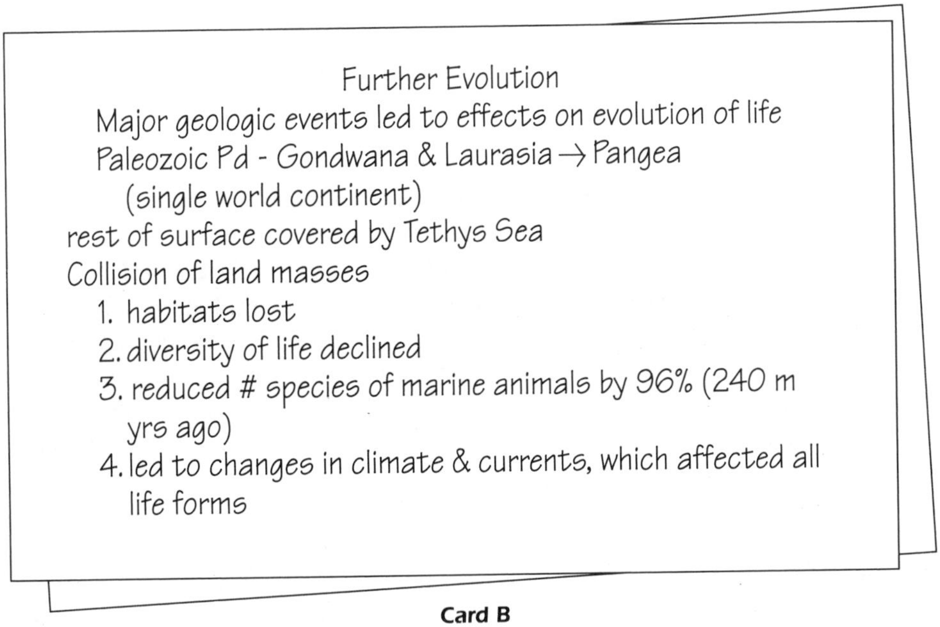

Further Evolution
Major geologic events led to effects on evolution of life
Paleozoic Pd - Gondwana & Laurasia → Pangea
(single world continent)
rest of surface covered by Tethys Sea
Collision of land masses
1. habitats lost
2. diversity of life declined
3. reduced # species of marine animals by 96% (240 m yrs ago)
4. led to changes in climate & currents, which affected all life forms

Card B

cal terms, though; you can write down names, dates, theories, formulas, and even diagrams in the same way.)

OUTLINING

Another popular method of taking notes on text material is outlining. Outlining can be very effective for taking text notes as long as you don't get caught up in the formatting and lose sight of what you are trying to accomplish. If you find yourself trying to decide whether to use an A or a 1, you're distracted—you're not concentrating on what you are reading.

If you have been using the outline method for taking lecture notes, you already are familiar with the basic format for informally outlining text material. When you take notes on your text, you can rely on the author's organization or you can create your own. You can use the chapter subdivisions as your main points. You don't have to use every heading as a main point; some of them may be combined or omitted. Write the heading next to the left margin and then indent to indicate supporting information. You don't need to use any numbers or letters in your informal outline.

Don't forget, your outline will be much more helpful if you write meaningful phrases instead of just key words.

MAPPING

Maps are visual displays of text information. They are a way of organizing the key information in the text into easy-to-read and easy-to-remember pictures or sketches. Although there are many different types of maps, only *hierarchical maps, semantic webs,* and *line maps* will be described in this chapter. You may find that mapping is a great way to take notes. When taking exams, you may find that this strategy helps you recall the information that you learned, because you can see a picture of it in your mind. Mapping is an even more active method than some of the others we've discussed, because you have to move outside the author's organizational framework and create your own.

Hierarchical Maps

One of the most common forms of maps is the hierarchical map. You often see this form of mapping in science texts in the form of flowcharts or process charts. To create a hierarchical map, write the main heading or topic at the top of the page and put a box around it. Then, draw lines to indicate the subdivisions (the next level of headings) and write and box each of them. You can then further divide each of these points into one or more supporting points. Look at the hierarchical map that Kendrick developed from his psychology textbook (Figure 8.3). You can see the natural progression from the main topic of the selection down to the supporting details.

Semantic Webs

One of the newest styles of mapping is the semantic web. Instead of using a top-down display, as in the hierarchical map, semantic webs radiate from a central focal point. There are four main components in a semantic web: the Core Question or Concept, the Web Strands, the Strand Supports, and the Strand Ties. The Core Question or Concept is the main focus of the text chapter or section. It may be the title of an article or chapter or the heading of the section that you decide to map. To start your web, write this word, phrase, or question in the center of a piece of paper and draw a circle around it. The second component, the Web Strands, are the subordinate ideas that describe the Core Concept. They are the main points

Figure 8.3 Kendrick's Hierarchical Map

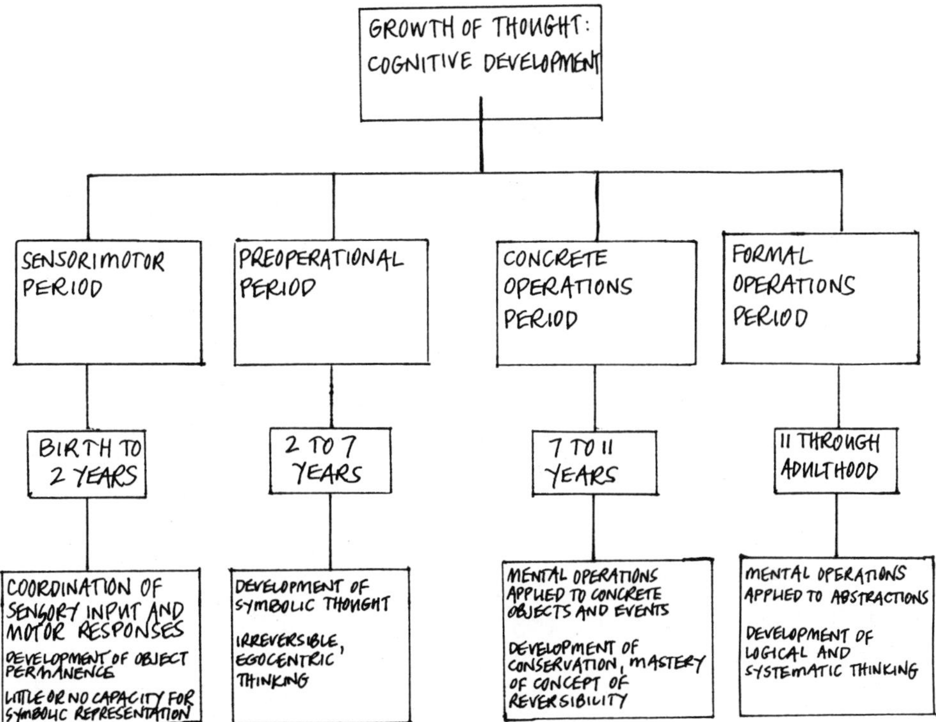

that the author makes about the topic. They are joined to the central focus by lines that radiate from it. Circle each main point as well. The Strand Supports do just what their title implies; they support the Web Strands. They include information that provides details related to the words or phrases that are designated Web Strands. Finally, the Strand Ties are words or phrases that are written on the lines that connect all of these pieces of information. They define the relationship between the Core Concept, the Web Strands, and the Strand Supports.[1]

Look at the semantic web that Kelly produced from a section of her text chapter on drug use (Figure 8.4). Can you locate each of the components mentioned above? First, what is the Core Concept? If you look at the center of Kelly's web, you

[1]Adapted from Freeman, G., and Reynolds, E. G., "Enriching Basal Reader Lessons with Semantic Webbing," *The Reading Teacher* 33 (1980): 677–684.

Figure 8.4 Kelly's Semantic Web

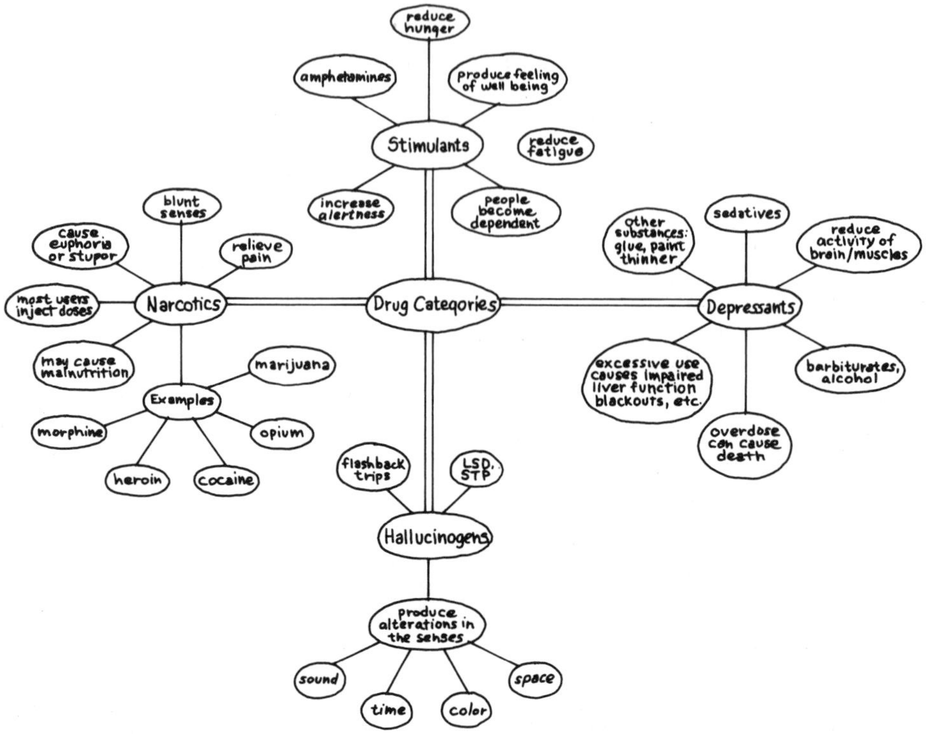

will see that she used the phrase "Drug Categories." It also is easy to find the four Web Strands, because Kelly used double lines to connect them to the center focal point. You may have noticed that Kelly uses several levels of Strand Supports. She moves from "Narcotics" (a Web Strand) to "Examples" (a Strand Support) to "Marijuana" (a detail supporting the strand support). Even though this last level of support was not in the "rules" for how to construct a semantic web, Kelly felt that the text information demanded further division. Don't leave out information you think is important just because it doesn't fit the formula for how to do the web. Instead, adapt the mapping technique to fit your text material. You may have noticed that Kelly didn't add Strand Ties to her map. She could have written "used to" on the line between "Narcotics" and "relieves pain," or "leads to" on the line that connects "Narcotics" to "blunt senses." You probably will find that strand ties are useful for certain types of information but can be omitted at other times. After you complete your web, review the information that you noted. If you aren't sure how some of your information relates to the information connected to it, you may need to add the strand ties to your map.

Line or Wheel Maps

If you don't like drawing circles or squares, you may find that line or wheel maps work well for you. You already may be familiar with time lines from Chapter 3 ("Time Management") and from history class. They are one form of line maps. To draw a line or wheel map for other types of information, write your topic in the center of the paper and then add subordinate points on lines that radiate up, down, or out from it. You can add supporting details by adding lines that extend out from the previous lines. Meira prepared a line map for a text excerpt on the same information shown in Kendrick's hierarchical map (see Figure 8.5). Could this same information be presented as a semantic web or an outline? Of course it could.

CHARTING

Another interesting method of note taking is charting. You can't chart an entire chapter of a textbook, but you may be able to create a chart for several sections of a chapter. If you have a collection of topics or headings that are all related (types or forms of something), you may find that creating a chart helps you organize the information while noting the similarities and differences of each topic. The information on the four drug categories and the four stages of cognitive development both lend themselves well to charting.

Look at the example in Figure 8.6, which shows a portion of a matrix, a chart designed with rows and columns. In order to create this type of chart from text material, you need to decide how many topics or categories you should include. The names of the categories are usually quite easy to identify. They are the main topics that are described in your text material. For example, the text material may focus around three types of rocks, four stages of cognitive development, or three types of maps. If, for example, you were creating a chart on the three types of maps, you would write the names "hierarchical," "semantic web," and "line or wheel map" along the left column of your paper.

In order to determine the names for the headings of the columns of the chart, you need to think carefully about the kinds of information that the author provides about each of the categories. If the text material includes both similarities and differences for each of the categories, this information can help you determine the headings. For example, since this chapter includes information on the appearance of each type of map, you might label one of the headings as "Appearance" or even "Design." What other headings could you use? If you decided to chart the four drug categories, you would write their names along the left margin of your paper. Then

Figure 8.5 Meira's Line Map

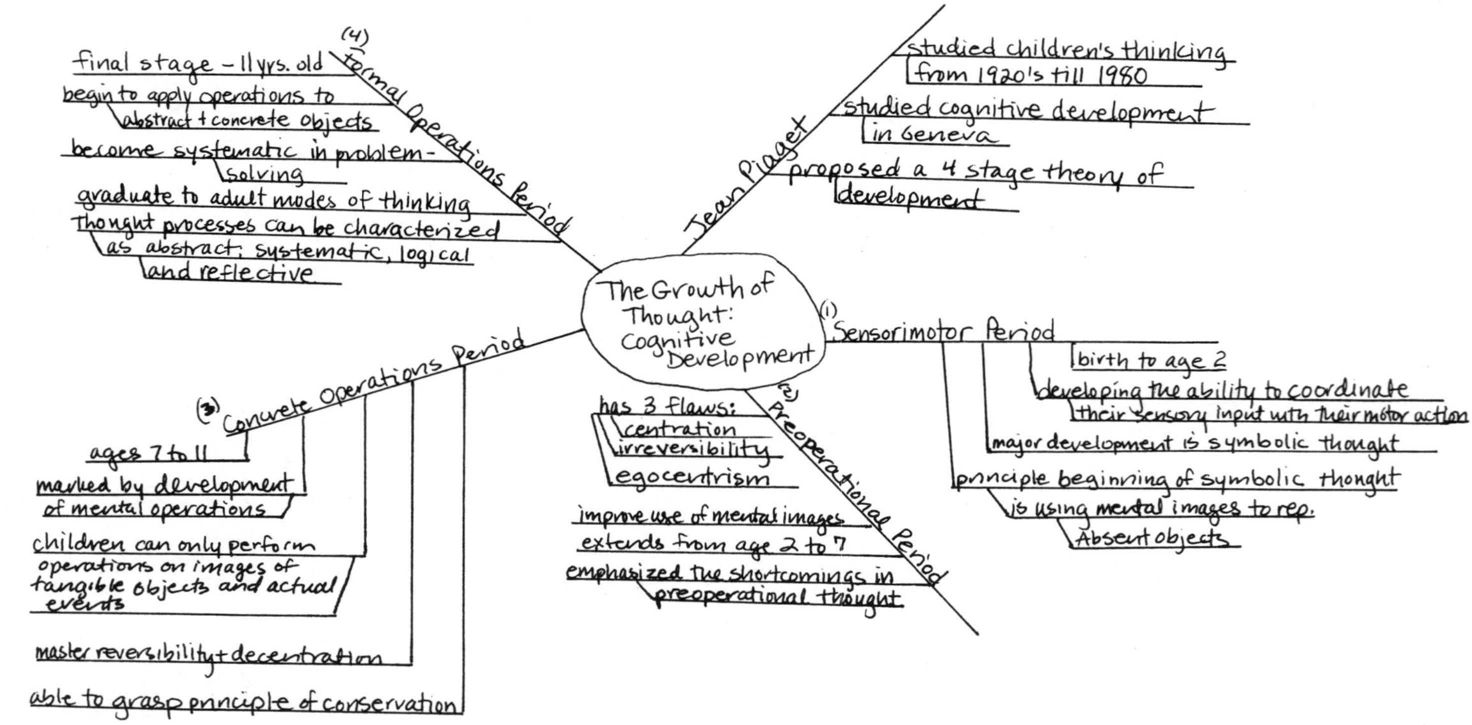
The Growth of Thought: Cognitive Development
Jean Piaget
studied children's thinking
from 1920's till 1980
studied cognitive development
in Geneva
proposed a 4 stage theory of
development
(1) Sensorimotor Period
birth to age 2
developing the ability to coordinate
their sensory input with their motor action
major development is symbolic thought
principle beginning of symbolic thought
is using mental images to rep.
Absent objects
(2) Preoperational Period
has 3 flaws:
centration
irreversibility
egocentrism
improve use of mental images
extends from age 2 to 7
emphasized the shortcomings in
preoperational thought
(3) Concrete Operations Period
ages 7 to 11
marked by development
of mental operations
children can only perform
operations on images of
tangible objects and actual
events
master reversibility + decentration
able to grasp principle of conservation
(4) Formal Operations Period
final stage - 11 yrs. old
begin to apply operations to
abstract + concrete objects
become systematic in problem-
solving
graduate to adult modes of thinking
thought processes can be characterized
as abstract, systematic, logical
and reflective

Figure 8.6 Melissa's Chart

Overview of Piaget's Stage Theory

	Age	Definition	Development	Key Concept or Flaw
Sensorimotor period.	birth to age 2	Ability to coordinate sensory inputs with motor actions	Symbolic thought Behavior dominated by innate reflexes	Key concept: Object permanence. Recognizing that object continues to exist even when no longer visible
Preoperational period	age 2 to age 7	Improve use of mental images Preoperational because of all the weaknesses	Development of symbolic thinking Not yet grasped concept of conservation: quantities remain constant regardless of shape or appearance	Key flaws: Centration: Focus on one part of problem Irreversibility: Inability to undo an action Egocentrism: Inability to share other's viewpoints Animism: Believe all things are living

you would fill in the pertinent information from your text in order to complete each column.

TAKING NOTES ON SPECIAL MATERIAL

Note taking also is useful with special types of text material. You may prefer to take notes on outside reading assignments rather than photocopying all of the articles and then marking them. If you are in literature class, you also may find that note taking is a better method than highlighting for marking your text.

LIBRARY MATERIAL

You can summarize, outline, or even map outside reading assignments. List the title of the article at the top of the note card or in the center of your map. Be sure to include the author's name, because professors often refer to particular articles by the author's name. You also should jot down the source of the article and the date of publication in case you need to find the article again. Preview the article to get an idea of what it is about. After reading one paragraph or headed section, take notes. Try to include the main points that the author makes and some of the details. Professors generally want to know if you read the outside reading assignment. They tend to ask test questions that focus more on main points rather than on fine details. However, some instructors test on the finer points, so be prepared.

LITERATURE

If you're taking a literature class, you may have to read a large number of short stories, plays, poems, novels, or a combination of them. It's hard to remember all of the plot lines, characters, themes, and symbols that you read and discuss. You can improve your comprehension of literary works by taking notes as you read.

Any of the note-taking methods will work, but I have found that note cards work best for me. Put the title of the work at the top of the card and then add the author's name and the date of publication. Next, devise a list of categories of information that you want to record. You may want to include such topics as the setting, theme, main characters, symbols, and even the general plot line. (You could draw a brief time line on your card and write in the main points of action.) Jot down any other information that seems to stand out, and include your own thoughts about the work. It will be easy to review your cards and refresh your memory whenever you wish.

REVIEWING YOUR TEXT NOTES

There are two main ways to review text notes, but simply "reading over them" is not one of them. One way to transfer the information in your notes into your long-term memory is to recite it. First, practice the information by reviewing the main and supporting points. Try to recall and recite the pattern of organization that you used to set up the information in your notes. Then recite the actual information in your notes. Look back at your notes to see whether you are correct. Then cover your notes and practice again. If you made note cards, carry them with you. Review them whenever you have a few minutes to spare. Then look away and try to recite (or mumble) the information. Try taping your notes to a mirror, or tack them to a bulletin board. Review them in the morning and then try to recite them as you walk to class.

Another method for reviewing text notes is to replicate them. Take a blank sheet of paper and try to reconstruct your notes. If you mapped the information in the text, you probably will find that it's fairly easy to recall the visual image that you created; try to remember the map and also how you set it up. If you made a detailed map, practice drawing it one section at a time. You also can practice writing out your note cards, outlines, or charts. When you review charts or matrixes, don't try to learn all of the information at once. Work on one column at a time. Practice matrixes by starting with a blank sheet of paper. Write in the headings and the left column. Then try to fill in one column across or down. Keep working on the matrix until you can write it from memory.

EVALUATING YOUR TEXT NOTES

After an exam, you can evaluate your text notes in much the same way you did your text marking. Go through your notes for one chapter and put a "T" in the margin every time you find the answer to a test question. Then go back through your textbook to check for any other answers to test questions. If all of the answers to the questions from the book were in your text notes, you did an excellent job of taking notes. If a number of the answers were not in your notes, you may want to go over your notes with your professor. This is a good way to learn why the professor thought some of the points that you overlooked were important. You can then improve the set of notes that you take on the next group of chapters and be better prepared for the next exam.

You also may find that comparing your text notes to those of a classmate can be very helpful. For one thing, you may notice some information that you omitted, or even find out that you included a lot of unnecessary information. More important, you may get some new ideas about how to set up or organize the text information. Looking at how other students arranged and organized the same text information can help you evaluate your own notes.

ACTIVITIES

1. During the next week of classes, experiment with taking notes at different times. Try taking notes on one part of a text chapter as you first read the chapter. Then try taking notes on a different part of the chapter after the lecture. Finally, wait until the end of the week and take notes on another section of the chapter. Note the time it took you to complete each task. What did you find? Which set of notes do you think is most useful? Why?
2. Practice taking notes on some of your own text material using each of the note-taking methods described. Which method worked best for you? Why?
3. Use each of the mapping methods as you take notes on one or more of your textbooks. Which method did you find the most easy to construct? To remember? To replicate?
4. Create a matrix for a section of material from one of your textbooks. Did you find that you were able to organize the material in a more memorable way?
5. After your next exam, evaluate your text notes. Did your notes contain the information that you needed to answer the questions on the exam? What do you plan to differently the next time you take notes?

POSTTEST

Where Are You Now?

Now that you have completed Chapter 8, take a few minutes to answer *yes* or *no* to the following questions. Compare your answers with those in the pretest.

	YES	NO
1. Do you take notes on your textbook after you have highlighted the chapter or section?	______	______
2. Do you take text notes when you read the chapter for the first time?	______	______
3. Do you read the whole paragraph before you begin to take notes?	______	______
4. Do you evaluate your text notes after an exam?	______	______
5. Do you usually copy information from the text using the same wording that the author used in the book?	______	______
6. Do you recite your text notes when you review for an exam?	______	______
7. Do you create maps when you take notes on your textbook material?	______	______
8. Are your text notes a good summary of the text material?	______	______
9. Do you tend to write down only key words when you take notes?	______	______
10. Do you use formal outlining to take notes on your text?	______	______

Give yourself one point for each *yes* answer to questions 1, 3, 4, 6, 7, and 8, and one point for each *no* answer to questions 2, 5, 9, and 10. Now total up your points. Compare your score on this posttest with the score that you had on the pretest. Did you improve? In which areas? Where do you still need to improve?

CHAPTER 9

Preparing for Exams

"The Five-Day Study Plan has helped me a great deal. I used it for a Philosophy of Religion midterm. Instead of breaking the material down into chapters, I divided it into groups of philosophers and their similar beliefs. I had to learn various types of arguments for the existence of God, critique them, and state each argument. This was a very extensive exam, and this strategy helped me the most."

Kelly Mangan

USE ACTIVE STRATEGIES TO PREPARE FOR EXAMS

As you probably have discovered, college exams are different from high school tests; they cover more material and are given less frequently. These differences require you to prepare differently. Many new college students are shocked and disappointed when they get their first college exam back. They did exactly what they had done in high school to get an A, yet their college test grade was a C or D. What happened, they ask? Unfortunately, many students study for tests by only "reading over" the material. In order to do well on college exams, you must become actively involved with the material. You have to examine the material to determine what you know and what you don't know, write and recite to put information into your long-term memory, and then prompt your memory to check your mastery of

PRETEST

Where Are You Now?

Take a few minutes to answer *yes* or *no* to the following questions.

	YES	NO
1. When preparing for exams, is your primary study method to read over the material?	_____	_____
2. Do you tend to miss class the day before the exam?	_____	_____
3. After an exam are you unsure of how well you did?	_____	_____
4. Do you make up self-tests as a way of studying for exams?	_____	_____
5. Do you study by yourself and with a group before a very difficult exam?	_____	_____
6. Do you tend to study only the day or night before the exam?	_____	_____
7. Do you review your lecture notes and text material together according to the topic?	_____	_____
8. Do you often know the answer to multiple-choice questions even before you look at the alternatives?	_____	_____
9. Do you review by reciting out loud and/or making up study sheets?	_____	_____
10. Do you space your study time over a period of several days?	_____	_____

Give yourself one point for each *yes* answer to questions 4, 5, 7, 8, 9, and 10, and one point for each *no* answer to questions 1, 2, 3, and 6. Now total up your points. A low score indicates that you need to learn how to study for college exams. A high score indicates that you are already using many good test preparation strategies.

the material. These active strategies make the difference between "sort of knowing" the material and knowing it well. How you study, when you study, and what you study all affect how well you will do on your exams. This chapter includes strategies for planning and organizing your study time as well as active study strategies for learning course material.

GATHER INFORMATION BEFORE YOU STUDY

There are a number of things that you should find out before you begin to study for an exam. Learning about the type of test that will be given will help you know how best to prepare for it. In addition, knowing how you learn best can help you choose the most effective ways to prepare for an exam. Together this information can lead to better grades.

LEARN ABOUT THE EXAM

The first thing to do in preparing for an exam is find out what the exam will be like. If your professor has not already discussed the exam, ask about it. Don't feel afraid or foolish — the more you know, the better you can prepare. One of the first things you need to know is what type of questions you will be expected to answer. Ask whether the exam is objective or essay or both. If the exam is an objective one, find out if the questions all will be multiple choice or if some will be true-false, matching, or completion.

You also need to know how many questions will be on the exam. If you have 100 questions on four chapters of Life Science, you can expect about 25 questions on each chapter. On the other hand, if you have only 20 questions on the same four chapters, you will have only 5 questions per chapter. The more questions you have from each chapter, the greater the probability that they will cover not only main ideas but also less important points from the chapters and your notes. If there are only a few questions from each chapter, they are more likely to cover the main ideas or concepts. However, you can't depend on this. Some professors who ask only three or four questions per chapter still test on "picky little things." And, don't forget: Even one essay question can cover a great deal of material.

Many college students don't realize that professors test their understanding of the material at many different levels. Although most of the questions on your high school tests depended only on your ability to memorize, six different levels of questions are frequently found on college exams. Read the description of each in the list that follows.

1. **Knowledge**-level questions require only rote memory; they are the easiest type of question to answer. They include remembering terms, facts, dates, lists, and so on. To answer this type of question you need only to recognize or recall the information as it was written in the text or spoken in the lecture.[1]
2. **Comprehension**-level questions require you to do more than just recognize what was presented in the text or lecture. They require you to understand the material well enough to be able to identify concepts and issues even when they are phrased differently from the way you read them or heard them presented.
3. **Application**-level questions require you to apply the information that you learned to a new situation. Application questions are common in math and science courses, but they may appear on any exam.
4. **Analysis**-level questions require you to break down a complex concept into its components or parts. Many essay questions involve analysis.
5. **Synthesis**-level questions require you to bring information together into a single unit or whole. You also will find many essay questions that involve synthesis.
6. **Evaluation**-level questions require you to make judgments about the value or worth of an idea. In most cases, both analysis and synthesis are required to answer an evaluation-level question. They are the most difficult type of question to answer and require the highest-level thinking skills.

LEARN ABOUT YOURSELF

As you decide which strategies to use when you prepare and review for an exam, you also should consider how you learn best. Although there are a number of surveys and inventories that can help you determine your preferred learning style, you can get a pretty good idea of what it is by doing a few experiments. If someone told you to put together a birdhouse, for example, would you prefer to read and follow written directions? Would you rather listen to an expert explain how to put the birdhouse together? Or would you prefer to practice putting it together instead?

Think about a difficult class that you have taken. Did you find that you understood the material better when you read the textbook or when you listened to the lecture? Some students are auditory learners; they learn best by hearing the information. Other students tend to be visual learners; they learn best by seeing or visualizing the information. Have you found that you really understood the mate-

[1]Based on Bloom's Taxonomy. Bloom, B. S., ed., *Taxonomy of Educational Objectives: The Classification of Educational Goals. Handbook 1. Cognitive Domain.* (New York: McKay, 1956).

DRABBLE reprinted by permission of UFS, Inc.

rial after you performed an experiment on it? You may be a kinesthetic learner; you may learn best by doing. Until you discover what type of learner you are, you need to try different strategies for learning. Using a *combination* of visual, auditory, and kinesthetic strategies when you prepare for exams will guarantee that you are using your preferred style.

USE THE FIVE-DAY STUDY PLAN

Once you find out what the exam will be like, you can organize your study time. In this section, you will learn how to use the Five-Day Study Plan. This carefully designed study system emphasizes both spaced study and active learning strategies. Many students who have used this plan have reported dramatic improvements in their grades from one test to the next. The Five-Day Study Plan is not a magic solution to all of your problems; rather it is a well-structured plan that puts into practice what we know about how people learn and remember.

There are several main ingredients to this plan. First of all, you space out your learning over a period of days. During each day of the plan, you prepare a new chapter and then review the material that you prepared on all of the previous chapters. Next, you divide up the material so that you can work on it in small chunks. In addition, you use active learning strategies (writing and reciting activities) to study the material. Finally, you incorporate self-testing techniques into your study plan in order to monitor your learning.

SET UP A PLAN

After you determine what you have to learn, you need to start to think about how much time you need to learn it. One reason many new college students get low grades on exams is that they don't put in enough time on the material. How much time do you think you should spend studying for a four-chapter exam? How much time did you study for your last exam? Many students study for about one to three hours for an exam. Compared to the time they put in on high school exams, this seems like a lot. Remember, though, college exams may cover ten to twenty times as much information as high school tests. For most students, eight to ten hours of study may be required to achieve an A or B on an exam. Of course, this is only a general guideline. Some students constantly review material (daily and weekly) so that they don't need to put in quite as much time just before the exam. Other students may need to study even more. If you're taking a very challenging class (like anatomy and physiology, or organic chemistry), you may need to double or even triple the suggested study time. If you're having difficulty understanding the material in a required course outside of your major, you also may need to increase the amount of time for study. As you will see later in the chapter, it's not just the amount of time that makes the difference in your mastery of the material, but rather it's what you do with that time.

If you're trying to figure out when you can find time to study eight to twenty hours for one exam, don't panic. You don't need or really want to put in all of your study time on one day. It's much more effective to study over a period of several days than to cram one day before an exam. Research studies have demonstrated that we learn better by spacing out our study over time. Instead of trying to study for ten hours the night before an exam, try studying for two hours each day for five days before the exam. If you need to put in more time, add more time to each day's study session, or add more days to your study plan.

You can use time management strategies to "find" this extra time in your schedule. One of the best ways to clear time for study is to complete some of your regular assignments ahead of time. In Chapter 3, you learned to look ahead on your monthly calendar for "tough weeks." You can begin to free up study time a week in advance by doing reading or writing assignments during a "light" week. You also can put off some assignments until after the exam, if need be. Although it isn't a good idea to get behind in your reading, it's even more important to prepare well for your exams.

In order to set up your study plan, count backward from your exam date to decide when you should begin to study. For example, if you had an exam scheduled on Friday, you would count backward to Thursday, Wednesday, Tuesday, Monday, and Sunday. In order to get in five days of study before a Friday exam, you would need to start studying on Sunday. When would you begin to study for a Monday exam? If you said Wednesday, you are right. If you said Tuesday, you could still be right. This is a flexible plan. If you work or even if you party on Saturdays, you can still use this plan. Just count back one more day to make up for the day that you decide to omit. However, never omit the day right before the exam; it is imperative to do a final review the day before the exam.

DIVIDE UP THE MATERIAL

The next step is to divide up into chunks the material that will be on the exam. Make a list of the chapters, lecture topics, and outside readings that will be on the test. Then group or chunk them so that you review the lectures and readings covering the same topic at the same time. If your professor gave three lectures that covered or related to the material in Chapter 1 of the text, you should study those lectures at the same time that you study Chapter 1. If your exam will cover four chapters, you can divide the material into four chunks, allowing one chapter per day, and then one additional day for a final review. How would you divide up the material if your test was on only two chapters? You could study the first half of Chapter 1 on day 1, the second half of Chapter 1 on day 2, and so on. What about six chapters or eight chapters?

STUDY THE OLDEST MATERIAL FIRST

Look at the sample Five-Day Study Plan in Figure 9.1. This plan includes both time to prepare a chapter and time to review that chapter several times before the exam. (Remember that "Chapter 1" means the text chapter, the lecture notes, and any other related materials.) When you set up your Five-Day Study Plan, be sure to start with the oldest chapter first. For instance, if your test were to cover Chapters 5, 7, 8, and 10, and you read and discussed Chapter 8 first, that should be the first one on your plan. When you look carefully at the study plan, you'll notice that the oldest chapters are given the most preparation time and the most review time. You need to spend more time on the old material because it's less familiar to you. Even though you may have read it, marked it, and even taken notes on it, much of that material may seem new to you when you begin to review. If you covered Chapter 1 four weeks ago, you won't remember very much of it when you begin to study for the exam.

In the sample, Chapters 3 and 4 are more familiar and, therefore, should require less preparation time and review. However, if Chapter 3 or 4 happens to be an especially difficult chapter, you may need to modify the plan and add some additional time for preparation and/or review. Remember, this plan is only a model. It can work as it is written for many of your exams, but it may need to be adjusted for other exams.

Figure 9.1 Sample Five-Day Study Plan

Tuesday		
	Prepare CH 1	2 hrs
Wednesday		
	Prepare CH 2	2 hrs
	Review CH 1	30 min
Thursday		
	Prepare CH 3	1-1/2 hrs
	Review CH 2	30 min
	Review CH 1	15 min
Friday		
	Prepare CH 4	1 hr
	Review CH 3	30 min
	Review CH 2	15 min
	Review CH 1	10 min
Sunday		
	Review CH 4	30 min
	Review CH 3	20 min
	Review CH 2	10 min
	Review CH 1	10 min
	Self Test	1 hr

PLAN ACTUAL TASKS

How you prepare and review for your exam is just as important as when you study. If you don't plan actual tasks for the hours that you set aside for study, you may accomplish very little. Many college students know only one way to study for a test. They sit and read over the material until they know it (at least they think they know it). Reading the material over and over and over is not only ineffective, it is also boring. If you have been rereading your text and lecture notes for hours before an exam and still not getting the grades you want, you need to change your strategy. Unlike reading over the material, writing and reciting strategies are excellent ways of putting information into long-term memory. Many recitation tasks also let you practice getting the information back out of memory, too.

Figure 9.2 Actual Tasks for Five-Day Study Plan

Wednesday	
Prepare CH 2	1. Re-mark highlighting 2. Make study sheets 3. Make word cards 4. Make question cards
Review CH 1	1. Review re-highlighted material *unknowns (recite main points) 2. Mark and recite study sheets 3. Recite word cards 4. Recite question cards
Thursday	
Prepare CH 3	1. Re-mark highlighting 2. Make study sheets 3. Make word cards 4. Make question cards
Review CH 2	1. Review re-highlighted material *unknowns (recite main points) 2. Mark and recite study sheets 3. Recite word cards 4. Recite question cards
Review CH 1	1. Make a list of info still not known from text or study sheets—recite 2. Recite cards still not known 3. Make self-test questions

PREPARE A CHAPTER

In Figure 9.2, you can see some suggested types of preparation and review tasks for Wednesday and Thursday of the Five-Day Study Plan. Unfortunately, most students can't learn all of the important information in their notes and in the chapter by going over it just one time. That's why it's so important to prepare the chapter and notes and then spend some time over the next few days reviewing that same information. You can prepare a chapter for review by going through it and picking out the material that you think you still need to learn.

Pretend that you're following this plan for an exam. Open one of your textbooks to Chapter 2, and open your notebook to the first lecture that covered Chapter 2. Reread your highlighting and your lecture notes. Re-mark your text and your notes, or take notes on them as you review. Next, go through the material and make up study sheets on some of the main topics that you want to learn. You might also make up word cards and question cards. Each of these strategies will be discussed in detail later in the chapter. All of these preparation strategies are writing strategies. They make you dig through the material; they force you to make decisions about what's important and about what you still need to learn. They also help you condense what you need to review again. Don't just use one strategy, though. The more different ways that you study for an exam, the more likely it is that you will learn and retain the information.

REVIEW A CHAPTER

Now look at the tasks that are listed for reviewing Chapter 1. You could reread the material you re-marked in Chapter 1 or review the notes you took. This time you could put stars next to the information that you still want to review again. You also could cover the text material and try to recite it from memory. You should review your study sheets by trying to recite the information from recall words, questions in the margin, or from the headings. Use your word and question cards as you would flash cards and recite the definitions or answers. Most of the review strategies involve reciting what you prepared the day before. Each day, as you review the material, you continue to condense what you still don't know.

BE CREATIVE IN DESIGNING YOUR OWN PLAN

The tasks that are listed in Figure 9.2 are just examples of the types of tasks that you could use to study for an exam. The menu of preparation and review strategies includes a number of other good strategies that you may want to include in your plan (see Figure 9.3). You also may develop some excellent strategies of your own. Varying the activities you use when you study can keep you from feeling bored. You also may discover that many of these active strategies are fun and make learning interesting and exciting.

Figure 9.3 Menu of Actual Tasks to Add to Your Study Plan

Preparation Strategies	Review Strategies
develop study sheets	recite study sheets
develop concept maps	replicate concept maps
make word cards	recite word cards
make question cards	recite question cards
make formula cards	practice writing formulas
make problem cards	work problems
make self-tests	take self-tests
do study guides	practice study guide info out loud
re-mark text material	take notes on re-marked text
make a list of 20	recite list of 20
do problems	do "missed" problems
outline	recite main points from outline
take notes	recite notes from recall cues
summarize	recite out loud
chart related material	re-create chart from memory
list steps in the process	recite steps from memory
predict essay questions	answer essay questions
plan essay answers	practice reciting main points
write essay answers	write essay answers from memory
answer questions at end of chapter	recite answers
prepare material for study group	explain material to group members

ACTIVE STUDY STRATEGIES

In this section, you'll learn about a variety of active study strategies. Some of these strategies lend themselves to the preparation stage and others lend themselves to the review stage. You won't use all of these strategies to study for one exam; there are just too many of them. What you should do, however, is try each of them as you prepare for different exams during the semester. You probably will find that some strategies work better for you than others. You also may find that certain strategies work well for one class but others are better for another.

REREAD AND RE-MARK

A good way to start preparing for a test is to reread your highlighting. You'll stay actively involved in your reading if you re-mark the text as you read it. You can further condense the material that you'll need to review again by determining what you do know and what you don't know. It certainly is possible that after several weeks of class, some of the information in the early chapters will be "old hat." You may not have to spend any more time on it at all. Don't spend time rereading the material that you didn't mark, though. Some students have trouble skipping this unmarked material, but you must learn to trust the marking that you did.

Because you practiced marking and re-marking the text in the previous two chapters, only a few brief notes will be included here. If you highlighted in yellow, for example, you could re-mark the text in pink. You also could underline, use parentheses or brackets, or make check marks in the margin to indicate information that you want to review again. You should also mark your lecture notes as you review them. Use these same strategies to re-mark the important information in your lecture notes as you reread them. You can condense them just as you did your text material. You may want to go through the chapter and your notes and reread the newly marked information the next day, too. This time, use another one of the methods to again condense what you need to learn. You can continue to reread and re-mark your text material and lecture notes every day. However, this is just the first step in learning the material. Remember, you need to write and recite to get the information into long-term memory — to learn it at the *recall* level of learning. At this level, you'll be able to recall the information without any additional cues.

If you took notes as you read or after you marked, you should review your notes and mark them as your first step. However, if your professor tends to ask picky questions on small details, you may benefit from one quick rereading of your highlighting. This can be especially helpful if your exam is a multiple-choice test. In order to answer multiple-choice questions correctly, you often can rely on *recognition*-level learning. That means, you don't have to be able to recall the actual answer; you need only to *recognize* it from among the answers listed on the exam. If you have recently read that material, the answer may stand out or seem familiar to you. Of course, if your exam is completion, short answer, or essay in design, that quick rereading won't help at all.

After you have reread and recondensed the information in your text and notes, you should begin the process of learning the information. You can use many techniques to accomplish this process. You may want to prepare study sheets, develop self-tests, make up word and/or question cards, or use other strategies that you find effective. You also need to spend time practicing the information by writing it and reciting it in order to learn it.

PREPARE WORD CARDS

Think back to the last objective test that you took. How many of the questions on that test required you to know the meaning of a word that was part of the specialized vocabulary for that unit of material? You may have been surprised to find a technical term somewhere in the stem of the question or in at least one of the possible answers. Many students don't spend much time on technical terminology because they know that they won't have to actually write out the definition for an exam. What they don't realize, though, is that they are expected to know the meaning of those terms, and this understanding is necessary for answering many of the questions on the exam.

How do you learn all those terms? One way is to make word cards. By going through the chapter and writing out word cards, you are actively involved with the material. Just the process of writing the terms and their definitions will help you learn them. Put the word on the front of a three-by-five card and then write a brief definition on the back. Put only one word on each card. You want to use them like flash cards, so they shouldn't be cluttered with information. If you're trying to save money, cut your cards in half.

You can make word cards for just about any subject. If you're in a psychology class, you may have forty or fifty technical terms for just one chapter. In addition, you may want to make cards for famous psychologists and what they did, theories, or even research studies that were emphasized by your professor. In history, put people, dates, events, treaties, or anything else you need to learn onto the cards. Make formula cards for math and science classes. Put the formula on one side and the name of the formula or when it is used on the other side. Of course, word cards are a great way to learn foreign language vocabulary terms. Some students even put diagrams or sketches of things that they will have to identify on the front of the card, and the explanations on the back. Look at the examples of word cards from history, biology, and psychology (Figure 9.4). Word cards are easy to make, and they're quite effective in getting information into long-term memory.

If, like some students, you make as many as fifty word cards for just one chapter, you may find that this activity takes up most of your preparation time. If this is the case, you may want to make your cards before you begin to study. Some students make word cards even before they read a chapter for the first time. They use this activity to help them get acquainted with the material and the new terminology.

Figure 9.4 Sample Word Cards

HISTORY CARDS

(Front)	(Back)
Ziggurats	Sumerian buildings large brick platforms with terraces
Hammurabi	Babylonian king law– code of justice carved on stele

PSYCHOLOGY CARDS

(Front)	(Back)
Stress Holmes def	event that presents difficult demands (situation) ex: divorce
Stress Selye	response of physiological arousal elicited by troublesome events (person)

Making word cards provides you with an excellent preview before reading and allows you plenty of time to learn all of the definitions.

After you do make your word cards, you need to learn them. Although you will learn some of them just from writing them out, you won't learn all of them. Study

Figure 9.4 (continued)

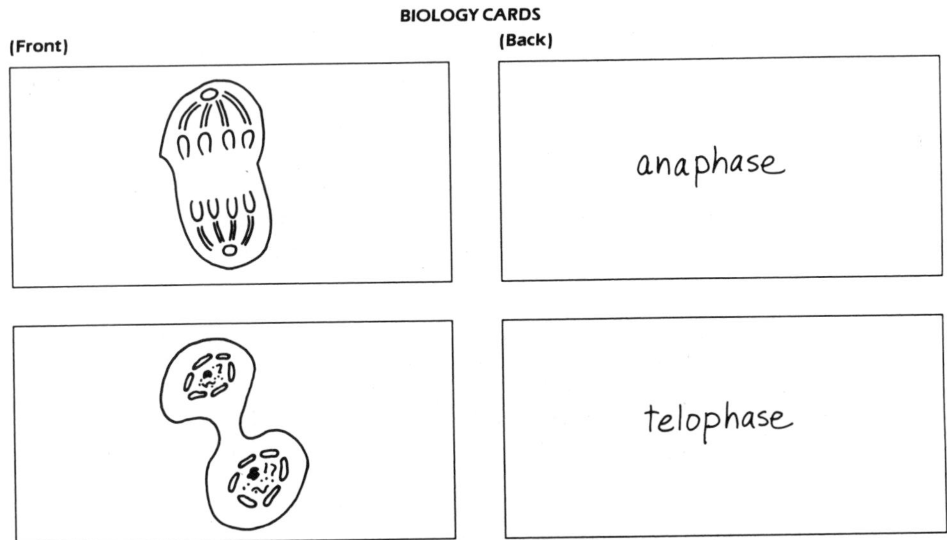

them by practicing ten or fifteen at a time. Carry them around with you and recite or mumble them whenever you have a few minutes to spare. After you know that group, start on the next pack of fifteen.

Hold the stack of cards in your hand and look at the first term. Try to recite the definition out loud. Turn the card over to check your answer. If you were right, set that card aside. If you couldn't think of the answer or were not completely correct, read the definition out loud. Then put it on the bottom of the pile. Continue practicing the cards until you have none left in your hand. After you know all of the terms, shuffle the cards to check your learning. Sometimes, you remember the definition of one word because you got a clue to it from the previous term. Although it is good to learn information in chunks, sometimes you need to separate closely related information in order to make sure that you can distinguish among similar terms. If you also include the note card information in your maps, charts, study sheets, or outlines, you will find that you also can tie the information to a major concept. This will help reduce the effects of learning the information in isolation.

MAKE QUESTION CARDS

Making question cards is another active strategy for preparing for exams. Instead of just concentrating on terms, names, dates, and events, you can dig through your text and notes and write questions on all types of information. By making question cards, you actually are predicting what type of information you may need to know for the exam. You also may approach the material in a slightly different manner and focus more on understanding rather than on simple memorization.

You can make question cards on any type of information. Write the question on the front of the card and then write the answer on the back. Make as many of them as you can. If you already have prepared a stack of word cards for the chapter, concentrate on different information for your question cards. Focus more on how things relate or how they differ. Look at the sample question cards for business, history, and biology (Figure 9.5). These questions emphasize steps in a process, lists of things, and causes and effects.

Using question cards is especially helpful for students taking math and science classes. If you will have to solve problems on your exams, you may find that making formula cards and problem cards is essential to getting a good grade. Have you ever started a math, chemistry, or physics problem on a test and realized you

Figure 9.5 Sample Question Cards

(Front)	(Back)
What are the steps in using a matrix model?	1. Identify steps 2. Develop a series of steps 3. Evaluate the competition 4. Consider factors that aren't addressed by matrix 5. Develop a target portfolio Ch 6

Business Card

(Front)	(Back)
What were the relief measures of the new deal?	1. Federal Emergency Relief Administration 2. Civilian Conservation Corps 3. Home Owners Loan Corp.

History Card

(Front)	(Back)
What is PKU? What causes it?	phenylketonuria Severe mental retardation one symptom One single missing gene transmitted as a recessive gene—parental carrier to 1/4 of offspring

Biology Card

weren't sure which kind of problem it was? Even though you knew how to do all of the problems when you reviewed, their random order on the exam may have left you confused.

Learn to recognize the special features of each problem so that you will be able to identify the problems when they appear out of context on a test. One way that you can do this is by creating your own test bank, a series of sample problems on cards. After you have studied for the exam, make three index cards for each kind of problem, with one sample question on the front of each index card. Don't put any other information on the front of the card; you don't want to give yourself any clues that won't be there on the test. Then, on the back of the card, put four things. First, at the top of the card, write the type of problem that it is. After that, write the first step that you need to take to solve the problem. Then put the answer or solution on the card. Finally, in the bottom corner put the page number where you got the problem or where you can go for help.

After you have prepared all of your cards, shuffle them to mix them up. Go through the cards orally a few times. Look at each problem and try to state the type of problem it is and the first step you would have to follow to solve it. If you're wrong, look at the problem and try to determine a way to remember which type of problem it is. Don't try to memorize the solution or page number; they are there only for reference. If you have prepared well, you should be able to solve the problem once you identify its type. Next, test yourself by solving the problems on paper. Take the stack and work each problem as though it were a test question. Turn the card over and check your work. Continue until you can do all of the problems. Problem cards provide an excellent self-test. They require you to solve problems outside the context of the text. They also can be saved for final exams and for a quick review before taking subsequent courses.

MAKE STUDY SHEETS

Preparing study sheets is one of the best ways to prepare for an exam. A study sheet is a one-page summary of the important ideas or concepts on a particular topic. The sample study sheet on Mesopotamia (see Figure 9.6) is the first of four study sheets that were prepared for the first chapter in a western civilization course. How many study sheets you prepare depends on how you organize or divide the information that you need to learn. If you were preparing for a history exam, for example, you could make a study sheet on each main topic that was covered in the lecture or each main subdivision of the chapter. You might have four study sheets for one chapter, or you might have ten.

Figure 9.6 Sample Study Sheet

Mesopotamia
I. Sumer (3500– 2350 BC)
agricultural settlements T& E valley formed towns
first system of writing
(signs on clay tablets - cuneiform)
led to trade → cities
center of life - temple
religion - seasons - fertility Great Mother
ex. Lady of Warka
govern - priests
Epic of Gilgamesh (most famous ruler) fiction
pessimistic (life struggle against disaster – no afterlife)
1. quest – human is a questioner (ultimacy)
2. death – pos & neg moments
3. story – human is a mythmaker
II. Semitic King Sargon ruled (2350 to 2150)
Akkadian Culture
art - bronze head of Nineveh
Stele of Naram - Sim
buildings - ziggurats

You also can use a number of different formats in designing your study sheets. You may use a modified outline format like the Mesopotamia sample, a chart (or matrix) format, or even a map format. If you already have been using one or more of these techniques for taking notes, you'll find that it doesn't take long to prepare your study sheets.

It's easy to make study sheets. After you choose your first topic, go through your textbook and your lecture notes looking for information about that topic; then combine the information as you prepare your study sheet. You also should include diagrams, formulas, and even sample problems on your study sheet. If you already have made word cards for the technical terms in the chapter, you don't need to put them on your study sheet.

There are two real advantages to developing study sheets. First, just making the study sheets requires you to dig through the material and think critically about each point. You also have to combine, organize, and condense the information from the text and the information from your notes into a single study sheet. In order to complete these tasks, you must synthesize the material in a way that makes sense to you. This processing of the information at a deeper level can aid in your retention of it.

Although you benefit from the process of developing study sheets, you also benefit from the result. The second advantage of preparing study sheets is that you have concise summaries of the information, which can be used for review. Study sheets provide a quick way to review as you progress through your Five-Day Study Plan and are useful when preparing for comprehensive finals. After you prepare your study sheet, use it to review the important information. Practice reciting the information. Cover the sheet and see how much of the information you can remember. If you have a lot of information on your sheet, focus on the main headings first. Learn them and then use them to help you recall the details. File them away after the exam until you're ready to study for your finals.

MAKE SELF-TESTS

Making self-tests is another active way to prepare for an exam. In order to make a self-test, you have to decide what information you need to know for the exam and then formulate questions about it. Most students tend to write questions that are either short answer or completion. Although both of these types of questions do help you focus on important information and do test your recall of that information, they are not the types of questions that typically are on exams.

If you predict and prepare for questions only at the knowledge level, you may be unable to answer higher-level questions. That may explain why you may have felt well prepared for an exam, but couldn't answer some of the questions. If you will have to answer comprehension- or application-level questions on an exam, you should try to write questions at that level for your self-test. Writing higher-level questions does require more time and effort than writing knowledge-level questions, but it will better prepare you for the types of questions that you will actually have to answer.

You can benefit even more from your self-tests if they are composed of the same types of questions as will be on the exam. For example, if you're going to have an exam in Psychology that is composed of fifty multiple-choice questions, you may be able to improve your score by writing multiple-choice test items rather than completion items. One advantage of actually making up multiple-choice items is that you have to generate three or four wrong answers in addition to the right answer. This can help you improve your score on the exam, because you are learning to distinguish between the correct answer and several possible but incorrect answers. In a sense you are predicting the incorrect answers or distractors that your professor may also use. If you choose the same ones that are on the actual test, you will be able to eliminate them immediately.

In the same way, writing your own true-false items can help you tune in to key words that can be used or changed to make the statement false. Making up matching tests helps you make fine distinctions among terms, concepts, people, and so on. If you will have to answer essay questions, you need to prepare by predicting and practicing possible essay test questions. A detailed discussion of how to prepare for essay tests will follow in Chapter 12.

No matter which type of questions you decide to write, you should never put the correct answers on the test page itself. Instead, write the answers on another sheet of paper or on the back of your self-test. Once you mark the answers on the test, you have changed your test into a study sheet. One of the benefits of making self-tests is that you can use them over and over again to test your knowledge of the information. As you prepare the chapter, make a self-test, and then take the test as a way of reviewing what you have learned. Some students like to make up test questions as they prepare for the exam and then answer all of them the night before the test. This can provide an effective final review. Be sure, however, to leave some time to learn those items that you don't get right. Then test yourself again just to be sure.

RECITE

If you've been practicing your word or question cards, you've probably discovered that reciting is one of the best ways to get information into long-term memory. If you like using recitation strategies, there are a number of them that you can try. First, practice the important information by reciting it from your notes, text, or study sheets. Cover the information with your hand or look away, and then try to recite it, or use the recall column to test your memory. Seeing, saying, and hearing the information helps you put it into long-term memory.

Teaching the information to someone else is another effective recitation strategy. If you're lucky enough to have a friend or relative who is willing to be your "guinea pig," you can take on the role of instructor and explain everything you know about the subject to him or her. One advantage of a human partner is that he or she can easily signal understanding or confusion. If your partner doesn't understand the information, you can try to explain it in another way. This may force you to rephrase the information in your own words, which helps you learn it, too.

Sometimes you can't find (or keep after one session) a human "student." This isn't a problem; you can teach the material to anything — a dog, a plant, or even a stuffed animal. Explaining the material out loud helps you clarify the information for yourself. Sit with your book and notes open and pretend that you are trying to explain the information to someone who doesn't understand it. Pretend that someone asked you a question about a particular topic, and answer it.

If you're being tutored or are part of a study group, remember one thing: The person who does the talking is the one who does the learning. Just listening to someone else explain something is a passive activity. When I was taking statistics in college, I would walk to and from the parking lot with another classmate. I would ask questions about something we had just covered, and he would explain it to me. He would then ask if I understood, and I always said "yes," but often I was still not sure I did understand. Finally, one day I stopped my friend in the middle of explaining something and said, "Wait a minute. Let *me* explain it to you. If I make a mistake, stop me." After that I did the explaining. I found that I truly understood the information because I was able to put it into my own words.

PRACTICE CHARTS, DIAGRAMS, AND MAPS

The best way to study charts, diagrams, or maps for an exam is to actually re-create them. If you're going to have to fill in a chart as part of an exam, prepare by starting with a blank chart and fill it in from memory. Many students in biology classes, for example, have to identify specific structures in diagrams. Your text or notes may contain a nicely labeled diagram similar to the one in Figure 9.7. Do you remember trying to learn all of the bones in health class? I remember trying to cover all the names with my hands and arms and then trying to recite the names out loud. No matter how fast I covered them, I could still see some of those words. Instead of trying to study a labeled diagram, you should photocopy, trace, or draw the diagram and cut out, blacken, or white out the names. Number each line, and you will have created an effective study sheet or self-test. Put the names on the back or keep a copy of the original as your answer sheet. Practice out loud until you can correctly identify all of the numbered sites. Then practice writing the correct names and check your work.

Figure 9.7 Sample Diagram

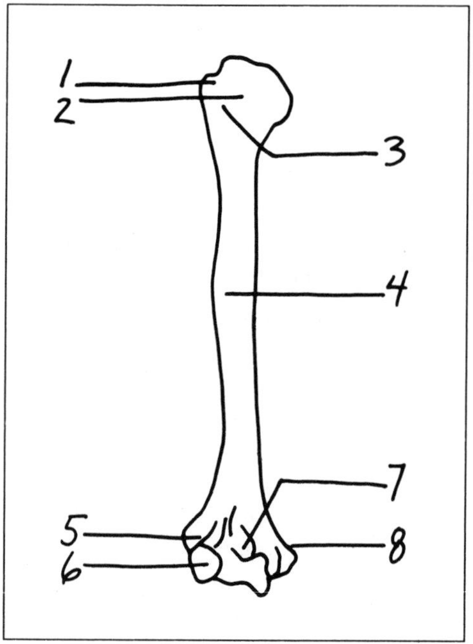

STUDY IN A GROUP

Many students who are taking difficult classes form study groups. They feel that by working together each of them can help and be helped by others in the group. Study groups work the best if all members are committed to working hard. One advantage is that each member can share information. Not everyone has identical notes or can do all of the problems. By working together, group members help each other fill in gaps in their learning. By taking turns explaining information or by throwing out questions to other members of the group, each person gets a good review of the material. Sharing predictions about what will be on the test also can help all of the group members prepare.

The best way to work in a study group is to work as a group throughout the semester. If, however, you decide to work as a group just for exams, schedule your first meeting at least a week before the exam. Spend a few hours deciding what each member of the group should do in order to prepare for the next meeting. You may decide to divide up the material so that each group member is responsible for one chapter and the related materials. For example, each member could prepare study sheets for the chapter (with photocopies for all other group members), predict test questions or make a self-test, and be prepared to discuss or explain the main topics in the chapter. Everyone else should still review all of the chapters, but with one person responsible for each chapter, the group will benefit from the in-depth preparation that would have required more time than each of them had.

During the next meeting, each student should present a short overview of the material and then drill the group on his or her portion of the material. If everyone works together, all members of the group should be well prepared for the exam. Remember, though — group sessions don't replace preparing alone. In many cases, they provide a clearer understanding of what you still need to learn on your own.

CONDUCT A FINAL REVIEW

Conducting a final review the day before your exam will help insure your recall of all of the important information. You can review all of your word or question cards, you can recite all of your study sheets, or you can check your understanding by making charts or maps for all of the important topics. However, there are a few other review strategies that you may want to add to your study plan.

Make a List of 20

One of the last things I like to do before taking an exam is make up a list of twenty things that I think will be on the test. This is a good final review because you have to go back through all of the material to decide what twenty pieces of information to put on your list. Write the actual information you will need to know on your list; don't just list the topic or idea.

Your List of 20 can be used like a final study sheet. When you go to take the test, review it as often as you can before the professor tells you to put away your materials. After the exam, you'll be able to evaluate how well you predicted what would be on the test. Each time you take an exam, try to predict what the professor will ask. You'll find that you get better each time you do it. The best that I ever did was eighteen out of twenty; that's 90 percent. If you become skilled in predicting what will be on the exam, you can focus on those things that you think will be on the test and spend less time on other things.

Use Study Guides

Sometimes professors hand out a study guide or study sheet before exams. Generally, this guide is a list of information that you need to know for the exam. It rarely contains the actual information itself. It's your job to use it to guide your preparation and review. If you have a list of terms to identify, write them on cards or on a separate paper; don't try to write the answers on the study guide sheet. Make up test questions and study sheets for concepts or topics that are stressed. Then, before the exam, use the study guide itself as a self-test to check your preparation.

Some texts come with study guides that the author has prepared to help you master the material. The instructor usually recommends that you fill in the study guide as you read or after you read the chapter. This helps you monitor your comprehension of the material. However, what could be an excellent "test" before the exam then becomes just something that you can "read over." Instead of filling in your study guide (especially the kind with the blanks scattered through the text material), number each blank and write the answers on a separate sheet. Then you can use the study guide like a self-test.

Use Old Exams

Sometimes old versions of a test are made available by the professor. Old exams can be helpful because you can get an idea of the types of questions that the professor will ask. Although you may not face exactly the same questions on your exam, they may cover the same material. If old tests are available, use them to test your preparation. If you miss some items, be sure to spend extra time on that information. Then take the test again as a final review. Old tests cannot replace proper preparation, though. If you study only the items on the old test, you won't be very well prepared for your exam, and you won't learn very much about the course.

ACTIVITIES

1. Use the following exercise to test your learning style. Jot down three lists of five words each and their definitions. Be sure that the lists are comprised of unfamiliar but similar words (that is, all five words in a list should be of similar difficulty). Try to learn the definitions in the first list by reading over the list. Test yourself. Then try reciting the words in the second list out loud. Test yourself again. Finally, try writing the definitions of the words in the third list. Test yourself again. Which method was the most effective for learning the word lists?
2. Set up a Five-Day Study Plan for an exam that you have coming up in the next few weeks. Select some actual tasks to add to your study plan from the menu in Figure 9.3, but feel free to create other strategies of your own.
3. Make a series of study sheets for a chapter from one of your texts. Be sure that you combine the information from your text and your lecture notes.

4. Make a self-test on some of your own text material. Include five multiple-choice questions, five true-false questions, and five completion questions.

5. Select two headed sections from one of your texts. Review one section by reading over it a few times. Then, review the second section by reciting the information or "teaching" it to someone or something else. Write a short paragraph explaining how well you learned using each technique.

POSTTEST

Where Are You Now?

Now that you have completed Chapter 9, take a few minutes to answer *yes* or *no* to the following questions. Compare your answers with those in the pretest.

	YES	NO
1. When preparing for exams, is your primary study method to read over the material?	_____	_____
2. Do you tend to miss class the day before the exam?	_____	_____
3. After an exam are you unsure of how well you did?	_____	_____
4. Do you make up self-tests as a way of studying for exams?	_____	_____
5. Do you study by yourself and with a group before a very difficult exam?	_____	_____
6. Do you tend to study only the day or night before the exam?	_____	_____
7. Do you review your lecture notes and text material together according to the topic?	_____	_____
8. Do you often know the answer to multiple-choice questions even before you look at the alternatives?	_____	_____
9. Do you review by reciting out loud and/or making up study sheets?	_____	_____
10. Do you space your study time over a period of several days?	_____	_____

Give yourself one point for each *yes* answer to questions 4, 5, 7, 8, 9, and 10, and one point for each *no* answer to questions 1, 2, 3, and 6. Now total up your points. Compare your score on this posttest with the score that you had on the pretest. Did you improve? In which areas? Where do you still need to make improvements?

CHAPTER 10

Improving Memory

"For several years I have used catchwords to aid my memory, but this semester I started using catchphrases and found that they work well also. The most important thing that I learned, though, is that you must know the material in the first place. These tricks won't do any good without already having the knowledge."

Peter Caroff

MEMORY: STORAGE AND RETRIEVAL

Doing well on exams requires an effective study plan, active study strategies, and a good memory. What you typically think of as learning involves storing information in your memory so that it will be available later when you need it. In this chapter, you will gain a better understanding of how information is stored in memory. You may begin to understand why many of the exam preparation strategies described in Chapter 9 helped you learn and retain course material. "Having a good memory," however, involves both putting information into memory *and getting it back out*—both storage and retrieval. Although this chapter includes some additional strategies for storing information, the focus of the chapter will be on strategies and techniques that you can use to retrieve or get that information back out of memory when you take an exam.

PRETEST

Where Are You Now?

Take a few minutes to answer *yes* or *no* to the following questions.

	YES	NO
1. Do you often know the answer to a question but find that you can't think of it?	_____	_____
2. Do you organize or group information to help you remember it?	_____	_____
3. Do you take self-tests in order to check your learning?	_____	_____
4. Do you make up rhymes or words to help you remember some information?	_____	_____
5. Do you use deep processing strategies?	_____	_____
6. Do you try to memorize all of the information that you need to know for an exam?	_____	_____
7. Do you often find that you get confused by closely related information?	_____	_____
8. Do you often forget a lot of the information that you studied by the time you take the test?	_____	_____
9. Is the TV or stereo on while you study?	_____	_____
10. Can you learn and remember information just by making up a rhyme, word, or other memory aid?	_____	_____

Give yourself one point for each *yes* answer to questions 2, 4, and 5, and one point for each *no* answer to questions 1, 3, 6, 7, 8, 9, and 10. Now total up your points. A low score indicates that you need to improve your memory. A high score indicates that you are already using many good memory strategies.

UNDERSTANDING MEMORY PROCESSES

Can you recall a time when you thought you had studied a particular topic well enough that you knew it for the exam, only to find that you were unable to remember the information during the test? Perhaps you never really got the information

Figure 10.1 Information Processing Theory

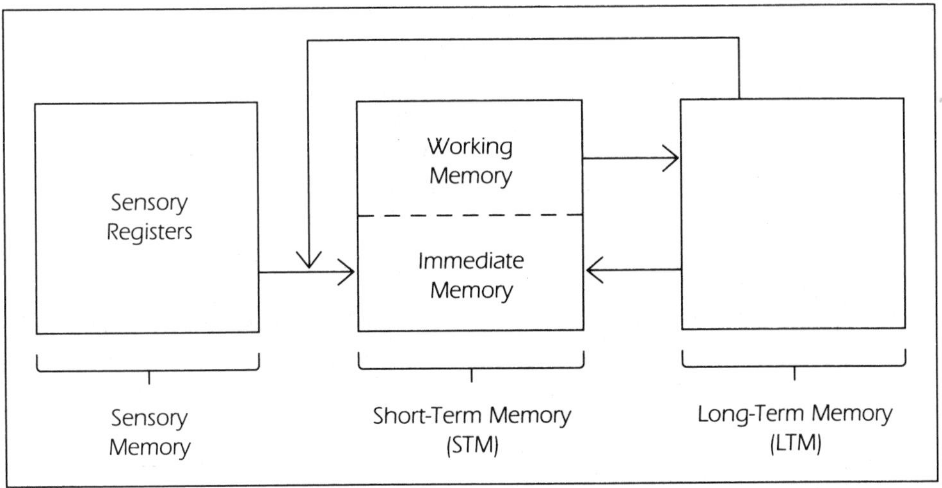

into your long-term memory, or perhaps you simply were unable to recall it when you needed to. Why do we forget? How do we learn? Many students really don't understand how memory works. Do you? Learning about how we store and retrieve information will help you understand why some study strategies work and others don't. Over the years, psychologists have tried to develop theories to explain how memory works. One of the most useful of these is the Information Processing Model.

INFORMATION PROCESSING MODEL

The Information Processing Model suggests that memory is complex and consists of various processes and stages. For example, there are at least three types of memory: sensory memory, short-term memory (STM), and long-term memory (LTM). In addition, there are three important memory processes: encoding, storage, and retrieval. Figure 10.1, which was adapted from a model developed by Bourne, Dominowski, Loftus, and Healy,[1] shows the three types of memory (represented as boxes) as well as the memory processes (represented as arrows).

In order to learn and remember, we must encode, store, and retrieve information. The first step in this process is encoding. Encoding involves interpreting information in a meaningful way. Suppose you want to remember what a cloud looks like.

[1]Bourne, L. E., Dominowski, R. L., Loftus, E. F., & Healy, A. F., *Cognitive Processes,* 2nd ed. (Englewood Cliffs, NJ: Prentice-Hall, 1986).

Clouds are amorphous (without a definite shape) and lack any clear structure. You might find it difficult to remember exactly how a cloud looks after observing it briefly. However, if you notice that the cloud looks somewhat like an elephant, you will be better able to remember its shape later simply by picturing an elephant. In order to be remembered, information must be encoded; it must be interpreted in a meaningful way. The second step in the memory process, storage, involves working on (for example, repeating) and organizing information so that it can be placed into long-term memory. Information doesn't automatically move into long-term memory unless we work to store it there. Much of what we think of as studying involves storage processes. The third step, retrieval, involves getting back information from our long-term memory storehouse. As you will see, retrieving a memory is very much like going into your basement to find the badminton set that you know is there, somewhere—you may have to hunt for awhile, but eventually you'll come upon a clue that will lead you to your goal.

Sensory Memory

You probably have heard about short-term and long-term memory. However, sensory memory, also known as the sensory registers, may be new to you. Essentially, our senses (vision, hearing, smell, taste, and touch) are always very busy. We hear, see, smell, taste, and touch hundreds of stimuli each moment. Most of these stimuli are unimportant and are, therefore, quickly forgotten. However, some of the stimuli are important to us and worth remembering.

At one time scientists believed that we remembered, somewhere in our brain, everything that we ever saw, heard, smelled, tasted, or touched. We now realize that such a feat would be nearly impossible; our memories quickly would fill up with billions upon billions of bits of useless information. Instead, we remember only those stimuli that we decide are important, those to which we choose to pay attention.

Short-Term Memory

Once we decide to remember material, we immediately have to move it into short-term memory. However, in order to do this the material must be encoded. Encoding, as you know, involves making information meaningful, making sense out of it.

Short-term memory has two components, *immediate memory* and *working memory*. Immediate memory is related to the concept of consciousness. Whatever we currently are thinking about is in our immediate memory. Think of your immediate memory as being similar to a small desk. In a two-hour study session you may work on a number of tasks at your desk. However, because your desk is very small, you can place only a limited amount of material on it at any one time. If you want to work on something new, you need to move aside the material on which you were just working. Immediate memory is similar to this because you can remember only the material that is "sitting on your desk" at any one time. Because immediate memory is very limited, we typically can retain only about seven (plus or minus two) chunks of information on our "desk." Furthermore, without some additional help, those seven chunks can stay on the "desk" for only twenty to thirty seconds before they slip away.

Consider the following example. Suppose you want to order a pizza from the new pizza parlor. You have to call directory assistance for the number, because it isn't yet listed in the phone book. The operator tells you that the number is 837-6204. You hang up and immediately dial 837-6204 and get a busy signal. You decide to wait thirty seconds and call again. In the meantime you notice the dog's water bowl is empty, and you fill it up. When you try to call again after thirty seconds, you find that you can't remember the number. We can't hold information in short-term memory for more than thirty seconds *unless we continue to rehearse it*.

In order to hold on to information and get it into your long-term memory, you must first move the material into the other part of your short-term memory, the working memory. This part of the memory system is aptly named, because you really have to "work" on the material to make it meaningful, memorable, and easy to remember. There are a variety of strategies that you can use to move information into your working memory, but all have one thing in common. The harder you work on the material, the greater the probability that you will put the material into long-term memory in a place where you can find it again.

Long-Term Memory

Once material has been processed in working memory it can be moved into long-term memory. What is so remarkable about long-term memory is that it has an almost unlimited capacity. We have not yet discovered anyone who has completely filled his or her long-term memory. In fact, the more we learn, the more capacity for learning we appear to have. Building long-term memories appears to provide a structure for adding new memories. The more we learn, the easier it is to continue learning. Long-term memory also is remarkable because we appear to hold on to most of our memories indefinitely.

Long-term memory can be compared to a warehouse full of filing cabinets. Both the cabinets in the warehouse and the material within the cabinets are arranged in a logical order; each cabinet drawer is labeled, and there are dividers within each drawer. Materials (memories) are placed in specific folders, in specific sections, in specific drawers, in specific file cabinets, in specific sections of the warehouse. However, the warehouse (your long-term memory) is enormous. Unless the material is carefully classified and placed in the correct file, it can easily be misfiled. Once material is misfiled, or just poorly classified and filed, it is much more difficult to retrieve. Only when we really work to appropriately classify it are we able to retrieve it easily.

RETRIEVAL AND FORGETTING

If we can hold on to memories indefinitely, why do we forget? As you might guess, there are a number of reasons for forgetting, some of which are related to retrieval. At times, we think that we have forgotten information, but in fact we never really got it into long-term memory at all. Either we worked on it too little to store it in long-term memory, or we did such a poor job of organizing it that although it's in long-term memory, it's in a form that is unrecognizable and unusable.

Many memories are available to us in our long-term memory; however, they aren't readily accessible. In order to access a memory, we need to know how to find it. Many times we need a key term, or what psychologists call a cue, to unlock the memory. Memories that we use frequently are typically stored with a number of cues, thus making them easier to remember. However, at times we store memories with only one or two cues. Unless we hit upon those cues, we are unable to retrieve those memories. Clearly, the more ways we devise for material to be remembered, the more cues we develop that make the material more accessible to us.

Other processes also affect retrieval. For example, organization affects retrieval. Memories that are well organized are easier to retrieve than material that is not well organized. Anxiety also affects retrieval. When we're anxious it's more difficult to recall cues and retrieve important information, because anxiety affects our

PEANUTS reprinted by permission of UFS, Inc.

ability to focus and concentrate. Many of us have had the experience of being unable to retrieve a memory during an examination and then remembering the material once the exam is over and our anxiety is reduced.

Interference theory, another memory model, also is important to the concept of forgetting. Interference theory states that memories can interfere with one another during the retrieval process. Over the years we tend to learn many things that are similar to one another. Unless we make each of these memories distinctive, there is a strong likelihood that one memory will interfere with another. It's well worth the effort to develop some unique cues that will help to make each memory distinctive.

Other types of interference also affect our ability to store and retrieve information. Watching television or studying with the stereo on can prevent you from concentrating on the material you are trying to learn. Even though you think you are working on learning the material, you may instead be "working" on the distractions around you.

Due to a combination of failing to store information appropriately in long-term memory, using too few cues, and interference, we tend to forget newly learned material rapidly if we don't rehearse it. The next part of this chapter will discuss attending to information, maintaining information in short-term memory, encoding information for storage into long-term memory, and retrieval strategies.

WHY DO YOU NEED MEMORY STRATEGIES?

Now that you understand how information is encoded, stored, and retrieved, you may wonder why you need to learn specific strategies to aid your memory. According to Donald Norman, "To remember is to have managed three things successfully: the acquisition, retention, and retrieval of information. Failure to remember means failure at managing one of those steps."[2] In order to perform well in college courses, you need to use strategies that aid the acquisition, retention, and retrieval of the information that you want to learn. In college, learning to get back information from memory is just as important as learning to put that information into memory.

Let's try an experiment to find out what kinds of strategies you already use. Can you name all fifty states? Write down the first ten that you can remember in the

---

[2]Norman, D. A., *Learning and Memory* (New York: W. H. Freeman, 1982), p. 2.

margin or on a piece of scrap paper. How did you remember the states that you wrote down? What method did you use to remember them? Look at the first couple of states that you wrote down. Do they follow some type of order? Did you use alphabetical order to list the states, or did you use geographical order, like Maine, New Hampshire, Vermont, or Washington, Oregon, California? Although these are the two most common ways that students tend to remember the states, many students use other strategies. How you remembered the states really isn't important. The important thing is that you probably used some strategy to recall information that you most likely learned a number of years ago.

If you learned the states in alphabetical order, it would be easier for you to retrieve that information alphabetically than geographically. On the other hand, if you learned the information geographically, by doing maps or by travel, you may find it difficult to list the states alphabetically. From this exercise, you should have learned that the method you use to organize information during study will in some way determine how effectively you can retrieve that information. In addition, the more associations you develop for particular information, the easier it will be to retrieve. In this section, you'll learn some general and specific strategies that will help improve your ability to learn and retrieve information.

GENERAL STRATEGIES FOR IMPROVING YOUR MEMORY

You already may be using a number of the following general strategies to help you acquire, retain, and retrieve course information. However, you may find it useful to take another look at them now that you have a better understanding of how memory works.

SPACED PRACTICE

There are many benefits to using spaced practice instead of massed practice. Massed practice, like cramming, involves studying all of the material at one time. Spaced practice, on the other hand, involves distributing your study time over a longer period, with breaks between practice sessions. Studying for short periods of time, such as one fifty-minute session, prevents boredom, helps avoid fatigue, and improves motivation. If you space out your study over a period of days (as recommended in the Five-Day Study Plan), you gain several additional benefits. First of all, you delay forgetting. As we discussed earlier, even when you think you have learned the information, some information usually is "forgotten" due to ineffective encoding, insufficient rehearsal, interference, or poor organization. By reviewing the same material the next day, you have a chance to find out what you have forgotten and go over it again. In addition, you benefit by reviewing and reinforcing the information that you previously studied. By spacing out your learning, you can delay or prevent some of the forgetting that would occur before an exam.

Spaced practice or distributed practice, as it is also known, allows time for the information to consolidate or jell in long-term memory. If you try to shove too much information into memory at one time, you won't be able to retrieve very much of it. One explanation for this is that the longer you study, the more inhibitions you develop (feeling tired, bored, and so on) that decrease your efficiency for storing the material in long-term memory. With massed practice, you may get to the point where you are just reading over the material rather than "working on it" to learn it.

Another problem that may occur is that you don't organize the information well enough to find it again in your long-term storehouse. Allowing breaks between learning sessions gives you time to think about what you have been studying and structure or organize it according to what you already know about the topic.

BREAKING DOWN TASKS

When you study small amounts of material at one time (as recommended in the Five-Day Study Plan), you can do a better job of organizing it in order to place it into long-term memory. It's easier to stay focused and actively involved in your learning when you're dealing with small units of material. Trying to learn large amounts of material at one time can become overwhelming.

REPETITION

Spaced learning also works because it involves repetition of the material. Each time you write or recite the same information (especially if you do it in a slightly different way), you strengthen your memory of it. An early theory of how memory works described traces or pathways in the brain. Although developing a memory really is not like wearing a path in the brain, you may find that this analogy helps you understand how learning and retrieval occur. Each time you work on the material (by writing, reciting, or even thinking about it), you strengthen the path that leads to your long-term memory. Here's another way to look at it. Imagine that each time you practice the same piece of information, you open a particular file in one of the drawers of your long-term memory filing cabinet. The more times that you open that same drawer and pull out that same file, the easier it is to do it the next time; you know just where to go in the warehouse and exactly where in the filing cabinet to look. Repetition, especially spaced over several hours or days, can help you strengthen and maintain your memory of important material.

OVERLEARNING

Overlearning involves continuing to work on material even after it is learned. This practice is very helpful in improving your memory. Each time you review the material, you help reduce forgetting and strengthen the path to your long-term memory. Overlearning also may provide additional benefits. It may lead you to review the material in other ways. You may form different cues for, or associations with, the material each time you review it. You may even find that as you continue to work on the material, you gain a better understanding of it.

Overlearning also can help you cope with test anxiety, which interferes with your ability to retrieve information from long-term memory. If you're worrying about an exam, you may have difficulty identifying or remembering the cues that you need in order to locate the information that you stored. Overlearned material is less susceptible to the debilitating effects of anxiety, because you can retrieve the overlearned information without having to think very much about it. You can count on overlearned information to help you get started during the exam. Answering questions that cover overlearned information is a good way to use your test time efficiently until you calm down.

SPECIFIC MEMORY STRATEGIES

In addition to the general strategies that were described above, there are many specific learning strategies that are effective in developing your memory processes. Weinstein and Mayer describe five groups of learning strategies: *rehearsal* strategies, *elaboration* strategies, *organizational* strategies, *comprehension monitoring* strategies, and *affective* and motivational strategies.[3] Each of these categories includes a variety of learning strategies that can be used to improve the various memory processes. Let's look at some of them.

REHEARSAL STRATEGIES

Rehearsal strategies include tasks such as repeating information in a list, underlining or highlighting, copying, and even taking selective verbatim (word-for-word) notes from the text. If you originally learned the list of the fifty states simply by writing them over and over or saying them again and again and again, you were using a rehearsal strategy. You also are using rehearsal strategies when you prac-

[3]Weinstein, C. F., and Mayer, R. F., "The teaching of learning strategies," in M. C. Wittrock, ed., *Handbook of Research on Teaching* (New York: Macmillan, 1986).

tice your word or question cards, when you cover your notes and then try to recite the information, or when you read or write your study sheets over and over again. You probably already have discovered that this strategy works fairly well for simple tasks, but is not as well suited to some of the more complex learning tasks that you need to use for college classes.

As you discovered in Chapter 9, rehearsal strategies are an important component of your test preparation repertoire. Rehearsal strategies such as reciting are very important for moving information from short-term to long-term memory. Also, when they are combined with one or more of the other learning strategies described below, they can be effective tools for making material memorable. If you want to remember the five learning strategies, which rehearsal strategy could you use?

ELABORATION STRATEGIES

Elaboration strategies involve forming associations or determining how new information relates to what you already know. Paraphrasing, summarizing, explaining, answering questions, forming mental images, and using mnemonics (ni-mon-iks) are all elaboration strategies. Effective note taking requires you to embellish or refine what the professor or the author has said. When you take notes in your own words and add comments or make connections, you're using an elaboration strategy. One of the chief advantages of elaboration strategies is that they help you create more associations with the material to be learned, thereby providing you with more routes for getting to the information during retrieval. Explaining the material out loud, preparing study sheets, and making maps also are examples of elaboration strategies that you probably are using already. Because you already are familiar with how to use those strategies, in this section we'll focus on some other elaboration techniques, especially the use of mnemonics.

Mnemonic devices or techniques often are referred to as memory tricks. However, many of these techniques aren't tricks at all. They are, instead, techniques that can help you remember things when you can't seem to remember them any other way.

This brings up a very important point. Mnemonic devices are aids to retrieval, but they do not guarantee that you will know the material. You can't just decide that you are going to remember Weinstein and Mayer's five categories of learning strategies by remembering the "word" REOCA (Rehearsal, Elaboration, Organizational, Comprehension monitoring, Affective). Before you can use "REOCA" to help you list or discuss these strategies, you have to practice the connection between the mnemonic and the information to be learned. Although this section focuses on the use of mnemonics, it's important to remember that you must use the other elaboration strategies to learn the information in the first place. The mnemonics will then be useful in retrieving what you have learned.

According to Kenneth Higbee (1977), "A mnemonic system may help you in at least three ways when you are trying to find items in your memory: (1) It will give you a place to start your search, a way to locate the first item. (2) It will give you a way of proceeding systematically from one item to the next. (3) It will let you know when your recall is finished, when you have reached the last item."[4] You will learn more about how to make those connections and use mnemonics as retrieval aids as you examine the use of rhymes, associations, acronyms, acrostics, and imagery.

Rhymes

One of the earliest forms of mnemonics that you probably learned to use was the rhyme. What do you think of if someone asks you how many days there are in the month of June? I immediately think of the rhyme:

> Thirty days hath September, April, June, and November...

Can you think of any other rhymes that you learned in elementary school? Perhaps you learned the alphabet song, the song for how to spell "encyclopedia," and "i before e, except after c." You may have learned many others but don't even think about them until you need them. As you will see, one of the benefits of mnemonics is that we tend to be able to remember them for a long time. Even though many mnemonic devices are common ones that we all learn in elementary school, couldn't you make up some to help you remember information for your college exams? Of course you can. Heidi devised the following rhyme to help her remember the steps to follow in writing an essay answer.

> Answer question right away
>
> List in margin, that's the way.
>
> Budget time, plan ahead
>
> Make sure that the question's read.

---

[4]Higbee, K., *Your Memory: How It Works and How to Improve It* (Englewood Cliffs, NJ: Prentice-Hall, 1977), p. 78.

Associations

Forming associations is always important when you're trying to remember something. We use this technique every day. You also can use association to help you remember details for exams.

When I was in eighth grade, we were studying longitude and latitude in geography class. Every day for a week, we had a quiz, and I kept getting longitude and latitude confused. I went home and almost cried because I was so frustrated and embarrassed that I couldn't keep them straight in my mind. I stared and stared at those words until suddenly I figured out what to do. I told myself, when you see that *n* in longitude it will remind you of the word *north.* Therefore, it will be easy to remember that longitude lines go from north to south. It worked; I got them all right on the next quiz, and the next, and on the exam.

When I tell this story in class, some of my students laugh because it seems silly to them that anyone could get longitude and latitude confused. However, some of us do get confused about things that may seem simple to others.

Acronyms or Catchwords

Acronyms are "words" that are made up of the first letters of other words. Acronyms are so commonly used today that most of us don't even realize that they aren't real words. "SCUBA," "NASA," "FBI," "COD," and "AIDS" are all quite familiar. We don't even think of them as standing for self-contained underwater breathing apparatus, National Aeronautics and Space Administration, Federal Bureau of Investigation, cash on delivery, and Acquired Immune Deficiency Syndrome; they all are well understood in their abbreviated form.

John Langan used the term *catchword* to describe an acronym.[5] In a sense, acronyms do help us catch or hold on to the information that we have learned. Catchwords, or acronyms, can be real words or nonsense words. You probably can name all of the colors in the spectrum because someone taught you to use the catchword "ROY G. BIV" (red, orange, yellow, green, blue, indigo, violet). "REOCA" also is an example of a catchword; each letter stands for the first letter in a list of other words. Can you say them now? Try it.

Catchwords are useful for learning lists of information. You can use catchwords to remember the four kinds of fossils that are listed below.

---

[5]Langan, J., *Reading and Study Skills,* 4th ed. (New York: McGraw-Hill, 1989), p. 207.

1. Actual Remains
2. Petrified
3. Imprint
4. Molds and Casts

You might create a catchword like "PAIM" (sounds like pain but with an M instead; it would be painful to become a fossil) or "IMAP" (fossils are my maps of the past). In both cases your catchword also provides an *association* with the material to be learned. You also can use catchwords to remember longer lists of information. Look at the five general principles of nonverbal communication listed below.

1. Nonverbal communication is multichanneled.
2. Nonverbal communication is relatively spontaneous.
3. Nonverbal communication is relatively ambiguous.
4. Nonverbal communication may contradict verbal messages.
5. Nonverbal communication is very culture-bound.[6]

In order to make an acronym, or catchword, you first have to identify a key word in each statement. Go back and underline the following words: *multichanneled, spontaneous, ambiguous, contradict,* and *culture-bound*. These words should work well as hooks or tags to help you remember the entire list of principles. Next, list (or underline) the first letter of each word: M, S, A, C, C. "MSACC" doesn't sound as though it will be very memorable, but by simply rearranging the letters you could form the catchword "MACCS" or "SMACC." Both of these are fairly easy to recall.

Your work is not done, though. In order to form associations and really learn the material, you need to practice connecting the catchword to the key word and then the key word to the entire phrase. Reciting or writing will help you form the connections. If I were going to use the catchword "MACCS," I would rehearse the information this way: "M" stands for "multichanneled," and "multichanneled" stands for "nonverbal communication is multichanneled." "A" stands for

---

[6]From Weiten, W., Lloyd, M. A., and Lashley, R. L., *Psychology Applied to Modern Life,* 4th ed. (Pacific Grove, CA: Brooks/Cole, 1991), pp. 159–160. Used with permission.

"ambiguous," and "ambiguous" stands for "Nonverbal communication is relatively ambiguous" (and so on). Of course, you still have to be sure that you understand what the terms *multichanneled* and *ambiguous* mean in this context. Students who say that mnemonics don't work for them often think that simply constructing the mnemonic should firmly embed the information in long-term memory. Unfortunately, the mere construction of a word or phrase doesn't replace learning the information. Your catchword will help you retrieve the information from memory only after it is learned.

Acrostics or Catchphrases

Acrostics, or catchphrases, as Langan calls them, are phrases or sentences that are made up of words beginning with the first letters of other words. Catchphrases are especially useful if you have to remember the information in a special order or if you can't form a memorable word from the letters available to you (for instance, you may have all consonants, with no vowels). If you had to learn the five principles of nonverbal behavior in order, you might find that "Many students answer Conrad curtly," "Mark saw a clever calf," or "Meira saves all cubic centimeters" is more memorable than "MSACC."

Each of the above examples can provide us with some additional tips for creating acrostics or catchphrases. You may have noticed that in the first example ("Many students answer Conrad curtly"), the two "c" words have the same second letters (the vowels *o* and *u*) as the original key words (*contradict* and *culture-bound*). When you have two key words that start with the same letter, it is helpful to use the second letter to show which one comes first. The second example ("Mark saw a clever calf") demonstrates another good strategy to use; make your mnemonic sentences outrageous, silly, or humorous. We tend to remember funny or outrageous catchphrases better than dull and boring ones. All three examples also provide a visual image that can aid your recall. Try to visualize Meira scooping up all those cubic centimeters. After a little practice, you will find that you can use catchphrases to help you recall information for many of your college courses.

Whenever you are using catchwords or catchphrases to help you learn and remember text material, consider the following five rules.

1. Select a key word to represent each piece of information.
2. Underline or write down the first letter of each key word.
3. Form a catchword or catchphrase.

4. Practice associating the letter to the key word and then the key word to the actual information that you need to know.
5. Use the mnemonic to test your memory for the original information.

Imagery

You've already seen how effective visual imagery can be in helping you remember catchphrases. However, you can create visual images to remember course material without writing catchwords or catchphrases. Semantic, hierarchical, line, and wheel maps all can be used to present a visual display of material that you need to remember. After developing and practicing a map, you may be able to recall much of the information by visualizing the map itself.

You also can paint visual pictures in your mind to remember main points and supporting information. If you were studying the Boston Tea Party, for example, you could remember many of the details about this historic event just by visualizing what happened. Picture Boston Harbor with three of the British ships (you can see the flag on each) carrying the tea shipments. Can you see the chests (340 of them) full of tea? What is that written on the side of one? It says, "Property of the East India Company" and lists the date as "December 16, 1773." Of course, these words were not printed on the real chests, but you can imagine they were in order to create a more helpful mental picture. Can you see the colonists, many disguised as Indians, throwing the chests overboard? By incorporating names, places, dates, and so on into your visual image, you can recall a great deal of information about your topic.

ORGANIZATIONAL STRATEGIES

Organizational strategies include tasks such as listing, ordering, grouping, outlining, mapping, or diagramming. In each of these types of activities, you act on the material that is to be mastered. With outlining or mapping, for example, you organize the material in a way that shows how each component is related to the others. One of the advantages of organizational strategies is that by structuring the material, you provide yourself with new ways to remember many of the details. If you can remember the structure — the main headings of the outline or the web strands of your map, for example — you will be able to remember many of the details.

Look at the following list of words for sixty seconds; then cover it with your hand or a piece of paper and try to write the words in the margin or on scrap paper.

newspaper, pencil, bus, automobile, book, pen, boat, magazine, comic book, chalk, crayon, train

You may have found that it was difficult to remember all twelve of the items. Do you know why? Earlier you learned about the capacity of short-term memory. If you recall, you can remember only about seven pieces of information at one time. You can, however, increase this capacity by chunking (grouping) the information. You probably will be able to remember all twelve items if you group them as follows:

Things You Read	**Things You Write With**	**Things You Ride In**
newspaper	pencil	bus
book	pen	automobile
magazine	chalk	boat
comic book	crayon	train

With this grouping, you have three pieces or chunks of information to remember instead of twelve. It's easy to remember three things, right? You also can remember the four items in each category quite easily because the headings help trigger your memory. Now look at the three groups for sixty seconds and try to write down as many of the items as you can.

You can improve your ability to learn and recall a large amount of material by grouping or chunking it. However, you should follow some basic guidelines when setting up your groups. First, never set up more than seven groups. Why? If you make up ten or fifteen groups, you won't be able to remember all of the group headings. For the same reason, limit the number of items in each group to seven. Second, be sure you use a simple system. If your plan for remembering the information is extremely complex, you won't be able to remember it (the plan), and then you won't be able to remember the information itself. Third, you can't learn the information just by looking at it. You need to write or recite the lists and then test yourself. Remember, the more organized the information is when you put it into long-term memory, the more easily you will be able to retrieve it later.

Before her exam in Computer Literacy, Heather organized the information on the five different programming languages by using an informal outline and mnemonic sentences (Figure 10.2). She pulled the important information out of her text and notes and structured it in such a way that she could learn and remember it. Then, she created catchphrases to prompt her memory. Her first sentence, "Corey Finds Bobby Playing Alone," provides hooks for the five programming languages. The

Figure 10.2 Heather's Informal Outline (with Mnemonic Sentences)

	Computer Programming Languages	
Corey	1. COBOL	Corey
	-widely accepted	wins
	-English statements, business applications	every
	-processes, records, produces	program.
Finds	2. FORTRAN	Fanny
	-solve science, math, engineer problems	Smith
	-programming	plays
	-widespread use, science-engineer communities	walleyball
	-solve problems	Saturdays.
Bobby	3. BASIC	Bobby
	-teaching tool	tells
	-easiest	everyone
	-programming language	Pat
	-Apple, IBM	ate
	-data structure—FORTRAN	dirt.
Playing	4. PASCAL	Pat
	-preferred teaching language	prefers
	-teaching tool	tulips.
Alone	5. ADA language	All
	-general purpose	girls
	-most advantages	must
	-structures—PASCAL	stay
	-strong type	strong.

other five sentences are designed to help her remember the details about each language. By organizing the information and practicing the connections between the catchphrases and the material she wanted to learn, Heather insured her ability to recall the information.

COMPREHENSION MONITORING STRATEGIES

Comprehension monitoring strategies allow us to keep tabs on our learning. They help us monitor our progress in mastering the material and allow us to evaluate the effectiveness of the strategies that we use to gain that mastery. Setting goals and then assessing your progress, self-questioning, self-testing, and even just asking yourself whether you understand something are all examples of comprehension monitoring strategies.

Comprehension monitoring strategies help us determine when learning or understanding breaks down. For example, you may find, as you read and take notes on one of your textbooks, that you can't figure out how to summarize the information under one of the headings. At that point, you should realize that you did not comprehend or understand that section of the text. Being unable to summarize serves as a signal that you need to reread the material or ask your professor to explain it in more detail.

When you use self-testing activities, you're monitoring your learning. If you find that you don't really know the information as well as you thought you did, you can review it again. Self-testing also allows you to practice retrieving the information from long-term memory in a test-like situation. Some students become frustrated when they take exams, because they spend hours and hours studying but can't seem to recall the information during the exam. Although they may have worked on acquisition and retention, they probably didn't spend much time working on retrieval of the information. Each time you self-test, you practice getting the information back out of memory. This provides you with an opportunity to practice the cues and strategies that you intend to use during the exam and to monitor their effectiveness.

Comprehension monitoring strategies also help us examine and evaluate the strategies that we are using to acquire, retain, and retrieve information. By taking a self-test, for example, you may discover that you don't really know as much as you thought you did about a particular section of the text and lecture material. Again, your discovery that you haven't learned that material provides you with some feedback on your progress in preparing for an exam. However, it also may allow you to evaluate the strategy that you originally used to "learn" that material. You may realize, for example, that just reading over the material wasn't very effective for getting it into long-term memory, or that just reciting the information from your notes didn't prepare you to write an essay about it. Once you determine that your study strategies aren't effective, you can modify the way you learn, and select more effective strategies to use.

AFFECTIVE AND MOTIVATIONAL STRATEGIES

Affective and motivational strategies also can influence the way we learn and remember. Many of the strategies that you used for setting goals, managing time, and improving concentration are examples of affective and motivational strategies. These strategies help prepare us mentally for studying and create a positive learning environment. Setting realistic, moderately challenging goals helps get you motivated to study and learn. Using "To Do" lists, planning rewards, and taking breaks are just a few of the motivational strategies that you probably are using on a regular basis. They help you keep up with your daily assignments and give you a sense of accomplishment at the end of the day. When you have a long-range project that requires more time and effort, such as writing a term paper or studying for an exam, get started on it quickly, even if you don't have time to do much right away.

Your attitude about learning the material can influence how well you will attend to it, organize it, and store it. If you are trying to prepare for an exam, it's important that you feel interested in the material and motivated to learn and remember. Establishing a purpose for studying, seeing the relevance of the course, and using active learning strategies can all help increase your motivation. If you think studying won't help, you won't be very motivated to study. On the other hand, if you discover that using active learning strategies helps you learn and remember the material, you'll be more willing to put in the time and the effort to prepare for an exam. Did you find that you liked studying more when you used active study tasks? Many students actually enjoy studying for a test using these strategies, because they end each study session feeling good about what they have accomplished.

Monitoring your learning also can be an effective motivational device. If you test your learning by covering the material and trying to recite the information, you'll be able to evaluate your storage and retrieval processes. You also can accomplish this by reciting from a recall column, taking self-tests, reproducing maps or charts, and so on. One advantage of reciting is that it allows you to test your memory. If you're able to remember the information that you're reviewing, you feel good — you know you're learning. Successful recitations motivate you to continue to study and to continue to use that learning strategy because it worked. If you have difficulty remembering the information when reciting or taking a self-test, you may be motivated to work even harder to get it into memory, especially if you got some of the answers correct. Changing to a different learning strategy or studying for a longer period of time may be necessary in order to implant the "missed" information into memory. When you know you know the important information for a test, you develop more confidence in yourself as a student, and this can affect your performance on the exam.

Your state of mind during the exam affects how well you are able to retrieve the information. If you experience test anxiety, you may not be able to concentrate on the exam questions. You may find that you're so upset that you can't think of the answers. Knowing you're well prepared for an exam reduces and, in some cases, eliminates feelings of test anxiety. As you know, most test anxiety stems from not knowing the material well enough or not being sure that you know the material well enough. Spacing your study, using active learning strategies, and practicing retrieval all help you prepare well for the exam. If you begin the exam with positive feelings about your preparation and expect to do well, you increase your probability for success.

When you get your test back, use it to evaluate how well your study plan and strategies worked for you. Go over all of the test items, both the correct and incorrect ones, to examine your preparation and test-taking skills. Instead of being discouraged by a poor test grade, find out why you made the mistakes that you made. Plan ways to avoid making the same mistakes again. Think of a good test grade as a reward for the hard work that you did. High scores on exams don't just happen; they are the result of hard work.

ACTIVITIES

1. Choose one of your own text selections and organize the information that you need to learn. Group, outline, or map the information to make it more meaningful. Then devise a strategy for remembering the main headings and relevant details that you included.
2. Which of the memory strategies did you find most effective for helping you learn and retrieve information in Activity 1? Describe how you used each one and explain why it worked for you.
3. List at least five affective and motivational strategies that you used during the past week. How did they help you improve your memory?

4. Choose a chapter or part of a chapter in one of your textbooks, select the material that you think you need to learn for an exam, and organize it on a separate sheet of paper. Then determine how you would go about learning the material. Finally, test yourself to monitor your learning. Write a paragraph or two describing the process that you used to learn the material and how you decided to monitor your learning. Describe your results.
5. Analyze the preparation and test-taking strategies that you used on your last exam. Which ones worked? Which ones didn't? When during your study sessions or even during the exam did you feel proud of your performance? When were you angry at yourself? What did you do about it?

POSTTEST

Where Are You Now?

Now that you have completed Chapter 10, take a few minutes to answer *yes* or *no* to the following questions. Compare your answers with those in the pretest.

	YES	NO
1. Do you often know the answer to a question but find that you can't think of it?	_____	_____
2. Do you organize or group information to help you remember it?	_____	_____
3. Do you take self-tests in order to check your learning?	_____	_____
4. Do you make up rhymes or words to help you remember some information?	_____	_____
5. Do you use deep processing strategies?	_____	_____
6. Do you try to memorize all of the information that you need to know for an exam?	_____	_____
7. Do you often find that you get confused by closely related information?	_____	_____
8. Do you often forget a lot of the information that you studied by the time you take the test?	_____	_____
9. Is the TV or stereo on while you study?	_____	_____
10. Can you learn and remember information just by making up a rhyme, word, or other memory aid?	_____	_____

Give yourself one point for each *yes* answer to questions 2, 4, and 5, and one point for each *no* answer to questions 1, 3, 6, 7, 8, 9, and 10. Now total up your points. Compare your score on this posttest with the score you had on the pretest. Did you improve? In which areas? Where do you still need to improve your knowledge and use of memory strategies?

CHAPTER 11

Taking Objective Tests

"Before reading this material, my test-taking skills were not very good. This text has helped me learn different strategies that have helped me improve my test grades. Before, I used to do the questions in order and would get frustrated when I didn't know one of the answers. Now I do the ones that I know and come back to the others. Crossing off wrong answers and underlining key words both help me determine the right answers."

Amanda Fisher

PREPARATION ISN'T EVERYTHING

You know that in order to perform well on objective tests, you have to be well prepared. However, although proper preparation is the most important criterion of good test performance, several other factors also may contribute to your success or failure. One of these factors often is referred to as your "test-taking ability." Some students are more skilled at taking tests than others. They have learned strategies and techniques that improve their performance on exams. Another factor that can affect test performance is your level of comfort when you take an exam. Some students view exams as everyday events, while other students consider them to be

PRETEST

Where Are You Now?

Take a few minutes to answer *yes* or *no* to the following questions.

	YES	NO
1. Do you always read the directions before you begin to answer the questions on an objective exam?	_____	_____
2. Do you eliminate wrong answers on multiple-choice exams?	_____	_____
3. Does text anxiety interfere with your performance on exams?	_____	_____
4. Do you ever leave blanks on exams?	_____	_____
5. Do you use strategies to help you figure out the correct answer when you are unsure of it?	_____	_____
6. Do you ever find that you are unable to finish an exam before time runs out?	_____	_____
7. Do you go back over the entire exam before you turn it in?	_____	_____
8. After your exam is returned, do you go over it to evaluate your preparation and clarify your errors?	_____	_____
9. When you get your exam back, are you often surprised by the grade that you received?	_____	_____
10. Do you usually make careless errors on your exams?	_____	_____

Give yourself one point for each *yes* answer to questions 1, 2, 5, 7, and 8, and one point for each *no* answer to questions 3, 4, 6, 9, and 10. Now total up your points. A low score indicates that you need to develop some new skills for taking objective tests. A high score indicates that you are already using many good strategies.

monumental obstacles that must be overcome. These different attitudes toward exams may be, in part, a result of students' varying levels of test anxiety. A final factor that may influence your performance on objective exams is how well you're able to learn from your exams. In this chapter you'll learn both general strategies for approaching objective exams and specific strategies for improving your performance on various types of test questions.

GENERAL STRATEGIES FOR TAKING OBJECTIVE TESTS

Now that you have developed many good strategies for test preparation, you need to learn how to approach and take objective tests. Learning how to approach tests in a calm, logical way can help you increase your score. However, good test grades depend, first of all, on good test preparation, so let's quickly review some of the ways that you can prepare for your exam.

PREPARE WELL

In the previous two chapters, you learned a wide variety of general and specific strategies for how to study for a test. Rather than review all of the strategies, let's focus on just a few. First, in order to acquire information or learn it, you must use active learning strategies. You need to spend the majority of your study time writing and reciting the information. Although reading the information out loud and copying your notes does help you encode the information, you will gain a better understanding of the material if you use elaborative strategies such as mapping, note taking (in your own words), and explaining the information to someone else. Second, organizing the information so that it's more meaningful to you makes it easier to learn and remember. Third, spacing your study over a period of days, working on small units of material at one time, and planning additional opportunities for rehearsal or repetition all help you learn more effectively and reduce forgetting. Fourth, monitoring your progress by taking self-tests allows you to evaluate what you know and what you still need to learn, as well as how effectively your selected strategies for learning are working. Finally, it's important to be in good physical condition when you take an exam. You should be well rested and properly nourished.

REDUCE TEST ANXIETY

Some students come into an exam feeling well prepared, well rested, and well motivated. Other students, however, feel uncertain about their level of preparation and anxious about their performance on the test. We could say that they are experiencing test anxiety. Test anxiety involves both physical responses, such as rapid heart beat or shallow breathing, and emotional responses, such as worry and negative thoughts. What are some other common symptoms of test anxiety? The following list of symptoms was suggested by college students.

nausea	fainting	throwing up
light headedness	going blank	shaking
sweaty palms	worrying about failing	headaches
butterflies	trouble concentrating	feeling tense
heart pounding	diarrhea	crying

Of course, not everyone exhibits all of these symptoms of test anxiety, but some students do experience one or more of them. Can you think of any others that could be added to the list?

Although many students experience test anxiety, we don't know for sure whether test anxiety really causes some students to perform less well on exams. The connection between test anxiety and poor test performance still is being investigated by many researchers. However, test anxiety does appear to be related to poor test performance in students who exhibit very high levels of anxiety. For most of us, though, test anxiety alone does not cause test failure. Instead, lack of preparation (which can contribute to text anxiety) is the real cause of test failure.

What Causes Test Anxiety?

What causes some students to experience test anxiety while others appear calm and collected on exams? Although there is no real answer to this question, several possible explanations may help us understand the problem. For some students, past experiences during exams lead to anxious feelings about subsequent exams. Failure accompanied by embarrassment and frustration in one testing situation can lead to anxiety in the next. Failure, by the way, does not mean the same thing for every student. When most people talk about failing an exam, they mean getting a grade that is below passing. For some students, however, getting a C or even a B is like failing; they failed to get the grade they wanted or needed. Excellent students often exhibit high levels of test anxiety because of the pressure they (or others) put on themselves to be the best.

The amount or level of anxiety that students experience also may depend on the value that they place on the exam. If doing well in the course is very important to them personally or professionally, they may view the exam as a critical or "must win" situation. On the other hand, if the class is seen as having little value or being unimportant to their future, the students may experience little anxiety associated with it. This may explain why some students suffer from test anxiety in one class but not in others. Often, the greater the risk, the greater the stress.

Sometimes the type of test being given can lead to test anxiety. Some students become anxious during exams that require them to demonstrate their knowledge in ways in which they do not feel comfortable. For example, some students panic when they find that they have to take essay tests. Others become anxious over oral exams. And some, like me, hate true-false tests. Different types of tests cause feelings of anxiety for different people.

Some professors also make students anxious because of things that they do during the exam. Telling the class that the test is the hardest they've ever made up or that no one in the other class got above a D can lead to feelings of anxiety.

Is Test Anxiety Normal?

With all of these factors contributing to test anxiety, it's hard to believe that any student doesn't feel some level of anxiety. Actually, just about everyone does experience some test anxiety. It's perfectly normal to be anxious about an exam. If you weren't a little anxious about your performance, you probably wouldn't study at all. A small amount of test anxiety is good. We can describe this state of anxiety as *facilitating test anxiety* — anxiety that facilitates or helps motivate us to prepare before and work hard during the exam. On the other hand, a high level of test anxiety can interfere with your performance on an exam. We call this type of anxiety *debilitating test anxiety.* Like a debilitating illness, it prevents us from functioning in a normal way. High levels of test anxiety may interfere with your ability to concentrate on the exam or even to prepare for it.

Some students find that they really can't prepare for exams because they are so anxious about them. The closer they get to the exam without preparing, the more anxious they become, because they think that now they don't have enough time to prepare adequately. When they begin to study, they start to think about the exam, and they experience some of the physical and mental symptoms that we've discussed. They have difficulty concentrating on the material during the study session in much the same way that they do during the exam. Sometimes, they spend half of their study time worrying about what will happen to them after they fail the exam. This leads to poor preparation, which then leads to a poor test grade, and so the cycle begins. Although only a small number of students have such high levels of test anxiety that it interferes with their study, many students use test anxiety as an excuse for not studying.

How Can You Cope with Test Anxiety?

There are a number of ways that you can learn to cope with test anxiety. First of all, remember that some test anxiety is good, so your goal should be to reduce anxiety to a level that becomes facilitating. One way to lower your anxiety level is to be well prepared for the exam and to know that you are well prepared. By using active study strategies like writing and reciting, you can master the material for your exam, and by monitoring your learning through self-tests, you can feel confident about your preparation. Use time management strategies when you're studying to reduce stress and keep yourself on task. Plan exactly what you intend to do each day, and reward yourself for completing your tasks. Begin to prepare early enough (use the Five-Day Study Plan) to adequately prepare yourself and, therefore, reduce debilitating anxiety.

During an exam, use relaxation exercises to help reduce your anxiety level. Use breathing or muscle-relaxing techniques to calm yourself. Just taking a few deep breaths can help you calm down. If that doesn't work, try taking a breath and then blowing it out very slowly as if you had built a house of cards and didn't want to knock it over. Do this a few times until you find that you're able to control your breathing.

One of the most common problems that students experience during exams is negative thoughts. They find that they begin to think about failing the test, they start worrying about whether they studied the right material, and they tell themselves that they are dumb or don't belong in school. All of these negative thoughts interfere with their ability to concentrate on the test itself. The Information Processing Model can help explain how these negative thoughts interfere with your ability to perform well on the exam. If your attention is occupied by the negative thoughts, you can't effectively process the questions and retrieve the answers that you need to complete the exam. The negative thoughts compete with and distract you from thinking about the exam.

One of the most successful ways to deal with negative thoughts is to eliminate them. Unfortunately, just telling yourself to stop thinking negatively doesn't work. Instead, you need to prepare a positive mental script to substitute for the negative one. After you study for the test, write down a positive statement or script. Practice saying it over and over again and think about why it is true. Everyone's script will be different, but yours might go something like this: "I'm going to do well on this exam because I really know this stuff. I studied for twelve hours for this exam, and I got A's on all of my homework papers and on my self-test. I know how to take tests and I'm well prepared." As soon as you begin to think any negative thoughts during the exam, yell "STOP" or "STOP IT" in your mind, and then immediately start to repeat your positive script. Some students actually write their positive statements at the top of their exam papers. Whatever technique you use, try to eliminate negative thoughts so that you can completely focus your attention on the exam.

FOLLOW DIRECTIONS

Reading the directions before beginning an exam can make the difference between getting a good grade and failing the exam. The directions give you information on how many questions to answer, what form the answer must take, and special directions for some parts of the test. The directions for all parts of an exam are not necessarily the same. Some sections of a multiple-choice exam, for example, may ask you to choose the best answer. Other sections may ask you to select all the correct answers or the only incorrect answer. Marking only the best answer when all correct choices are required may cost you two or three points per question. Occasionally, students lose points on true-false exams because they don't read the directions. A student may mark the statement false without correcting the false statement (as required in the directions), and he or she may not get credit for the answer. Errors like these can result in test failure.

BUDGET YOUR TIME

If you budget your time during a test, you should be able to complete the entire test before time runs out. However, some students lose track of time or spend too much time on one part of the exam and end up leaving some questions undone. Being unable to finish even five 2-point questions on a test can mean the difference of one letter grade. Pacing yourself during the test also helps you maximize your score by letting you devote the most time to those parts of the exam that have the highest point values.

Previewing the exam gives you an idea of what you need to accomplish during the test period. Count the total number of questions that you have to answer. Then look at each section of the exam and check the point value for each question. Some students ignore the differences in point value among questions and treat all questions as if they were of equal weight. Occasionally, this has disastrous effects. If you use the following rule, you will always be able to determine how much time to spend on each question or section of the test.

> **Rule:** Percentage of the total points = Percentage of the total time

Sometimes, however, you still may not be finished with the exam when time runs out. If you have one or two questions left to do, ask the professor for a few more minutes. Even though some professors are sticklers about time, they may allow you to finish the exam while they gather up their materials. If you still have a lot to do, talk to the professor. Ask if you can come to his or her office to complete the exam. If you know that you often have difficulty completing exams in the required time, try to discuss this with your professor ahead of time. Some professors allow students to arrive early and begin the exam before the rest of the class. If you have a reading problem or if English is your second language, you often can make special arrangements through your campus learning center or academic dean. Most professors are willing to make accommodations to help you succeed on exams, but you need to tell them what your needs are.

ANSWER THE EASIEST QUESTIONS FIRST

Another strategy for improving your grade on an exam is to answer the easiest questions first. By immediately answering all of the questions that you know, you can maximize your score on the test — if you do run out of time, you'll be sure to receive points for the questions that you did know. In addition, you can reduce your test anxiety by answering the easiest questions first; by the time you go back to work on the more difficult questions, you'll feel more relaxed. This is because you build up your confidence as you complete the easy questions — you know that you know at least some or even many of the answers. One student reported that she used this strategy on an algebra exam. By the time she went back to the "difficult" questions, they didn't seem nearly as hard. Because she was more relaxed, she was able to think through the problems more logically and solve them correctly.

Some students panic if they read the first question on the test and realize they don't know the answer. Instead of allowing yourself to start thinking negative thoughts, just tell yourself "This is a hard question" or "This is tough — I'll come back to it later." These types of positive thoughts allow you to focus on the rest of the test.

As you move through the exam, skip the questions you aren't sure of and go on to the easier questions. If you know that you don't know an answer, don't spend a lot of time on the question. Mark the questions you skip by putting a dash or question mark in the margin or by circling the number. After you complete the rest of the test, go back to them. (If you're using an answer sheet, be sure you skip the same space there, too.) When you return to the question you skipped, try to figure out the answers strategically. Think through each question. Eliminate any answer that you know is wrong and then try to figure out the correct answer. Do a memory search to try to retrieve the information about the topic. Ask yourself questions about the material. Try to determine whether the answer came from the lecture or from the text. Try to remember where you saw it on the page, where it was written

PEANUTS reprinted by permission of UFS, Inc.

in your notes, or what the professor was talking about just before or after that topic was presented. By searching your memory, you often can recall the information. Later in this chapter we'll discuss a number of other strategies that should help you eliminate wrong answers and recognize correct ones.

Many times students find clues to previous questions as they move through the test. You may even find that the answer to an early question is one of the possible answers to a question three pages away. Even if you don't find the answer itself, you may find a clue or cue that helps you answer the question. You may read a word in another question or in another possible answer that triggers your memory and helps you retrieve the information that you need. Occasionally you may come across information that allows you to eliminate an answer that you previously had considered for another question. You also can use the objective part of an exam to give you ideas or gather details for essay exams. Professors often test on the same topic in both objective and essay formats. Even if you pick up a clue to only one or two questions as you move through the test, that can often make a difference in your grade. Some students have found that they were able to improve their grades significantly by using test clues to help them answer or retrieve information for other questions.

SPECIFIC STRATEGIES FOR OBJECTIVE TESTS

If you prepare well, reduce test anxiety, read and follow directions, pace yourself, and answer the easiest questions first, you should do well on exams. However, some students pick up additional points by learning some test-taking strategies for particular types of objective exams. Some of these strategies involve ways to approach the questions and figure out the answers. Others include "test-wise" tricks or gimmicks that can help you improve your ability to guess the right answer when you still aren't sure of it. Many students are fascinated by these tricks for multiple-choice, matching, or true-false tests. However, they are not the focus of this chapter, nor should they be the focus of your approach to taking objective tests. Use them when all else fails; use them when you don't know the answer, and use them only *after* you try every problem-solving and retrieval strategy you know.

STRATEGIES FOR MATCHING TESTS

With proper preparation and test-taking strategies, you should be able to get top scores on matching tests. Matching tests require you to recognize the correct answer from a list of alternatives. The answers to all of the questions are given; you don't have to "pull" the answer from memory. Before beginning a matching test, be sure that you read the directions. Usually you're instructed to use each possible answer only once, but some matching tests allow for or require the repeated use of some answers.

Work from One Side

Matching tests often include a list of names or terms in one column and then a list of accomplishments or definitions in the other column. When you take a matching test, you should always work from one side only. Crossing off items in both columns leads to confusion and often results in careless errors or wasted time. Also, work from the column that has the most words. If you work from the term column, you have to scan more words in the definition column to find a correct match. If, instead, you work from the definition column, you have to scan fewer words on each pass, because the term column contains fewer words. Working from the column with the most words can save you time when you're taking an exam.

Answer the Questions You're Sure of First

In the case of a matching test, it's crucial that you answer the questions or make the matches that you are absolutely sure of first. By skipping through the list and answering only the ones you're sure about, you improve your chances for a high or perfect score. If you make an error early in a matching test, you probably will make several more. Moreover, by eliminating all of the choices that you're sure of, you can narrow the alternatives for the remaining choices.

Eliminate and Cross Off Alternatives

In matching tests, each possible answer or definition usually is associated with a letter (A, B, C, and so on). As you go through the list of definitions, cross off the letter associated with each one that you use. Just put one diagonal line through the letter so that you can recheck your matches later. If you can eliminate five of the ten alternatives on your first pass through the list, you have improved your chances of getting the others right.

After you match all of the items you're sure of, start with the first unmatched definition that you have and try to match it with each remaining term. If you're sure of a match, make it; if not, skip over that definition and go on to the next one. Continue down the list until you can make one more match. Then go back through the list again. Having eliminated one more alternative, you may find that only one other term could possibly be correct for one of the definitions. Through the process of elimination, you should be able to make all the matches.

Recheck Your Work

After you have matched all of the items in the list, go back and check to be sure that you have not accidentally used the same letter twice. Going through the letters and crossing off each one again can help you avoid careless errors. If you do find that you have one term left and one definition left, and you know that they don't match, you need to go back and recheck your work, because it's unlikely that this is your only error. Go back through the list looking for any term that could fit the remaining definition. If necessary, rewrite the letters next to the original list and cross them off again.

STRATEGIES FOR TRUE-FALSE TESTS

Many students like true-false tests because they provide excellent odds for guessing correctly. However, some students have difficulty dealing with this type of test. Professors use many different methods to write incorrect true-false items. In order to make a statement incorrect, they may change key words, omit key words, add absolute or qualifying words, add one or more negative words, add extraneous information, and so on. Because there are so many ways to make a statement "false," students must consider all of them as they examine each statement.

Use the following basic guidelines to determine whether statements are true or false.

1. *Always read the directions before beginning a true-false test.* Some instructors are very particular about how they expect students to mark true-false items. If you don't complete the exam according to the directions, you may not get credit for your answers.
2. *In order for a statement to be true, it must be all true.* If any part of the statement is false, the entire statement is false. Even if a statement is com-

posed of two or three parts or entire sentences, if one part or even one word is incorrect, the entire statement is false.

3. *True-false items are not all tricky.* Some students start to look for "tricks" or read too much into the question when a true-false item seems "too easy." If you're properly prepared for a test, some true-false items should appear to be easy.

4. *Identify the key words or phrases.* By identifying and verifying the accuracy of key words, you can more easily decide whether a statement is true or false.

5. *Statements containing absolute words are usually false.* Words like *always, all, none, never, only, every,* and *no* are examples of absolute words. Each of these words implies that there are no exceptions. Although the inclusion of these words in a true-false item does not guarantee that it is false, it usually indicates a false statement. In fact, other than changing one or more key words in the statement, this is one of the most common ways to turn a true statement into a false one.

6. *Statements containing qualifying words are usually true statements.* Words like *usually, often, may, can, sometimes, frequently, rarely, most, some, many, few,* and *generally* are examples of qualifying words. These words qualify or "temper" the statement to allow for exceptions and make the statement less extreme and absolute. Just as absolute words are not always indicators of false items, qualifying words are not always indicators of true statements. However, they generally are associated with true statements. If you know that a statement is false because it contains an incorrect explanation, for example, mark it *false,* even if it contains a qualifying word.

7. *Statements that contain negative words often are tricky and require careful attention.* Be sure that you underline or circle negative words like *not* when they appear in a true-false statement. Double negatives, which generally include the word *not* plus another word that contains a negative prefix, such as *incoherent, illogical, irresponsible, unhelpful,* and so on, often confuse students. If a statement contains a double negative, cross off the word *not* and the negative prefix (*in, il, ir,* or *un*) and then reread the statement in order to determine whether it is true or false.

8. *Always underline the word or words that make a statement false.* If you can't identify and mark the actual key words, absolute words, qualifiers, and so on that cause the statement to be incorrect, assume that it is correct and mark it true. This rule is especially effective for students who tend to read too much into true-false items. There is one exception, however. If you know that a statement is false by omission (because a key word or phrase has been left

out) mark the statement *false* even though you can't actually underline the words that make it false.

9. *Professors usually include more true items than false items on an exam.* If you absolutely can't figure out whether a statement is true or false, mark it true, because many professors use tests to reinforce the main ideas that were presented in the course. Watch for patterns on each test. If you notice that your instructor tends to divide the items equally between true and false, count the number of true's and false's in order to determine how to mark the ones that you can't figure out.

STRATEGIES FOR MULTIPLE-CHOICE TESTS

The most common type of objective test is the multiple-choice test. Multiple-choice tests allow instructors to test students' knowledge of the course material at various levels of understanding. Many new college students have difficulty on these exams because they expect all of the questions to be at the knowledge level. They prepare by memorizing the material and often don't take the time to really learn and understand it. If you're able to recall the correct answers from memory without cues, multiple-choice exams will be easy for you. Most multiple-choice exams contain a *stem,* which is comprised of a question or an incomplete sentence, and several *alternatives* or possible answers.

Many strategies are effective for taking multiple-choice exams. However, these strategies come in two different forms. The first group includes problem-solving strategies that can help you identify the correct answer from the various distractors or decoys. The other group involves tricks or gimmicks that should be used only after you have tried all of the logical strategies first. Some students think of these tricks as rules; they aren't. They should be used only in a guessing situation. After you read the directions and budget your time, use the following strategies for multiple-choice items.

Problem-Solving Strategies

1. *Read the question and all of the answers before you select the "correct" answer.* Some students lose points on multiple-choice exams because they never read all of the possible answers before selecting the one that they think is correct. Many times the first or second alternative may appear to be the correct answer but, in fact, one of the other answers may be an even better choice.

2. *Work to eliminate incorrect alternatives rather than looking for the "right" answer.* After reading the question and all of the alternatives, begin looking for those that you know are wrong. When you are sure that one possible answer is a distractor, cross it off. Continue eliminating choices until only one answer remains. If you can eliminate all of the alternatives except one, you know you have found the correct answer.

3. *Connect the stem of the question to each alternative answer; then treat each statement as a true-false item.* If there are four alternatives, you will have four true-false items to consider. In a way, all multiple-choice exams are really composed of a series of true-false items. If you're good at taking true-false tests, use the strategies for true-false tests for the multiple-choice items. Identify key words, underline words or phrases that make the statement false, and watch for absolute, qualifying, and negative words. By examining each alternative as a separate true-false statement, you may be able to improve your test score.

4. *Read the question, cover the alternatives, and think of the answer.* Some students find multiple-choice tests difficult because they allow the alternative answers to confuse them. Some professors are so good at writing distractors that even if you know the correct answer, you begin to have doubts about it after reading the alternatives. To avoid this problem, read the question and think of the answer. Then read each alternative and ask yourself, "Does this mean the same thing as the answer that I know is correct?" This strategy is especially effective when the question is written at the comprehension level. In this situation, the information is rephrased or put in different words. By comparing your answer to each of those listed, you should be able to identify the correct choice.

5. *Use caution when "all of the above" and "none of the above" are included as choices.* Some professors save on test preparation by using these alternatives for every item on the test; if a test has five possible answers for each question stem, the professor then needs to write only two distractors in addition to the correct answer for each item. Although it is easier for professors to add "all of the above" and "none of the above," it is more difficult for the students who are taking the test. When you're faced with this kind of question, look carefully at the individual alternatives. If you can eliminate even *one* alternative, you can eliminate "all of the above" as the correct answer. Similarly, if you are sure that at least one choice is correct, you can eliminate "none of the above." If you have three alternatives and you know that two of them are correct but aren't sure of the third, "all of the above" must be correct (assuming you can choose

only one answer). If "all of the above" or "none of the above" are used only occasionally on the test, they are probably the correct choices. Watch for patterns like this on each exam.

Test-Wise Strategies

Use test-wise clues or tricks to help you determine the correct choice. Many courses that are designed to prepare students to take the SAT's or other standardized tests seem to specialize in these "test-smart" strategies. Some of them are very helpful; others are not as useful. The key to using these tricks or clues is to use them sparingly. Never follow a test-wise strategy that would require you to select one alternative when you are fairly sure that another alternative is the correct answer. Use these strategies only when you can't determine the correct answer by using the more conventional strategies. Some of the more effective and useful test-wise strategies are presented below.

1. An answer that contains more specific, detailed information probably is correct. Vague or general alternatives are often used as distractors.
2. An answer that contains the most words, especially if it also contains the most specific information, probably is correct.
3. An answer that is in the middle probably is correct, especially if it has the most words.
4. An answer that is about in the middle numerically probably is correct. Instructors often surround the correct choice by a range of lower and higher alternatives.
5. An answer that contains an unfamiliar term probably is wrong. Instructors often make up words or take terms from other material in order to generate additional distractors.
6. An answer that contains a "typo," especially if there are very few typos in the test, probably is wrong.
7. An answer that is grammatically correct probably is right if the other choices are not grammatically correct.
8. An answer that contains a form of the word or a word similar to one in the stem of the question may be correct.
9. If a question contains two opposite alternatives, one of them is probably correct.

WHEN IN DOUBT, GUESS

Even if you are well prepared for a test and use good test-taking strategies, you still may find that you can't answer some of the questions. When none of your strategies works, then you have to guess. Strategic guessing can make a difference in your grade. Let's say there are four questions that you can't figure out on a fifty-item multiple-choice test. Because each of those questions is worth two points, your unanswered questions add up to eight points or almost one letter grade. Not answering them will result in at least an eight-point loss in your grade. Guessing does not guarantee that you'll get all of the questions right, but it certainly improves your odds of getting some of them right.

What is a guess anyway? Some students describe a guess as just putting down any letter they can think of to fill the slot. They choose randomly from among the alternatives. For other students, however, guessing involves more active processes. Some students think they are guessing when they aren't sure of an answer but "kind of think" they know which one is right. These guesses may not really be guesses at all; they may be incomplete retrievals. When you read one of the alternatives and it sort of sounds familiar or looks right, you may be making a faint connection to your long-term memory. You may be picking up on a cue different from the one that you previously used to retrieve the information, or you may be responding to the material on a different level. Nevertheless, your selection of that particular alternative may be more than a random guess.

In the following two activities (see Figures 11.1 and 11.2), you have a chance to see how well you guess. Remember that before you actually get to the point of guessing, you should use strategies such as eliminating wrong answers, looking for key words, using test-wise clues, and so on in order to identify the correct answer.

Take a true-false test and then look at the answer key at the end of the chapter and check your score. Your score before you guessed was 72 out of 100, a low C. Add up the number of guesses that you got right and multiply that number by 4 (the point value for each question). Add your total points to 72 to get your new score. Were you able to increase your score by one letter grade (80 to 89 is a B) or by two letter grades (90 to 100 is an A)? When tests like this one are done in class, students frequently raise their score by one or two letter grades.

Did you use any strategies to guess the correct answers? Some often-used strategies include looking for patterns in the answers, counting the number of true and false choices already used, and marking all true or all false to get at least some

Figure 11.1 Guess at True-False Questions

Pretend that you answered all of the easy questions on the following exam and then went back and figured out a few more by using test-taking strategies. There are still seven questions that you can't answer. In the spaces below, write T for true or F for false for each of the unanswered questions. Since you don't know the actual questions, you will have to guess the correct answers.

1. T	6. F	11. T	16. ____	21. F
2. ____	7. F	12. T	17. F	22. F
3. F	8. ____	13. F	18. F	23. T
4. F	9. T	14. ____	19. F	24. ____
5. ____	10. F	15. T	20. ____	25. T

What strategies did you use to figure out the correct answers?

additional points. In the case of this test, you would have done well if you had marked all of the blanks *true*, because five of the seven answers were true. You would have improved your score by 20 points, which would give you a 92—an A. Although guessing is not a recommended strategy for early in a test, it certainly can help you pick up a few points when you absolutely don't know the answer. Now try the multiple-choice test in Figure 11.2.

Look at the answer key at the end of the chapter and check your score on the multiple-choice test. Again, your score before you guessed was 72 out of 100. Add up the number of correct answers and multiply by two (each question is worth two points). Then add your total points to 72 to get your new score. Did you improve your score? How much? You may be disappointed that your score is lower this time than it was for the true-false test. However, the odds of guessing correctly on this multiple-choice test were only one in four; on the true-false test you had a fifty-fifty (or one in two) chance of being correct. You can increase your odds of guessing right on multiple-choice exams by eliminating answers that you know are wrong. Many students are able to narrow the odds to one in two by eliminating two of the distractors. They then have the same chance of guessing correctly as they did on a true-false test. When you can't find the correct answer and have eliminated wrong answers, use strategic guessing to pick up a few additional points.

Figure 11.2 Guess at Multiple-Choice Questions

Pretend that you answered all of the easy questions on the following multiple-choice exam and then went back and figured out a few more by using test-taking strategies. There are still fourteen questions that you can't answer. In the spaces below, write A, B, C, or D for each of the unanswered questions. Because you don't know the actual questions, you will have to guess the correct answers.

1. A	11. B	21. D	31. ___	41. ___
2. ___	12. A	22. D	32. B	42. C
3. C	13. C	23. A	33. ___	43. ___
4. C	14. ___	24. ___	34. B	44. D
5. B	15. B	25. A	35. D	45. A
6. D	16. ___	26. C	36. ___	46. B
7. C	17. C	27. A	37. ___	47. A
8. ___	18. C	28. B	38. D	48. ___
9. B	19. D	29. D	39. A	49. D
10. D	20. A	30. ___	40. ___	50. C

What strategies did you use to figure out the correct answers?

Some professors always balance their answer keys; they use exactly the same number of A's, B's, C's, and D's. If you find that there are three or four questions that you can't answer, count how many of each letter you have already used. You may find that you have fewer A's than any other letter. By marking your remaining answers "A," you probably will pick up several additional points. Although this sounds like a great strategy, it works only if the professor has balanced the answers. By looking at old exams or watching for patterns on each exam that you have in the course, you will be able to determine whether or not you can use this strategy.

Remember, guessing strategies are designed to help you pick up a few additional points when you absolutely can't figure out the correct answer any other way. They are *not* designed to replace proper preparation or substitute for more active problem-solving strategies that can lead you to the correct answer by providing you with clues or aiding your recall of the answer.

END-OF-EXAM STRATEGIES

Just because you've answered all the questions on your exam, that doesn't mean you've done everything you can do to get the best possible grade. By remaining in the classroom and using strategies like reviewing the entire exam and rethinking and redoing difficult questions, you can improve your score on objective exams.

DON'T LEAVE THE ROOM EARLY

Many students leave the classroom long before the exam time is up. Often, these students receive the lowest grades, not the highest grades. They "fly" through the test, answering the questions impulsively, giving them little thought and using few problem-solving strategies. Other students hurry to finish the test because they notice that others are leaving. They rush through the test because they are afraid they will look dumb if they are among the last to leave. This pressure to finish first or at least not last hurts them, because they don't put the necessary effort into working on the exam. By leaving the test early, all of these students negate the effort that they put into preparing for the exam.

I have noticed that over the course of the semester, as students learn how to use test-taking strategies, they spend more time on exams. In most cases, this additional time results in higher test scores.

GO BACK OVER DIFFICULT QUESTIONS

If you have any additional time, use it to rethink or redo difficult questions or problems. On a math or science exam, put your hand over your original solution and rework the problem. Compare your answers. Many students don't pick up minor mathematical errors when they just "look over" the problem. However, they usually don't make the same error again when they rework the problem from scratch. If you find that your answers to the original and reworked problems are different, compare your solutions line by line until you locate your mistake.

When taking an objective test, go back and look at what each question is asking, check to see if your answer is the best answer, and be sure that you know why each of the other alternatives is wrong. Because you may be calmer and able to think more clearly at the end of the exam, you may catch errors that you made early in the test.

USE CAUTION WHEN CHANGING ANSWERS

Many students gain points from changing answers, but a number of students actually lose points because they change correct answers to incorrect ones. Although most researchers indicate that it is more common to change wrong answers to right answers, their findings reflect averages. That means that on the average, more students change wrong answers to right answers, but not all students do. Some of us tend to change right answers to wrong answers.

What kind of an answer changer are you? You need to find out so that you can determine whether this practice (if you use it at all) helps or hurts you. When you get your test back, count the number of answers that you changed and then how many of them you changed from right to wrong or wrong to right. Watch for repeated patterns on several exams to find out what type of answer changer you are.

Sometimes it's beneficial to change answers. Many students change answers because they find the correct answer somewhere else in the test, because they figure out the correct answer, or because they realize that they misread the question or one of the alternatives. In each of these cases, students gain points by changing answers. However, some students change answers because they begin to have doubts about the alternative that they chose. They have no reason to change their answer other than they just aren't sure anymore. Remember: In most cases, your first choice is the right one. It results from a memory connection caused by the cues in the stem of the question and in one particular alternative. If you find that you tend to change right answers to wrong answers, try using my rule: Don't ever change an answer unless you find the correct answer somewhere else in the test, figure out why the original answer is wrong, or realize that you misread the question. Monitor the success of following this strategy over the next several tests. You may be pleased with the results.

LEARNING FROM EXAMS

Many students think that once an exam is over, the only thing that matters is their grade. However, exams are learning opportunities. Professors often use them to help reinforce the critical concepts that they are trying to present. Reviewing an exam after it is returned can help you learn more about the course content and clarify any errors that you made. You also can learn a great deal about your professor's testing methods and about your own test-taking skills.

EVALUATE YOUR PREPARATION

Your graded exam can be used to help you evaluate your preparation. By finding out where each of the questions came from (the lecture or the textbook), you can determine whether you are focusing on the same topics and ideas as your professor. You also can check how well you mark and take notes by scanning the text or your text notes and looking for questions that were on the test. If you find that few of the test questions are contained in material that you highlighted or noted, you can adjust your marking for the next test. Determining how many of the questions came from the text and how many came from the lecture can help you determine how much time to spend on each type of material the next time you prepare. If, for example, your professor took 80 percent of the test questions from the lecture material, then you should have spent 80 percent of your study time on lecture notes and only 20 percent on text material.

You also can evaluate how well you were able to anticipate or predict test questions. Compare your exam to the self-tests that you designed. How many of the test questions did you predict? Think back to how you felt as you took the exam. Did you feel surprised by many of the items, or did you often find yourself thinking, "I knew this would be on the test"?

Finally, evaluate your test-taking skills. Did you read the directions, budget your time well, and answer the easy questions first? Did you work through the difficult items in a logical, systematic way, eliminating wrong answers? Were you able to identify key words in the questions that helped you figure out the correct answers? Did you review the exam and rework the difficult items? Knowing how effectively you were able to use the various test-taking strategies can help you improve your performance on the next exam.

LEARN FROM YOUR MISTAKES

Understanding why you were wrong about a particular answer can be critical to your success on the next exam. In some cases, you may need to clarify or correct some of the information that you learned. By discussing your mistakes with your professor, you may find that you hadn't really understood the material after all. By examining your errors you also can determine whether they resulted from poor preparation or from carelessness or poor test-taking strategies. Locating the questions that you missed in the text or in your notes can help you determine whether or not you spent enough time on that material. Never throw exams away; even if you didn't do well on an exam, you still can use it to review for finals.

Because you can learn a lot from exams, it's important to spend some time going over them. If you don't get to keep your exam, set up an appointment to review it with your professor. Unfortunately, too few students make use of their opportunity to review exams. Even if the professor goes over the answers in class, you need to see your own paper to analyze your errors. If you don't understand why something was marked wrong, ask the professor to explain it. You'll benefit by learning more about the subject and by getting a better idea of what the professor expected.

GET HELP BEFORE THE NEXT EXAM

If your grade on the exam isn't up to par, go for help immediately. Your first stop should be your professor. Set up an appointment to discuss your exam. Go over the exam question by question until you have a clear understanding of what you need to do to improve your grade for the next exam. Tell your professor exactly what you did to prepare, and ask for suggestions as to what you may need to do differently.

Your next stop should be your college learning center. Many learning centers offer individual assistance or workshops in test preparation, test anxiety, and test-taking strategies. You also may need to request tutorial assistance. If you don't have a learning center on your campus, ask where you might go to get this type of help. Some departments or organizations offer tutoring services to students. Waiting to see if you do better on your next test can be very risky. If you don't do any better, you'll have two low grades to pull up. By finding out what you did wrong, and by asking for help in correcting those mistakes, you can improve your performance on the next exam.

ACTIVITIES

1. Keep a log of all of the strategies that you use when you take your next objective exam. Which strategies were the most helpful? Why?
2. Describe the steps that you go through to figure out the correct answers when you take true-false, matching, and multiple-choice tests.
3. On which type of objective test do you do the best? Why? On which type of objective test do you have the most difficulty? What do you plan to do differently in the future?

4. Describe the anxiety symptoms that you experienced on a stressful test. Then list the methods that you used or plan to use in the future to help reduce your anxiety.

5. Review one of the exams that recently was returned to you. Write a paragraph or two discussing what you were able to learn from the exam. Include information about how the test was designed, your preparation, and about your test-taking skills.

ANSWER KEY FOR TEST ITEMS

Answer key to true-false test in Figure 11.1

2. T 5. T 8. F 14. T 16. F 20. T 24. T

Answer key for multiple-choice test in Figure 11.2

2. B 8. C 14. B 16. D 24. B 30. D 31. C 33. A 36. C 37. C 40. A 41. C 43. A 48. D

POSTTEST

Where Are You Now?

Now that you have completed Chapter 11, take a few minutes to answer *yes* or *no* to the following questions. Compare your answers with those in the pretest.

	YES	NO
1. Do you always read the directions before you begin to answer the questions on an objective exam?	_____	_____
2. Do you eliminate wrong answers on multiple-choice exams?	_____	_____
3. Does text anxiety interfere with your performance on exams?	_____	_____
4. Do you ever leave blanks on exams?	_____	_____
5. Do you use strategies to help you figure out the correct answer when you are unsure of it?	_____	_____
6. Do you ever find that you are unable to finish an exam before time runs out?	_____	_____
7. Do you go back over the entire exam before you turn it in?	_____	_____
8. After your exam is returned, do you go over it to evaluate your preparation and clarify your errors?	_____	_____
9. When you get your exam back, are you often surprised by the grade that you received?	_____	_____
10. Do you usually make careless errors on your exams?	_____	_____

Give yourself one point for each *yes* answer to questions 1, 2, 5, 7, and 8, and one point for each *no* answer to questions 3, 4, 6, 9, and 10. Now total up your points. Compare your score on this posttest with the score that you got on the pretest. How much did you improve? What areas do you still need to work on?

CHAPTER 12

Preparing for Essay Tests

> "The idea of constructing four to five questions for each essay that will be on the exam is great. I have predicted and planned up to six essays for one question. I enjoy this activity because it helps me guess the question and find the answer. Searching for the questions forces me to go through the material, which is a great review. Marginal notes work well for me, too, because they allow me to "see" my thoughts."
>
> Janeen Hurey

ESSAY TESTS REQUIRE EXTRA PREPARATION

Essay tests are more difficult than objective tests for many students because they require recall learning—you need to know what you're writing about. In addition, you need to be able to put what you know on paper in a rather short period of time. In order to prepare for an essay test, you should use many of the strategies presented in Chapter 9 for setting up a study plan and learning the material. Preparing for an essay test, though, involves more than just knowing the material. In order to write a good essay answer, you need to be able to organize your

PRETEST

Where Are You Now?

Take a few minutes to answer *yes* or *no* to the following questions.

	YES	NO
1. Do you study differently for essay tests and objective tests?	_____	_____
2. Do you generally plan out your answers in your head rather than on paper?	_____	_____
3. Do you always write out essays before the test if the professor gives you the questions?	_____	_____
4. Do you predict possible essay questions before an exam?	_____	_____
5. Are you usually able to predict accurately which essay questions the professor will include?	_____	_____
6. Do you use memory techniques to help you remember the main points that you want to make in your answer?	_____	_____
7. Do you tend to rely on old exams and hope that the same questions will be used again?	_____	_____
8. Do you prepare sample essay answers and ask your professors to evaluate them before the exam?	_____	_____
9. Are you generally well prepared for essay exams?	_____	_____
10. Do you know how to study for an essay exam?	_____	_____

Give yourself one point for each *yes* answer to all of the questions except 2 and 7, and one point for each *no* answer to questions 2 and 7. Now total up your points. A low score indicates that you need to develop some new skills for preparing for essay tests. A high score indicates that you already are using many good strategies.

thoughts and ideas rapidly and then present them in a well-developed and well-written form. All of these skills require training and practice. In this chapter, you'll learn some additional strategies for preparing for essay exams. Predicting, planning, and actually writing out answers before the exam all can help you improve your performance on essay exams.

PREPARE BY PREDICTING QUESTIONS

An essay test is a test that requires you to write paragraph-style answers to the questions. Sometimes you'll be asked to write about topics that were presented either in the lecture or in the text. Other times, you'll be required to pull together bits and pieces of information from one or more lectures, several sections of your text, or even information from both lectures and the text in order to answer the question. Essay tests may require you to focus on rather specific information or to synthesize a large body of information.

If you're not given the actual questions that will be on the exam, then the best way to study for an essay test is to predict test questions yourself. By anticipating questions that could be on the exam, you increase your chances of studying the same information on which you will be tested. Of course, it's also to your advantage to prepare the questions in essay form so that you study the information in the same format that you will be required to use on the test.

PREDICT EXTRA QUESTIONS

Deciding how many questions to predict is not as easy as it sounds. Many factors need to be considered. A test that covers two chapters may require more or fewer questions than one that covers six chapters; the difference involves the depth or breadth of the questions. A good rule of thumb is to try to predict at least four times the number of questions that will be on the exam. If you'll have to answer two essay questions on the exam, you should predict at least eight questions. The more questions you predict, the greater your chances of accurately predicting the questions that the professor will put on the exam. If you only predict two questions, you don't have a very good chance of selecting the same two questions that the professor will put on the exam. On the other hand, if you predict eight questions, you have a pretty good chance of picking one or more of the questions that will be on the test. Also, even if you don't predict the exact questions, you may find that you have predicted a question similar to the one on the test. In the process of studying to answer your question, you may learn the information that you need to answer the question that the professor asks. The more questions that you predict and prepare, the better you'll do on the test.

PREDICT THE RIGHT KINDS OF QUESTIONS

It's equally important to predict the right kinds of questions. You should predict broad, general questions if the exam will cover large amounts of material. However, if the essay test will include ten questions on only two chapters of text, the questions may be more specific and require more detail about a topic. If you go through your text and your notes, you should be able to come up with some ideas about topics that could become essay questions. Study guides (purchased guides or study guides provided by the professor) and end-of-chapter questions in the text also are valuable sources of essay questions. Your lecture notes are perhaps the best resource. Did the professor stress some particular topic? Were any comparisons drawn between one topic and a later one? Did the instructor ever hint that an understanding of one specific topic was critical to the mastery of the course? Asking the professor for sample questions and reviewing old exams can help you determine the types of questions that you should be predicting.

Questions that focus on why or how something happened often are too limited in scope. Most essay questions ask you to discuss causes and effects, compare and/or contrast, explain the steps in a process, and so on. You'll be able to predict and answer essay questions more effectively if you understand the terms that commonly are used in essay questions. A chart of frequently used terms is presented in Figure 12.1. Although you don't need to memorize the terms and their definitions, you should become familiar with them.

PREDICT CHALLENGING QUESTIONS

Predicting good essay questions requires some practice; they must be not only thoughtful but also penetrating and challenging. Many students predict only knowledge-level questions — questions that require only the repetition of the information as it was stated in the text or the lecture. Although some professors do include some of these short-answer essays, most ask questions that require analysis, synthesis, and application. Look at the three questions below:

1. What are two types of note-taking systems used for lecture classes?
2. Describe two types of note-taking systems that are used for lecture classes.
3. Compare and contrast the outline method and the paragraph method of taking notes in lecture classes.

The first question is not really an essay question at all. It requires only a short answer and little other information about the topic. The second and third ques-

Figure 12.1 Frequently Used Terms in Essay Questions

Term	Definition
compare	Tell how two or more subjects are alike; provide similarities. Some professors also expect you to discuss differences—ask.
contrast	Tell how two or more subjects are different.
define	Give the meaning or definition.
describe	Provide details or characteristics about a subject.
discuss or explain	Give a detailed answer that may include definitions, main and supporting points, reasons, and examples.
evaluate	Discuss both positive and negative aspects of the topic and then make a judgment.
illustrate	Explain by giving examples.
justify	Prove by giving evidence that backs up or supports a point.
list or enumerate	Number and list the information rather than writing in paragraph form.
summarize	Provide a brief review of the main points.
trace	Describe the events or steps in order of occurrence.

tions, on the other hand, require more in-depth mastery of the material. Several paragraphs or several pages may be needed to answer them properly.

In order to predict good questions, you have to know where to look for them. Although the questions themselves are not often found in your textbook or lecture notes, the clues to them are. Most essay questions center around main ideas or themes. The headings in the text provide clues to these main ideas. You often can rephrase the headings to come up with predicted questions. Unlike the recall questions that you may write in the margin, predicted essay questions should be a more general "summing up" of all the material under that topic. Look for clues such as lists of reasons (both positive and negative), similarities or differences, and sequences.

Students often get into the habit of predicting one essay question for each main topic or main heading in the text or lecture. One of the problems with this practice is that it may be too limiting for some essay tests. Learning the material in isolation, heading by heading, may not prepare you to answer a more general question that requires you to integrate the information. In order to prepare for tests where you may have only one or two long essays to write, you need to learn to connect two or more of the main topics. By learning to write broad, general questions that incorporate information in several sections of the chapter, you prepare yourself for the specific questions as well as the broad ones.

Look at some of the questions that one group of students predicted after reading a text excerpt on Federalism. Which of these questions are broad, general questions and which are specific?

1. Explain the impact of the Thirteenth, Fourteenth, and Fifteenth Amendments with respect to limiting state power for individual freedom.
2. What are the advantages and disadvantages of Federalism?
3. How does Federalism increase political participation?
4. Name the three amendments passed by the Reconstruction Congress and describe what each amendment did to delegate Congress's power of security.
5. Explain the differences between delegated and reserved powers.
6. Explain both Hamilton's and Jefferson's views on Federalism and the Constitution; tell which one you agree with and why.
7. What was the greatest crisis of the American Federal system? Why did it happen? What were the results?
8. Name the court case in 1819 that involved the state of Maryland and the National Bank and tell what it established.
9. What is Federalism? How does it affect the American people?
10. Discuss the 1954 Supreme Court case *Brown* v. *Board of Education.* What effect did this case have on civil rights in the United States?

Although almost all of the students included questions on the advantages and disadvantages of Federalism, they also predicted an impressive number of other essay questions from the material. Many of the questions were limited to headed sections, but others were broad questions that involved several headed sections.

Figure 12.2 Teri's Gathered Information

Question: What is Glycolysis?
Information:
Breakdown of glucose
Splitting of glucose
produces high energy products
occurs in the cytoplasm
highly exergonic
readies pyruvic acid for the next reaction
produces pyruvic acid
makes 4 ATP's
releases H_2O and 2NADH, $2H^+$

GATHERING INFORMATION

Predicting essay questions is not the end of your preparation for an essay exam. Instead, it is just the beginning. The next step is to gather information. You need to find the main and supporting points that are required to answer the question. You probably know some information to include in your answer, but you need to refer to your text and notes for more. This process of gathering information is valuable, because it forces you to dig through the text and your lecture notes looking for relevant information. Also, this active study technique may help you learn some of the other text information at the same time. Putting the information from the text and the lecture together also is a good technique for preparing for an essay test.

TREAT EACH QUESTION SEPARATELY

An easy way to gather information is to treat each question separately. Write each question across the top of a large piece of paper. Then open your text and your notes to that section of the material. Start to look for information that you would use if you had to answer that question. Pretend that it is an open book exam and you have the opportunity to look for the material that you are going to use. As you locate important points and details that would be useful in answering the question, write them down on your sheet of paper. Don't copy the information; rather, write it out in shortened form as you did in note taking. Look at the example of gathered information in Figure 12.2.

ORGANIZING INFORMATION

After gathering information for a number of questions, you may find that you have a huge amount of information to remember. By organizing the information and creating an outline for each question, you'll find it is easier to learn and remember the points you want to make for each question.

LABEL EACH POINT

You can organize information by *labeling* each point of the information that you gathered. Look at each piece of information that you wrote down, and decide where it should go in your essay. Find the point that you want to make first and label it 1. Any points that support it should be marked 1A, 1B, and so on, as shown in Figure 12.3. Because Teri didn't include her main ideas in her notes, she used labels only for the supporting points.

OUTLINE YOUR ANSWER

Although Teri was able organize the information by labeling (Figure 12.3), it still is not in a form that is easy to practice and remember. An informal outline may be more useful for remembering the points that you want to make for an essay

Figure 12.3 Teri's Organized Information

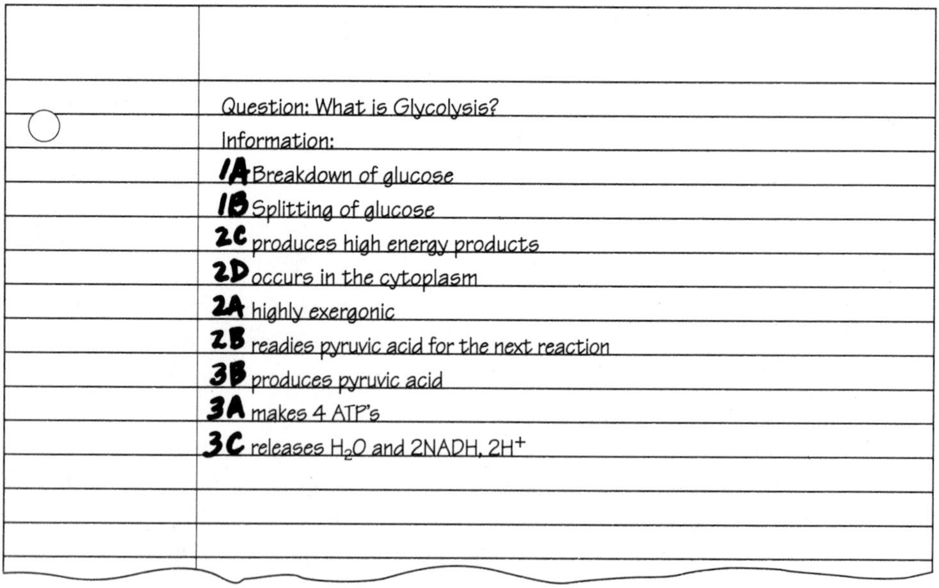

Question: What is Glycolysis?
Information:
1A Breakdown of glucose
1B Splitting of glucose
2C produces high energy products
2D occurs in the cytoplasm
2A highly exergonic
2B readies pyruvic acid for the next reaction
3B produces pyruvic acid
3A makes 4 ATP's
3C releases H_2O and 2NADH, $2H^+$

answer. The easiest way to outline your answer is simply to number each main point that you want to make and then list the supporting details underneath. Try to limit your main points to seven or fewer so that you can remember them. Three or four main points with good support for each should be sufficient for most answers. Of course, if you need to know the five causes of something, then you will have five main points.

Look at the outline that Teri developed from the information that she gathered (see Figure 12.4). Teri used formal outlining to organize the information that she had gathered. She could have used a more informal style in which she listed main or primary points (P) and then secondary or supporting points (S).

LEARNING INFORMATION

Gathering and outlining the information that you would use to answer a question is no guarantee that you will be able to replicate the answer on the test. The next step is to learn the information that you have gathered and organized. By learning the key points that you have selected, you increase your chances of maximizing your score on the exam. It is not necessary to memorize your outline word for word. Reciting the main points and then practicing the details that you wish to add should enable you to remember the material for your exam.

Figure 12.4 Teri's Outline

I. Glycolysis is
   A. Breakdown of glucose
   B. "Splitting" of glucose
II. What and where glycolysis is
   A. highly exergonic
   B. readies pyruvic acid for its next reaction
   C. produces high energy products
   D. occurs in the cytoplasm of a cell
III. Products
   A. makes 4 ATP's
   B. produces 2 pyruvic acid
   C. releases H_2O and 2NADH, $2H^+$

IDENTIFY AND LEARN KEY POINTS

Identify key points in your outline and then learn them. Use the same techniques that you used in Chapter 10 to select a word or phrase that can act as a memory tag for each main point that you want to remember. The best way to remember key points is to practice them over and over. Cover everything except the question with your hand or another sheet of paper. Ask yourself, What are the points that I want to make about this topic? Even better, try to write out your outline without looking back. By practicing (reciting and writing) the information over a period of days, you should insure that you'll be able to remember it at the exam.

USE MNEMONIC DEVICES

If you have difficulty recalling certain points or remembering them in order, try using a mnemonic device to improve your recall. Identify a key word in each of the main points that you made in your outline. Underline the word and then think of a way to remember it. You may find that acrostics, or catchphrases, are useful for essay tests, because they allow you to recall the information in order. Although these mnemonics don't replace learning the information, they do act as hooks or cues to help you recall what you learned. What mnemonics could you use to help you remember the main points in Teri's outline (Figure 12.4)?

WRITING OUT YOUR ANSWER

Some students know how to answer a question; they know the information. However, when they actually are in the testing situation, they just can't seem to put that information on paper. If this has happened to you before, the problem may be about writing rather than about studying. So that you can convincingly show the professor what you know, you may want to practice writing out the answers in paragraph form.

WHY SHOULD YOU WRITE OUT YOUR ANSWER?

Writing out your answer before the exam will help you overcome some of the problems that cause students difficulty during exams. One of the most common problems is getting started. By practicing ahead of time, you can avoid this problem. When the test begins, although you may not remember your first sentence word for word, you will know how to approach the question. Some students have difficulty deciding how to phrase what they want to say and how to tie their points together. Doing this before the exam will help you do a better job during the exam.

Again, don't try to memorize your answer word for word. If you forget one word or phrase, you may find yourself unable to complete your answer. You want to practice writing out the answer just to get the feel for how the whole thing fits together.

PRACTICE USING YOUR OUTLINE

Practice writing out your answer by referring to your outline with your book and notes open. Your goal here is not to test your memory of the information, but rather to practice stringing together your ideas. After you have successfully constructed an answer with the book open, try to write the answer again with the book closed. On the evening before the exam, practice writing out the answer one last time. By allowing yourself some time between your initial practice session and your final one, you test your ability both to recall the information and to present it in a well-written and well-organized manner. If you are able to construct a well-written answer without your notes the night before the exam, you will feel reassured when you begin the actual exam.

WRITE OUT ANSWERS FOR THE MOST DIFFICULT QUESTIONS

If you have predicted a large number of questions, you may not have time to write out all of your answers ahead of time. If this happens, write out only the ones that you think you would have the greatest difficulty explaining. If a number of your questions seem fairly straightforward, you can probably eliminate this stage. Just be sure you review aloud the key points that you would make and think about how you might start the answers. Choose more complex questions for written practice. If you can present the information in the difficult questions in a well-written form, you probably can do equally well or better on the easier questions. Figure 12.5 shows Teri's practice essay. Notice how she moved from one main point to the next in constructing her answer.

WRITE OUT ANSWERS TO SAMPLE TEST QUESTIONS

Some instructors pass out sample essay questions prior to an exam. These questions are a valuable source of information. Some students use them to get an idea of the kinds of questions that will appear on the exam. This is one way to use the sample questions; however, they can be used to even greater advantage. Each sample question can be planned, learned, and practiced using the strategies described above. In cases where professors hand out the exact set of questions that will be on the exam, those students who prepare ahead of time are almost assured of an excellent grade.

Figure 12.5 Teri's Practice Essay

The process of glycolysis is the breakdown of glucose. It is known as the "splitting" of the glucose molecule. This process makes glucose ready to produce energy for needed reactions.

Glycolysis is a highly exergonic process. The main reaction in glucose is getting pyruvic acid ready for its next reaction. The products made by glycolysis are of very high energy. This process occurs in the cytoplasm of a cell.

Glycolysis produces several things. 4 ATP's are made, along with 2 pyruvic acids. Glycolysis also releases water and 2NADH and 2 Hydrogens.

Even if the sample questions are not the ones on the actual test, chances are they are closely related. In the process of preparing to answer the sample question, the student probably will learn what he or she needs to know in order to answer the new question. A good general rule to follow is to always treat sample questions as if they were the actual exam questions. Don't assume, however, that you should focus your study only on those questions. Go ahead and predict some additional questions just in case.

After you have prepared several of the questions (written out the answers), go see your professor. Ask him or her to take a look at your predicted questions (or the sample test questions) and the answers that you wrote. Ask for feedback on how you approached the question and how you presented your answer. Don't expect your professor to "grade" the paper for you; instead, look for tips or suggestions for how you might improve your essay for the exam. A number of students have reported that getting feedback on their answers before the exam resulted in much higher test grades and a better relationship with their instructors.

ACTIVITIES

1. Predict three essay questions for an exam that you have coming up in the next few weeks. Write each question on a separate sheet of paper. Then plan all three questions by gathering information and outlining the answers on the three sheets of paper. Finally, take a fourth sheet of paper and write out one essay.

2. Make up a mnemonic in order to remember the main points that you selected for a question that you planned. Practice learning the main points out loud. Then review out loud, or write the supporting points that you would like to add. Try to replicate your outline in writing. How effective was your mnemonic in helping you recall the information in your outline?

3. Set up an appointment with your professor to discuss some of the questions that you predicted, planned, and wrote out. Write a paragraph describing your discussion and what you learned from the experience.

POSTTEST

Where Are You Now?

Now that you have completed Chapter 12, take a few minutes to answer *yes* or *no* to the following questions. Compare your answers with those in the pretest.

	YES	NO
1. Do you study differently for essay tests and objective tests?	______	______
2. Do you generally plan out your answers in your head rather than on paper?	______	______
3. Do you always write out essays before the test if the professor gives you the questions?	______	______
4. Do you predict possible essay questions before an exam?	______	______
5. Are you usually able to predict accurately which essay questions the professor will include?	______	______
6. Do you use memory techniques to help you remember the main points that you want to make in your answer?	______	______
7. Do you tend to rely on old exams and hope that the same questions will be used again?	______	______
8. Do you prepare sample essay answers and ask your professor to evaluate them before the exam?	______	______
9. Are you generally well prepared for essay exams?	______	______
10. Do you know how to study for an essay exam?	______	______

Give yourself one point for each *yes* answer to all of the questions except 2 and 7, and one point for each *no* answer to questions 2 and 7. Now total up your points. Compare your score on this posttest with the score that you got on the pretest. In what areas do you still need to improve?

CHAPTER 13

Taking Essay Tests

"I feel that I am better prepared for essay exams now. I never really knew how to study for them or how to write out the answers. Often I would just write down anything that came to mind. Now that I have learned to plan in the margin before I write, essay tests don't seem as hard as they did before. I plan to use this strategy on my future exams."

Kim Bednarski

THEY'RE NOT AS HARD AS YOU THINK

Most students think that essay tests are more difficult than objective tests. They are in some ways, but in other ways, they are actually a little easier. Essay tests do require you to recall rather than just recognize the answer. However, there are several advantages to taking essay tests. First of all, unlike objective tests, which often are filled with "trick" questions, essay tests are fairly straightforward; there usually is no confusion about what the question is really asking. Another advantage to essay tests is that there are no distractors (wrong answers) there to tempt you. In addition, you can get partial credit on essay exams. Rarely are essay answers all right or all wrong. In most cases students are given points for any and all information that they present. In some courses, professors provide students beforehand with sample questions, actual questions from which the test questions will be

PRETEST

Where Are You Now?

Take a few minutes to answer *yes* or *no* to the following questions.

	YES	NO
1. Do you always read the directions before you begin to answer the questions on an essay exam?	______	______
2. Do you generally plan your answer in your head rather than on paper before you begin to write?	______	______
3. Do you usually score lower on essay exams than on objective exams?	______	______
4. Do you ever leave blanks on essay exams?	______	______
5. Do you organize your answer before you begin to write?	______	______
6. Do you generally find that you are unable to finish the exam before time runs out?	______	______
7. Do you go back over the entire exam before you turn it in?	______	______
8. After your exam is returned, do you go over it to evaluate your preparation and clarify your errors?	______	______
9. When you get your exam back, are you often surprised by the grade that you received?	______	______
10. Do you know how professors grade essay exams?	______	______

Give yourself one point for each *yes* answer to questions 1, 5, 7, 8, and 10, and one point for each *no* answer to questions 2, 3, 4, 6, and 9. Now total up your points. A low score indicates that you need to develop some new skills for taking essay tests. A high score indicates that you already are using many good strategies.

PEANUTS reprinted by permission of UFS, Inc.

taken, or even the exam itself. Assuming they have properly prepared, many students find that they actually can get higher grades on essay exams.

HOW TO TAKE AN ESSAY TEST

There are a number of strategies for taking essay exams that can help you retrieve, relate, and organize the information that you learned. Reading the directions, budgeting your time, and planning before you write all can help you be successful on essay exams.

READ THE DIRECTIONS CAREFULLY

The first step in taking an essay exam is to read and follow the directions. Some students have actually failed essay exams, not because they didn't know the information, but because they didn't read and follow directions. Unfortunately, they just plunged into the exam without making sure they knew how to proceed. If you find that you tend to forget to read directions on tests, set up a special method to insure that you read them. Some students use strategies like circling or underlining key words in the directions. Others sign their names, write their initials, or put a check mark at the end of the directions. Some students even jot down the directions in their own words before beginning the exam. All of these are good strategies, because they help insure that you read the directions.

Find Out How Many Questions You Have to Answer

When you read the directions, be sure that you look to see *how many* questions you are expected to answer. On many essay exams, you are given a choice of questions to answer. Consider the following set of directions: *1. Answer two of the following questions.* (Six questions are given in total.) *2. Answer two questions from set A and two questions from set B.* (Three questions are included in set A, and three questions are included in set B.) Each of these types of directions limits you to a certain number of questions and, in the latter case, to a certain number of questions from two different sets.

Don't Answer Additional Questions

Sometimes students who have extra time at the end of an exam go back and try to answer additional questions (more than the directions indicated). This is often a mistake. If the directions indicated that you were to answer two of the six questions, your professor isn't going to read all of your answers and pick the best two on which to base your grade. In most cases, the professor will grade the first two answers and merely cross off or ignore the rest. This can really hurt your grade if your best answers were the fourth and fifth ones.

How Much Should You Write?

Although essay answers are often only one paragraph in length, they can range from a few sentences to ten pages long. The best guide for how much to write is how much space the professor provides on the examination paper. If there are three questions on one side of a page, a one-paragraph answer probably is expected. However, if you're not limited to just one side of the page, don't limit yourself to only the space that the professor has provided. Instead of trying to squeeze in or leave out additional information, continue your answer on the other side of the page. If there is only one question per page on your exam, the professor probably expects you to fill the page in order to provide a satisfactory answer.

BUDGET YOUR TIME

Budgeting your time during an essay test is extremely important; otherwise, time can become a major obstacle. If you move too slowly through the test, you may not have time to complete all of the questions. Therefore, it is very important to develop some strategies for spacing or budgeting your time. First, consider the total time that you have for the test. Then count the number of questions that you're expected to answer. After you do that, consider the point value of each of the questions. Take a minute or two to budget your time so that you allot the appropriate amount of time to each question and still have some time for a final review of the entire exam.

PLAN BEFORE YOU WRITE

If you take a few minutes to plan your answers before you write them, you'll find that you write better essay answers in a shorter period of time. When you first look at the essay test, read *all* of the essay questions before you decide which ones you want to answer. Circle the number of a question if you think you may want to answer it. Then jot down your ideas in the margin.

Jot Down Ideas in the Margin

As you read each question, make notes in the margin as the ideas for an answer pop into your mind. If you predicted one or more of the questions, jot down key words or main points from the outline that you planned. You'll be able to make a better decision about which question or questions you should answer after you look at your marginal notes. Look at the student example in Figure 13.1. Kesha listed all of the ideas that she thought of when she read the question. As you can see, she wrote down only key words and phrases.

Making notes as you read the questions can be very helpful. Sometimes it's hard to remember what you wanted to say about a particular question when you're ready to answer it. Reading the other questions and thinking about whether you should answer them can cause memory interference. Have you ever gone back to begin answering a question only to realize that you couldn't remember what you were going to say? If you think back to the analogy of your long-term memory and a filing cabinet, you may be able to understand better why this happens. When you read the first question, something in the question triggers an association that opens a particular file drawer for you and makes the information on that subject accessible to you. As you read other questions, however, that drawer is closed and others are opened. Sometimes, it's difficult to get the first drawer open again. Marginal notes help prevent this problem. In addition to aiding your memory, making notes in the margin helps relieve test anxiety. Once you know that you can answer the question, you can relax and feel more comfortable about the exam.

Figure 13.1 Kesha's Notes

Question: What general and specific strategies should a student follow when taking a matching test?

Notes in margin:

- work from one side to other
- usually longest first
- do not from side to side
- cross off answer if you use it
- do the ones you know 1st
- do not guess right away
- read directions
- read through all choices

Be Sure Your Notes Reflect All Parts of the Answer

After you have chosen to answer a question and have jotted your ideas in the margin, you should reread the question to make sure that your notes reflect all parts of the question. If you find that you've planned for only a part of the question, you should make additional notes in the margin. Some essays require you to answer two or three questions within one question. Consider the following essay question from a chemistry test. *What differences, if any, exist between morphine and heroin in terms of chemical makeup, pharmacological effects, legal availability, and abuse?* Because there really are four parts to this question, you could put a "1" above *chemical makeup,* a "2" above *pharmacological,* and so on.

Be Sure That You're Answering the Question That Was Asked

Also, at this point, you may want to go back to the question in order to make sure that your notes provide information that answers the question that was asked and not a different question. Some students lose points on essay answers because they have not really answered the question that the professor asked but instead have written an answer to a different question. In the case of the above example, you would need to be sure you were showing the differences between those drugs rather than just listing the chemical makeup of each. By rephrasing the question in your own words and then writing it below the professor's question, you can read both questions in order to verify your interpretation. Ask yourself, "What am I being asked to explain here?" After you plan your answer, go back and read the question again. As a final check, compare the information in your concluding sentence to the information required by the question. Even an excellent answer is wrong if it doesn't answer the question that was asked.

Organize Your Ideas Before Writing

After you jot down your ideas in the margin, you can organize your essay in just a few seconds. Simply number your ideas in the margin as Kesha did (see Figure 13.2). Look at the ideas that you jotted down and ask yourself, "What's the first thing that I want to talk about?" After that, you can decide what to put second, third, and so on. You also may decide that some of your ideas actually support some of the others. You can indicate that some of your ideas are supporting points by marking them with an "A" or "B" after the number.

Some students don't feel that they can take the time to plan their answers in the margin, because they feel pressured for time during exams. However, you should be able to plan and organize an answer in just one or two minutes. For a longer essay, you can organize your ideas even more by writing a brief outline in the

Figure 13.2 Kesha's Plan

Question: What general and specific strategies should a student follow when taking a matching test?

Notes in margin:

③ - work from one side to other
④ - usually longest first
⑤ - do not from side to side
- cross off answer if you use it
⑥ - do the ones you know 1st
⑦ - do not guess right away
① - read directions
② - read through all choices

margin. In addition to making it easier to write your answer, your outline also lets you see where you need to add supporting details. Taking just a few minutes to plan and organize your answer before you begin to write can help save you time and earn you extra points on the exam.

WRITE YOUR ANSWER

Getting started is often the hardest part of writing an essay answer. So, start with the easiest question first. Write your essay answer as you would write an essay for one of your English classes. State your first main idea and back it up with supporting details and/or examples. Then go on to your next main point.

Use a Basic One-Paragraph Design

The general format for a one-paragraph essay is shown in the left-hand column of Figure 13.3. Begin your essay with a topic sentence (TS) that states the central idea of your paragraph. After the topic sentence, state your first main point, also referred to as primary (of first order in rank or development) support (PS). After stating your first main point, back it up with one or more supporting sentences, or secondary (of second order in rank or development) support (SS). Each of these sentences may include details, facts, or examples that further explain your main point. Next, state your second main point, followed by a sentence or two of support. Your third main point should be made next, followed by relevant support. Additional main points and secondary information also can be included here. Finally, end your paragraph with a concluding sentence. A well-developed paragraph should be from eight to eleven sentences in length. Of course, a paragraph can be shorter or longer, but by writing at least eight sentences, you can insure that you are including both primary and secondary support (both main points and details).

Figure 13.3 Sample Essay Design

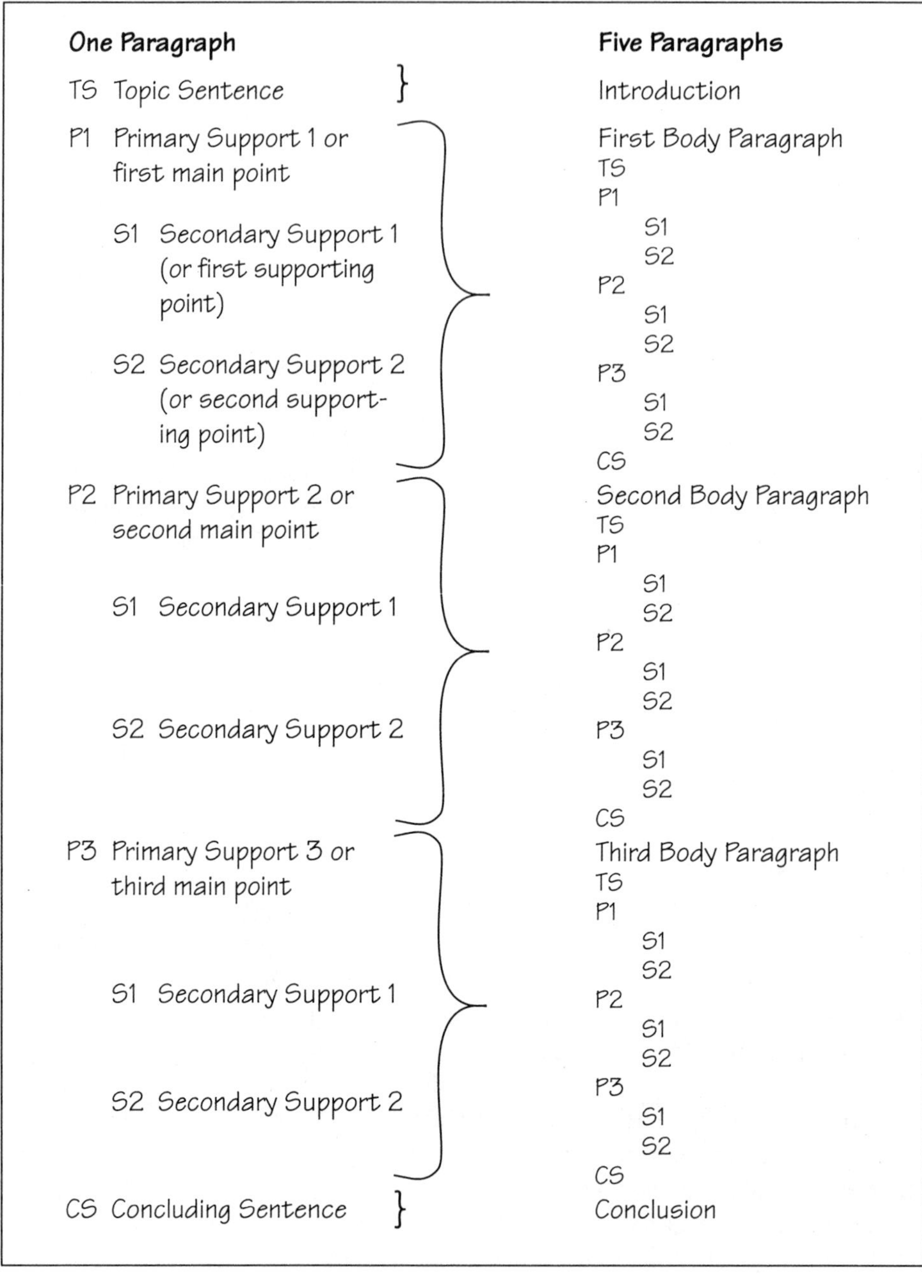

Modify the Design for Longer Essays

Not all essays can be answered in only one paragraph. You may be expected to write several paragraphs or several pages in order to answer a question properly. In that case, instead of having a topic sentence followed by several main points, each paragraph in your essay would focus on one of these main points. A one-paragraph answer easily could be expanded to a four- or five-paragraph answer simply by developing each point more fully. The topic sentence would be expanded to an introductory paragraph, each main-point sentence would be expanded to form a supporting paragraph, and the concluding sentence would become a concluding paragraph (see the right-hand column of Figure 13.3). A long essay, one of five or more pages, would be developed in much the same way. Remember, the shorter an essay answer is, the more general it tends to be. You can develop your ideas into a longer answer by adding more and more specific details and examples.

Turn the Question Into a Statement

One strategy that may help you get started is to actually take the question, turn it into a statement, and add your answer to it. The resulting statement will become either your topic sentence (for a one-paragraph answer) or your thesis statement (for a longer essay answer). Consider the following example. Question: *How did Greek architecture and sculpture reflect the Greeks' concern for order, reason, and the ideal? What rules did they follow?* This question can be rephrased in order to begin the answer in the following way. Topic sentence: *The Greeks valued architecture and sculpture and tried to make them reflect their concern for order, reason, and the ideal.*

By generating a topic sentence or thesis statement that includes your main points, you show your professor that you know the answer to the question. Turning the question into a topic sentence also helps you organize your own presentation of the material. In other words, you know where you are going with your answer.

Write Your First Main Point

The next step in writing your answer is to make your first main point. Take the idea that you labeled number 1 (or put first in your informal outline) and convert it into a sentence. Make it a general statement that can then be supported by details and examples. Look back at the sample plan in Figure 13.2. Kesha decided that "Read Directions" was the first main point that she wanted to make. She converted her notes to the following sentence: "The first and most important thing a student should do is always read the directions."

Support Your Main Points

After you write your first main point, you need to add one or more sentences that contain specific information to back up your main point. Next, add an example if you can. You may use an example that was presented in the text or lecture, or you could include an example of your own. By using examples, you demonstrate to your professor that you understand the abstract material. Don't stop after you make one good point. Continue with other main points and follow each of them with details and examples just as you did for the first one.

Even though Kesha didn't list any supporting points in her original plan, she did back up her first main point with several supporting sentences; her next two sentences explain *why* it is so important to read the directions: "Some students see that they have matching on a test and automatically start matching without reading the directions. Directions may help a student out, because not all answers are always used, and also because some answers may be used twice."

Add Transitional Devices

Add transitional devices to indicate each of your main topics and to help your reader move from one idea to the next. Words like *first, second, third, next,* and *finally* often are used to introduce the main points that you are making. They let your reader know that you're making a main point. *Moreover, in addition, also,* and *furthermore* tell your reader that you're adding support to the points that you already made. Occasionally, you may want to change direction or say something that contradicts the previous statement. In this case, you should begin your statement with a word or phrase like *however, but, on the other hand, nevertheless,* or *on the contrary.* Words like *consequently, therefore,* and *thus* indicate that you have reached a conclusion based on previous information.

You also can show connections by restating some of the key words in your question or topic sentence as you make additional points in your essay. If you're writing a long essay, it often is effective to restate parts of the question in each of your main points. You might say, for example, *The first main reason to answer the easiest question first is to maximize your points.* After explaining how that can be accomplished, you might restate the question in your second point as follows: *The second main reason for answering the easiest question first is to relieve test anxiety.* Each time you make a main point you can restate the question. Repeating key words and phrases helps to organize your essay and reinforces the points that you want to make.

Add a Conclusion

Finally, you should end your paragraph or essay with a concluding sentence or paragraph that reminds your professor of the main points that you made. Professors form opinions of essays as they read, but they don't assign an actual grade until after they have read the entire answer. If you have made some of your best points early in your answer, it helps to remind your professor of them just before he or she assigns a grade. Also, the concluding sentence or paragraph helps to bring the answer to a logical ending, making the entire essay appear well thought out.

Proofread and Revise Your Answer

Your job isn't done when you write the last sentence of your essay answer. If you take just a few additional minutes to reread your answer, you may catch careless errors in sentence construction, grammar, or mechanics. In addition, as you read your answer from start to finish, you may think of an additional point to make or a better way to phrase something.

Sample Essay

After reading the sample essay in Figure 13.4, try to determine why each sentence is included. Refer back to the sample essay design in Figure 13.3. Which sentence is the topic sentence? Which sentences present the main points? Which sentences provide the secondary support? Which sentence presents the conclusion? Are transitions used? Which ones?

FACTORS THAT INFLUENCE YOUR GRADE

Many factors can influence your grade. Although the content of your answer carries the most weight, other factors, such as the organization of your answer, the format that you use, your writing ability, and how neatly you write your answer all can affect your grade. Some professors are as interested in how well you present the information as they are in the information itself. Knowing what your professor will be looking for in your answer can help you write better essay exams.

CONTENT IS A FACTOR

Of course the information that you include in your answer is the most important factor in determining your grade. When you're planning and writing your answer, you should include as much relevant information as you can. Many students make

Figure 13.4 Sample Essay Answer

Question: How did Greek ①architecture and ②sculpture reflect the Greeks' concern for a. order, b. reason, and the c. ideal? ③ What rules did they follow? (30 points)

1 rules of proportion
3 Parthenon
2 human–ideal
4 perfect image
5 virtual image

Answer:

The Greeks valued architecture and sculpture and tried to make them reflect their concern for order, reason, and the ideal. First, the Greeks followed very careful rules of proportion in creating their sculptures of gods and heroes. Every human figure was seven and one-half heads tall. The distances from the head to the chest, the chest to the groin, and the ankle to the foot all followed exact proportional measurements that had previously been determined. Also, the Greeks followed careful "rules" in the way they portrayed man and the gods in their sculpture. All works were idealized. They showed only the best human features. Second, the Greeks used the rules of proportion and measurement in creating their works of architecture. The Parthenon provides an excellent example of this order. The columns were spaced in proportion to the others in order to create a "perfect" image for the viewer. The number of columns across the side was equal to twice the number across the front plus one. This provided a sense of balance to the Greeks. Also, all of the columns leaned inward in order to maintain the illusion that they were exactly parallel and vertical. They were also thicker in the middle so that from the bottom of the hill, they appeared to be perfectly straight. Other similar "corrections" were made to the floor and the decorations in the frieze in order to maintain that "virtual image" that was so important to the Greeks. Both sculpture and architecture reflected the Greeks' concern for order, reason, and the ideal.

the mistake of including only some of the information that they know. They incorrectly assume that their professor would think that some information is just obvious and should not be included in the answer. Assuming that your professor will know what you mean even with little explanation also may result in a lower test score. It's important to explain key terms and back up the statements that you make. One way to avoid being too general is to pretend that your professor doesn't know the answer to the question. If you tell yourself that you're writing the essay for someone who doesn't know anything about the topic, you'll be sure to include all the pertinent information. Remember, your job on an essay test is to show the professor how much you know about the question.

ORGANIZATION ALSO IS IMPORTANT

The way that you organize your essay answer also is an important factor in the grade you receive. When professors grade essay exams, they expect to read a well-organized answer. If they are looking for particular points to be made, they expect to find those points easily. Few professors will take the time to read an essay over and over again in order to *search out* the information that they are looking for. Some professors penalize students intentionally for poorly organized answers. They feel justified in giving a poorly organized answer a lower grade, because they think the student who wrote it didn't know the information as well as the student who wrote the more clearly organized answer. In other cases, though, students are *unintentionally* penalized because the essay answer is so jumbled that it becomes difficult to follow the argument, and the professor misses some of the information.

FORMAT IS ANOTHER FACTOR

The directions on an essay test are sometimes rather vague. Professors assume that students know how to write essays, and they don't go into detail about what form of answer they expect. Students, however, sometimes don't really know what is expected. In some classes, writing the correct information in list format would earn a student an A. In other cases, though, this student might be penalized for not answering the question in the appropriate form. Penalties for not using paragraph form vary greatly from one professor to another.

HOW YOU WRITE AFFECTS YOUR GRADE

Sentence structure, grammar, punctuation, and spelling all are factors that influence your grade. They probably are given more weight in English courses, but professors from every discipline — engineering professors, biology professors, business professors, and so on — are influenced by these factors. Poor sentence construction and grammar can make it difficult to understand the information that you're trying to relate. Even problems in punctuation and spelling affect how well your written answer matches what you wanted to say. Some essays include so many sentence structure and mechanics errors that it's difficult to locate the points that the student is making.

Your professors also may be influenced by these kinds of errors in less obvious ways. How well you are able to write your answer — how free of errors in mechanics it is — does say something about you as a student. Essay answers that include numerous errors in sentence construction, grammar, spelling, and punctuation can give your professor the impression that you're not a very well-educated student. Unfortunately, this impression can "spill over" to the evaluation of the content of your answer as well. This shouldn't happen, but it does. Some professors may find themselves thinking, "If this person can't even write a complete sentence, how can he or she understand philosophy (or psychology, sociology, history, and so on)?"

NEATNESS COUNTS

Neatness also may influence your grade. Most professors expect students to write clearly and neatly, observe margins, and present the material in a "professional" manner. Very few of them are willing to spend hours attempting to decipher messy handwriting. If your professor can't read your essay, you'll lose points simply because he or she will not be able to understand what you're trying to say. You also may lose points just because you make a "bad impression" by writing in an awkward and messy manner. Nicely written papers have been getting better grades than messy ones for years. Teachers seem to believe that good students care about their work and take the time to write in a careful and skillful manner, while poor students don't.

STRATEGIES FOR GAINING MORE POINTS

In this section you'll learn some strategies that may help you gain additional points on an essay exam. Even if you're well prepared, you may find that during the test you have difficulty getting what you know down on paper. Occasionally students draw a complete blank on an essay question, think of an important point after they have completed their answer, run out of time, or even run out of space. The following tips may be helpful if you find yourself in one of these situations.

USE THE EXAM AS A RESOURCE

Many college exams are a combination of objective and essay questions. Students sometimes overlook the objective questions, which are a valuable source of information. You may find a great deal of specific information that you can use in your essay in the multiple-choice, true-false, or matching questions. Don't be afraid to look back at them for names, dates, terms, or even key ideas. Professors often include in the objective part of the exam information that relates to the essay questions. In fact, some of these details may even be found in the incorrect choices for the multiple-choice items. Even if the actual information is not available, reading some of the questions and possible alternatives may help you recall some of the information that you need. Words or phrases in the questions may act as triggers for your long-term memory.

ALWAYS WRITE SOMETHING

There are times when even well-prepared students are surprised by an essay question and draw a complete blank. Before you give up and resign yourself to accepting a failing grade, try to think through the question. Look for key words in the question that might give you some clues to the answer. Think about the main topics of the lectures and the chapters that were covered. Try to recall the maps that you made, the study sheets that you prepared, and the questions that you predicted. Sometimes, you actually can recall the answer after you do a memory search. However, if you still have no idea what the answer to a question is, you should still write something. Many professors give students a few points for just trying. In addition, you may find that you know more than you thought. Even though you may not think you know the information the professor is looking for, you may be right on target. Also, sometimes in the process of writing "anything" to fill the space, you trigger something in your memory that suddenly makes the actual answer pop into your head. This has happened to a number of students who used this technique. They erased or crossed out their initial answer and continued writing the correct answer to the question.

It probably sounds strange to expect you to write an answer to an essay question when you don't know the answer. Essentially, you are preparing a well-written "snow job." Your goal is to make the professor think that you know the answer even if you don't. Doing this is not easy. Approach the essay by first writing a thesis statement. Of course it will be rather vague, but it still will be a beginning. Next, incorporate words or phrases that are used in the question into your answer. If you must, keep repeating the same thing over and over again using different words. This is not the correct way to write an essay answer, and with any luck, you may never have to use this strategy. Remember, though, that you get no points for a blank paper.

LEAVE EXTRA SPACE

When you're answering a question on the test paper itself, it's important to leave reasonable margins on all sides of the answer. First of all, this makes your answer look better. Also, it allows you to add information after you have completed your answer. If you must add further information at the end of your essay, place an asterisk (*) or number next to it and also in the paragraph at the spot where the information belongs. You may earn more points if the additional material is read within the context of the answer rather than if it is read at the end. You also benefit from leaving wide margins because your professor has space to provide you with feedback about your answer. If no space is available, professors tend to include comments only at the end or not at all.

If you're using a blue book for your answers, leave at least three lines between each answer. Again, you'll have room to write in another point if you think of something after completing the question.

WHAT IF YOU NEED MORE SPACE?

Sometimes you may find that you need even more space than is provided on the exam. You may write larger than other students or have more information to present. Before writing on the back of the page or on additional blue book pages, check with your instructor to see whether there are any space limitations. If your instructor has not limited you to one side of a page or to the space provided on the exam sheet, continue your answer on the back. Be sure to indicate that you are continuing your answer. Use an arrow, write the word "over," or write "continued on back." If you write several answers on the back, number them so that they will be easily recognizable.

WHAT IF YOU RUN OUT OF TIME?

No matter how carefully you budget your time, you occasionally may run out of time during an essay exam. The first thing you should do is ask your professor whether you can have additional time to complete the test. Some professors will allow you to continue working until the next class begins. Others may even allow you to come to their office in order to complete your test. If, however, your professor says that you must finish in the time allotted, you can still pick up most of the points on an essay answer. Let's say you have started writing your last essay answer out in paragraph form. When you have only about five minutes left, simply list the remaining points that you wanted to make. Add a little note to the professor that says something like, "I'm sorry that I didn't have time to finish my essay. These are the additional points that I wanted to make." Some professors will give you full credit for your answer, assuming it is a good one, even though you did not write all of it out. This is a better strategy than just writing until time runs out and answering only half of the question.

LEARNING FROM EXAMS

You can learn a great deal from your essay answers after the test is returned. You may think that once the test is over, you should simply move on and concentrate on the next unit of work. You probably think that if you just try harder the next time, you'll be able to do a better job. Unfortunately, some students just don't know how to write an "A" answer for some of their classes. They may do very well on the exams in one class, but for some reason that they can't explain, they just are not able to get the grades they want in another class. Looking carefully and analytically at your returned tests can provide you with information on how to improve your answers on future exams.

WHAT CAN YOU LEARN?

One of the most important things that you'll learn from your returned exam is how closely your answer matched what the professor wanted. If you scored a high grade on the exam, you probably are doing a good job of presenting the information that the professor wanted. If, on the other hand, your grade was lower than you expected, you need to find out where you went astray. It's important to understand why you got the grade that you did. You may want to evaluate your answer on the basis of the factors that influence grades (described earlier in this chapter) and then discuss it with your professor. Of course, the key to improving your score on subsequent exams is to find out what you need to do differently.

HOW CAN YOU EVALUATE YOUR ANSWERS?

There are several good ways to evaluate the quality of your essay answer. One method is to compare your answer with those of your peers. Sometimes just reading another student's essay can teach you a lot about what the professor expects. Find a student in your class who got an A on the exam. Explain to this student that you were disappointed in your grade and just want to get a better idea of what you should do differently. Ask the student to explain how he or she answered the question and ask whether you may read his or her essay.

Once you get a better idea of what the professor expected, set up an appointment to discuss your test with your professor. Don't go into the meeting with the expectation of getting extra points. Instead, focus on finding out how you should have answered the question in order to gain the maximum number of points. In this way, you and the professor are on the same side; you're working toward the same goal. Often, when you "fight" for additional points, you and the professor may find yourselves acting as opponents or adversaries. If that type of atmosphere is generated, you may gain a point or two on the exam, but you will probably lose the opportunity to learn how to write a better answer.

Another place you should go for help is your college learning center. The learning center staff can provide you with help in evaluating and improving your essay answers. Also, the learning center may provide tutorial services in the course content area as well as help in correcting sentence construction, grammar, and mechanics errors.

REWRITE YOUR ANSWERS FOR COMPARISON

An excellent strategy for learning to write better essay answers is to rewrite your answers to the test questions after you get the exam back. Use your text and your notes to put together the best answer that you can. Take time to organize the information and check your sentence structure, mechanics, and spelling. Then go back to your professor and ask him or her to read your new answer. Ask what your grade would have been had you written that answer for the exam. You need to find out whether you understand what your professor expects for an "A" answer. If you still don't succeed in matching your professor's expectations, you now have another opportunity to discuss why your answer wasn't a good one. You may want to rewrite the answer one more time and then meet with your professor again to discuss it.

ACTIVITIES

1. Describe the steps that you generally use when taking essay exams. What new strategies do you plan to use on future exams? Why?
2. Analyze and critique the grade that you got on one of your essay answers from a recent exam. Write a short paragraph describing what you learned. Consider some of the following questions as you examine your answer. What factors influenced your grade? What mistakes did you make? What did you learn from your peers and your professor?
3. Rewrite one of your essay answers from a recently returned exam. Use your text and notes to locate the correct information for your answer. Improve or correct organization, sentence structure, grammar, spelling, and punctuation errors. What changes did you make in your revised essay? Meet with your professor to discuss your revised answer. What were you able to learn from this experience?

POSTTEST

Where Are You Now?

Now that you have completed Chapter 13, take a few minutes to answer *yes* or *no* to the following questions. Compare your answers with those in the pretest.

	YES	NO
1. Do you always read the directions before you begin to answer the questions on an essay exam?	____	____
2. Do you generally plan your answer in your head rather than on paper before you begin to write?	____	____
3. Do you usually score lower on essay exams than on objective exams?	____	____
4. Do you ever leave blanks on essay exams?	____	____
5. Do you organize your answer before you begin to write?	____	____
6. Do you generally find that you are unable to finish the exam before time runs out?	____	____
7. Do you go back over the entire exam before you turn it in?	____	____
8. After your exam is returned, do you go over it to evaluate your preparation and clarify your errors?	____	____
9. When you get your exam back, are you often surprised by the grade that you received?	____	____
10. Do you know how professors grade essay exams?	____	____

Give yourself one point for each *yes* answer to questions 1, 5, 7, 8, and 10, and one point for each *no* answer to questions 2, 3, 4, 6, and 9. Now total up your points. Compare your score on this posttest with the score that you got on the pretest. In what areas do you still need to improve?

CHAPTER 14

Preparing for Final Exams

> "Preparing for finals would have been so much harder had I not planned and spaced out my studying. I also set up a specific time to start studying and I stuck to it. I'm not even worried about finals because of this. When my friends are running around cramming for finals, I just have to check my calendar to see exactly what I have scheduled to do. It's so easy."
>
> Brian Shomo

FOLLOW A SPECIAL PLAN OF ATTACK

Final exams are a whole new experience for many first-year college students. Some final exams are simply routine exams covering the last unit of work. Other finals cover some new and some old material. Still others are comprehensive finals. In comprehensive finals, students are tested on all of the material that was covered during the semester.

Although preparing for four or five exams at the same time is a difficult task even for experienced college students, new college students may view this task as nearly impossible. However, it's not. Each type of final exam requires a different plan of attack. Preparing for all types requires both good time management skills and good test preparation strategies. This chapter presents strategies that will help you decide when to study, what to study, and how to stay motivated.

PRETEST

Where Are You Now?

Take a few minutes to answer *yes* or *no* to the following questions.

	YES	NO
1. Do you work ahead before finals to free up study time?	_____	_____
2. Do you tend to give up at the end of the semester and spend little or no time preparing for finals?	_____	_____
3. Do you usually score lower on final exams than on the other exams given during the semester?	_____	_____
4. Do you set up a plan to prepare for your finals?	_____	_____
5. Do you put most of your effort into the course in which you have the lowest grade?	_____	_____
6. Do you generally spend a lot of time partying at the end of the semester when you know you should be studying?	_____	_____
7. Do you review all of your old exams before your final?	_____	_____
8. Do you use a four- or five-day plan to prepare for each of your finals?	_____	_____
9. Do you put so much effort into one exam that you don't have the time and/or energy to prepare for one or more of the others?	_____	_____
10. Do you realistically consider your chances of success before preparing for final exams?	_____	_____

Give yourself one point for each *yes* answer to questions 1, 4, 7, 8, and 10, and one point for each *no* answer to questions 2, 3, 5, 6, and 9. Now total up your points. A low score indicates that you need to develop some new skills for preparing for final exams. A high score indicates that you already are using many good strategies.

WHAT ARE FINAL EXAMS?

Final exams are end-of-semester tests that help professors evaluate your progress in their course. They are used by some professors to monitor your mastery of the concepts and ideas presented in the course. Other professors use them to make decisions about the grades they should give, whether students should move on to the next class, or even to monitor their own teaching. Although final exams may be one of many routine exams given during the semester, they often are longer, both in number of questions and in time allotted for the test, and more difficult. Comprehensive final exams survey all of the material covered in the course. Final exams range in value from about 20 percent of your grade all the way up to 100 percent. In some courses they count as much as two regular exams; in others, they are the *only* exam and determine your grade entirely.

Many courses include only a midterm and a final, with each one determining half of the course grade. However, sometimes the final carries more weight in determining your grade, because it is the second exam. If you score higher on the final, you will probably receive a higher grade, and vice versa. Although finals are more challenging than most of the regular exams that you have during the semester, you can still use many of the same test preparation strategies that you used for your other exams. However, if you have four or five final exams in a one-week period, you need to begin your preparation even earlier — perhaps several weeks before your first exam.

HOW SHOULD YOU PREPARE?

Many students change their patterns of sleeping, eating, studying, socializing, working, and so on before final exams. For example, they may limit their time with friends, cut out television, and spend more time at the library so they can fit in extra study time. They believe that their performance on finals is critical to their ultimate success in one or more of their courses. You can improve your grades on final exams by starting your preparation early, managing your time efficiently, making academics your first priority, and putting your effort into appropriate courses.

START YOUR PREPARATION EARLY

Many students "blow" their finals because they don't start to prepare early enough. They don't think about all of the regular assignments that are due at the end of the semester that compete with the study time that they planned for finals. Even the student who has become adept at managing his or her time needs to make extra time to prepare for final exams. One way to free up this additional study time is to begin several weeks before finals begin.

MANAGE YOUR TIME EFFICIENTLY

You can make the end of the semester much less stressful by using time management techniques to reduce the overload that many students experience. Two or three weeks before your first final, sit down and make out a new calendar for the end of the semester. Write down all of the assignments, papers, projects, and exams that you still need to complete. Then make a list of all of your outstanding assignments and realistically estimate the amount of time that you think you will need to complete them.

Pick several assignments to complete early. Even if they aren't due for two weeks, finish them as soon as possible to reduce the amount of work that you will have to complete right before exams begin. You need to be able to begin to concentrate on your finals at least four days before the first one is scheduled. That means that you need to complete most of your regular work about a week before it actually is due. Doing some of your reading early, completing a term paper, or working ahead in several of your classes can help create extra time that you will need.

MAKE ACADEMICS YOUR FIRST PRIORITY

Many students get tired at the end of the semester. College is hard work and it takes its toll on many students. One of the biggest mistakes that some students make, though, is to decide to rest up before finals week. They slack off and even get behind in their work just when they need to be pushing harder to get ahead. Although they may feel better for a day or two after this hiatus from work, most of them realize too late that it was a mistake. Suddenly they have only a few days to complete all of the assignments that have piled up and, at the same time, to prepare for their finals. Needless to say, they feel overwhelmed and stressed out. Even though they push hard at the end, they just don't have enough hours in the day to do all of the work that needs to be done, so something suffers. Often they give up on one or more assignments or on one of their courses, and their grades drop.

Rather than easing off at the end of the semester, you need to push hard. If you work as hard as you can for one week about two weeks before your first final, you will be able to complete many of the assignments on your list and still have a few days to rest up before you begin to study for your final exams. During this week, plan daily tasks. Some students still like to use the "To Do" lists; others get really serious and use hourly calendars to schedule their assignments. In either event, schedule regular study hours and set daily study goals.

Two weeks before finals tends to be a rather slow period for end-of-semester projects, so it's a good time to get ahead in your work. Look at your assignment calendar and locate a "light" week near the end of the semester. It may be three weeks before finals for you. Whichever week is the lightest week for you, that's the week that you should choose to get a head start on your outstanding assignments. Don't forget to break down tasks, switch subjects, and plan rewards to help you stay motivated.

SET PRIORITIES FOR EXAMS

You also can increase your chances for academic success by setting priorities according to your course load. Take an hour or two to re-evaluate your goals for each of your classes. Look closely at where you stand in each course. You may be able to figure out exactly what your grade is by averaging all of your exams, homework, and papers. If you can't determine your grade on your own, set up an appointment with your professor to go over your grade. You need to know what your grade is before you can determine how much time and effort you need to put into your final exams.

Pretend that you have the following test grades in your classes so far this semester. The final exam in each class has the same weight as the other exams. For which final exam or exams should you work the hardest, put in the most time? Make a decision before you go on with your reading.

Class A	82	84	83
Class B	81	76	79
Class C	74	84	85
Class D	14	40	56

Most students think they should put the greatest amount of time and effort on the final for Class D. For the second most important final exam, some students select Class A and others choose between B and C. The majority of students, however, select A and D as the finals that they would put ahead of the others. Why? First of all, they realize that they are failing Class D. In order to pass the class, they need to get a good grade on the final.

Unfortunately, some college students actually let all of their other exams go (spend very little, if any, time on them) in order to "ace" the final in their worst class and "save" their grade. In most cases, however, students who have failed all of the previous exams in a course are unlikely to score high enough on the final exam to improve their grade. In this exercise, what grade would you have to get in order to pass Class D? Because each of the exams carries the same weight, it's easy to figure this out. Add up the points that you already have (14 + 40 + 56). After the first three exams, you would have accumulated 110 points in Class D. In order to score a passing grade (with 60 as passing), you would need a total of 240 points (4 times 60). What would you need to get on the final in order to achieve your goal of 240 points? If you said 130 points, you were right. As you can see, not only is it impossible to score 130 points, but it also is highly unlikely that any student with scores of 14, 40, and 56 would even score 100 on the final exam.

By setting your priorities appropriately, you actually may improve your GPA. You should put the greatest effort into the courses in which you have a borderline grade, in courses where the final actually can make a difference. Many students think that they would put their greatest effort into Class A, because it was the class with the highest grade (an 83 average). Although Class A is the course in which you have the highest grade, the grade is a pretty solid B. What grade would you have to get on the final in order to get an A (90 average) in this class? Look at the following problem.

360	what you need for an A (if all four exams are given equal weight)
− 249	the total points you now have in Class A
111	total points that you need

As you can see, here again it's impossible to gain enough points on the final to significantly affect the grade; an A cannot be achieved, even with a perfect score. The two classes where you should put your effort are the middle two classes (B and C). In each of these courses you have a borderline grade (78.6 in Class B and 81 in Class C). Because your grade is close to the cutoff for a B (80 average) in each of these courses, the results of your final exam would determine your grade. If you wanted to get a B in Class B you would need to score only an 84 (320 minus 236) on the final. With previous grades of 81, 76, and 79, an 84 seems to be a realistic goal requiring only a little extra effort. In order to keep the low B that you already have in Class C, you would only need to get a 77 (320 minus 243). Putting in the extra effort in Class C certainly could pay off.

ATTEND ALL CLASSES

You also can improve your performance on final exams by attending class. Many students cut classes at the end of the semester. They decide to use up any "cuts" that they haven't used (perhaps feeling that they would waste them if they didn't).

Although some professors have cut policies that allow students to miss up to three classes without it affecting their grade, this doesn't mean you *should* skip three classes. Professors are just trying to allow for emergencies and illness.

Missing class is never a good idea, but missing class just before finals is extremely unwise. Many professors squeeze extra information into their lectures during the last week or two of classes in order to present all of the material that will be on the final. Others review or discuss what will be on the final as well as what won't be on the final. Knowing what to study and also knowing what you don't have to spend time on can help you use your study time effectively.

REDUCE TEST ANXIETY

Don't let the thought of final exams make you panic. Some anxiety is a normal part of finals week. Although you can't expect to eliminate all feelings of anxiety, you can do things to keep test anxiety from interfering with your performance on exams. If final exams are a new experience for you, talk to your professor, advisor, or someone in your learning center about what to expect. Ask some of your friends to describe their experiences with final exams and how they compared to regular exams. The more you know about the exams, the more prepared you'll be for them. If one of your finals will determine your grade in the course, be sure to make that exam your top priority. The strategies for test preparation that you learned will help you be well prepared for the exam, and being well prepared is the best way to reduce your feelings of anxiety. Finally, get lots of rest, eat well, and plan some time to relax during finals week so that you don't feel stressed out. If you used some stress reduction exercises to help reduce your test anxiety on previous exams, use them again as soon as you feel anxious. Although test anxiety may be an obstacle during final exams, you have many resources to help you overcome it.

FINALS WEEK PREPARATION

Many students prepare for one final exam at a time. They study all day for one exam, take it, and then start on the next. Although cramming for finals is a common phenomenon, it's not the best method for preparing for finals. If you cram for finals, you may find that after one or two days it becomes very hard to maintain that kind of pace. You may get tired of the long days and nights of study and give up on later exams. Cramming makes inefficient use of your time, causes feelings of frustration, and results in lots of memory interference. It's a form of massed practice, and massed practice is not an efficient method of learning information. Spaced practice gives you much more opportunity to practice, to organize, and to test your retrieval of the information.

Cramming is especially ineffective when you have more than one exam on the same day. Few students actually have a finals schedule that includes only one exam per day; usually students have at least two exams on the same day. In most cases, then, cramming is not a useful strategy for preparing for exams. What alternatives are there? By spacing your study over several days, you can study for each of your exams using the Five-Day Study Plan and, at the same time, maintain your motivation throughout exam week.

MAKE A SCHEDULE FOR YOUR FINALS

One of the first things that you need to do is set up a schedule of your exams. Check your syllabi or final exam schedule several weeks in advance and write each exam on a calendar. Occasionally, students find that they have more than one exam scheduled for the same time. If this happens, check with your professors about alternative exam times. More often, students find that they have more than one exam on the same day. It is relatively common to have two exams on one day, but some students find that they have three exams (or more) on one day. Having too many exams on the same day can negatively affect your performance during finals. By the time you take the third exam, you may be exhausted, frazzled, or emotionally drained. To put it another way, you will not be at your best. Some schools have policies that help eliminate these conflicts; the faculty and administration recognize that students can't properly demonstrate what they have learned if the testing situation works against them. Check with your professor, academic dean, or someone in the registrar's office if you have exam conflicts.

SET UP A STUDY SCHEDULE

By setting up a study schedule, you can properly prepare for each of your exams without feeling rushed or anxious. Use the Five-Day Study Plan to space out your study. By dividing up your day, you can prepare for several exams at the same time.

Space Your Study to Aid Retention

Spacing your study as you prepare for finals is crucial to getting information into long-term memory in a logical and organized manner. Because of the large amount of information that you may need to master for a comprehensive final, you need to learn information in small chunks and review it often. If you try to cram fifteen chapters of biology into one long (eight- to ten-hour) study session, you may find that you only partially know the material. By studying one chunk of the material each day and then reviewing it again over the next few days, you can monitor your learning and reinforce the information that you still don't know.

Split Your Day When Preparing for Several Exams

Rather than studying for one exam at a time, you need to learn how to prepare for several exams at the same time. This is not an impossible task, as some students think, but rather one that requires a little planning and a lot of perseverance. Count back five or six days from each of your final exams to determine your starting date. You may find that you are on Day 3 of your study plan for Biology when you start Day 1 of your study plan for English Literature.

By splitting your day, you can effectively prepare for several exams at the same time. If you have your other work done, you should be able to devote all of your time to preparing for exams. This doesn't mean that you will study nonstop from the time you get up until the time you go to sleep. Rather it means that you should be able to schedule two or three blocks of time each day to prepare for your exams. Let's pretend that you have the finals schedule shown in Figure 14.1. If you use a five-day study plan, you shouldn't have to prepare for more than three exams at one time. Your hardest and busiest days on this schedule are Sunday, Monday, and Tuesday. By carefully planning your time, you can prepare for each exam and still have sufficient time for sleep, meals, and some relaxation.

Students often ask me to help them figure out when to study for finals. If I were helping you plan a study schedule, I would recommend that you divide your day

Figure 14.1 Final Exam Schedule

Algebra—Monday	December 14	9:00 to 11:00
English—Wednesday	December 16	9:00 to 11:00
Biology—Thursday	December 17	12:30 to 2:30
Sociology—Friday	December 18	12:30 to 2:30

Final Exam Study Plan

Wed Dec. 9	Thurs Dec. 10	Fri Dec. 11	Sat Dec. 12	Sun Dec. 13	Mon Dec. 14	Tues Dec. 15	Wed Dec. 16	Thurs Dec. 17	Fri Dec. 18
Day 1 Alg	Day 2 Alg	Day 3 Alg	Day 4 Alg	Day 5 Alg					
		Day 1 Engl	Day 2 Engl	Day 3 Engl	Day 4 Engl	Day 5 Engl			
				Day 1 Bio	Day 2 Bio	Day 3 Bio	Day 4 Bio	Day 5 Bio	
					Day 1 Soc	Day 2 Soc	Day 3 Soc	Day 4 Soc	Day 5 Soc
					Take Alg Final	No Exam	Take Engl Final	Take Bio Final	Take Soc Final

according to the three courses on which you are working. Assigning one exam to morning, one to the afternoon, and one to the evening allows you to study for each test in a regular time slot. By studying the same material at the same time of day, you can separate course material for one exam from that of your other courses and thereby prevent some of the memory interference that often occurs during finals week. It's also a good idea to work on your hardest subject early in the day, when you are the most alert. By the time you spend four to six hours on your other two classes, you won't be able to concentrate as well on the material from the third class.

Look at the sample study schedule shown in Figure 14.1. If this were your exam schedule, I would suggest that you set up your study time as follows (see Figure 14.2). Because you have several finals early in the final exam period, you should begin to prepare for your final exams during the last week of regular classes. You may still be busy completing reading assignments or even papers or projects that are due at the end of the semester. If you need to prepare for more than one exam during this week, you should try to complete your regular assignments early. By Sunday of exam week, you should schedule time to prepare for your final exams. Even in this schedule you have some flexibility. You could use the morning to study, and spend the afternoon on only one of your classes. There even is room in this schedule to spend three hours on each course or four hours on Biology and two on each of the others. Because Biology is a very difficult class, I would schedule that study time first. (Notice, incidentally, how each study block is followed by at least a one-hour break. You need time to rest and allow the information to "sink in" before you start to study again.) You also may notice that Day 1 of Biology is scheduled for Sunday rather than Saturday. Because the exam is scheduled for an afternoon time slot, you could (and should) do your final review that morning.

PREPARE FOR COMPREHENSIVE FINALS

Check to see if your final is comprehensive or if it covers only new material. Some professors include both old and new material on final exams. Knowing how much of the exam is based on old material is critical to effective preparation. If you have a comprehensive final, find out *how much* of the exam is comprehensive. Many instructors give final exams that are partially comprehensive. If, for example, you had an exam that covered twelve chapters (and accompanying lecture notes and so on), you would prepare differently depending on whether the exam was 100 percent comprehensive, 75 percent comprehensive, 50 percent comprehensive, or 25 percent comprehensive.

Figure 14.2 Final Exam Planning Calendar

	(9) Wednesday	(10) Thursday	(11) Friday	(12) Saturday	(13) Sunday	(14) Monday	(15) Tuesday	(16) Wednesday	(17) Thursday	(18) Friday	(19) Saturday
9:00	Class		Class			Algebra		English	Day 5	Day 5	
10:00						FINAL		FINAL	Bio	Soc	
11:00	Class		class	sleep		break		break	break	break	
12:00	Lunch	Lunch	Lunch			Lunch		Lunch	Lunch	Lunch	
1:00	class		class		Day 1	Day 2	Day 3	Day 4	Biology Final	Sociology Final	
2:00		class			Bio	Bio	Bio	Bio			
3:00		↓	Day 1	Day 2	break	break	break	break	break		
4:00			Engl	Engl	Day 3	Day 4	Day 5				
5:00	Dinner	Dinner	Dinner	Dinner	Engl	Engl	Engl				
6:00					Dinner	Dinner	Dinner	Dinner	Dinner		
7:00	Day 1	Day 2	Day 3	Day 4	Day 5	Day 1	Day 2	Day 3	Day 4		
8:00	Alg	Alg	Alg	Alg	Alg	Soc	Soc	Soc	Soc		
9:00					break	break	break	break	break		
10:00					OPTIONAL	OPTIONAL	OPTIONAL	OPTIONAL	OPTIONAL		
11:00					Study Time	Study Time	Study Time	Study Time	Study Time		

Preparing for 25 Percent Comprehensive Finals

Let's say that you're going to have an exam that is only 25 percent comprehensive. That means that 75 percent of the test questions cover new (not yet tested) chapters, while 25 percent of the test questions cover old (already tested) material. If the exam is composed of 100 multiple-choice items covering twelve chapters, how many of the questions will be on old material? Of course, twenty-five of them will be. That means that seventy-five of the questions will be on the new material, which, for this example, will be Chapters 10, 11, and 12.

If you were going to set up a five-day study plan for this final, which chapters would you study on each of the first four days, assuming that you save the last day for a final review and self-test? Many students make the mistake of dividing the material into four equal chunks (as they did for regular exams). In the case of a comprehensive final, however, this would result in very poor planning. Because 75 percent of the questions will come from the new material, 75 percent of your time should be spent on that material. It may seem strange to spend only 25 percent of your study time on the first nine chapters of the text (and accompanying lecture notes, and so on). However, that is the appropriate time to devote to the old material. Look at the two study plans shown in Figure 14.3. In the first plan, the student divided his or her study time equally. In the second plan, the proportion of time spent on each section of the material is more appropriately divided to reflect the weight (number of test questions and point value) of each of the sections. The correct way to divide your time would be to spend Day 1 preparing Chapters 1 through 9, Day 2 on Chapter 10, Day 3 on Chapter 11, and Day 4 on Chapter 12. Because each of the four chunks of material (1-9, 10, 11, 12) is weighted the same on the exam, they should be given the same preparation time.

The number of questions that are taken from each chapter often signals how detailed or specific each question will be. Typically, the fewer the questions from each chapter, the more general they tend to be. If you have only twenty-five

Figure 14.3 Sample Study Plans

Plan 1		Plan 2	
DAY 1	CH 1–3	DAY 1	CH 1–9
DAY 2	CH 4–6	DAY 2	CH 10
DAY 3	CH 7–9	DAY 3	CH 11
DAY 4	CH 10–12	DAY 4	CH 12

questions covering nine chapters of text, you have less than three questions per chapter on the exam. On the other hand, if you have seventy-five test questions based on the last three chapters, you have approximately twenty-five questions for each chapter. Although the student who spends three days preparing and reviewing the first nine chapters may know that material very well, he or she will not know the last three chapters well enough (with only one day of preparation) to achieve a high score on the exam. A quick review of the old material followed by intense study on the new material is necessary for exams that are only slightly comprehensive.

How can you review nine (or more) chapters of material in only a two- or three-hour study session? Obviously, you don't have time to reread all of your highlighting or even all of your lecture notes (and rereading is not a good way to review anyway). If you prepared properly for each of the exams that covered the comprehensive chapters, you should have summary sheets, maps, card files, and self-tests from which to study. The best way to prepare for those chapters, then, is to review the material that you already prepared when studying for the earlier exams. In addition, if you have copies of your old tests or are permitted to review them in your professor's office, do so. Many instructors use questions from the original exams again on the final.

Preparing for Other Comprehensive Finals

Now that you know how to divide your time correctly between old and new material for 25 percent comprehensive finals, let's look at other combinations. Let's say that you're going to have a final that will be 50 percent comprehensive. One half of the test questions will be based on Chapters 1 through 14 and the other half will come from the last four chapters in the text (15 through 18). How would you divide your study time assuming the same four days to prepare and one day to review? In order to figure out the proper ratio of time to chapters, think about how many chapters will be covered in each quarter of the exam. Because half of the test questions will come from the first fourteen chapters, you can effectively divide those chapters in two. You would prepare Chapters 1 through 7 on Day 1 and Chapters 8 through 14 on Day 2. You would then prepare Chapters 15 and 16 on Day 3 and Chapters 17 and 18 on Day 4. Remember to review each chunk of material on each of the succeeding days in order to aid retention.

An exam that's 75 percent comprehensive requires more time on old material than on new material. Let's use the following example. If you had 100 questions that covered nineteen chapters of text, how much time would you spend on the old material if only Chapters 16 through 19 were still untested? In this case, you would spend the first three days of your study plan reviewing the first fifteen chapters (because 75 percent of the questions will come from those chapters) and only the last day on the new material (because only 25 percent of the questions will be drawn from those chapters.) Even though you haven't yet been tested on the last three chapters, you shouldn't spend a disproportionate amount of your time on them, because so few questions will be taken from each one. By spacing your study and allocating the appropriate amount of time to each of the chapters, you can maximize your test scores on any type of comprehensive final exam.

USE ACTIVE STRATEGIES TO STUDY

Use active strategies when you review your text and lecture materials. Write and recite in order to move information into long-term memory. Test your understanding of the material by using flash cards, self-tests, and recitation. If you already took notes on your textbook and prepared study sheets combining the information from your text and your notes, you won't need to go back and review the text again. If you prepared word or question cards for each of your chapters, take them out again to review for your final. Rather than rereading the notes that you took and the study sheets or maps that you prepared, create new ones. This time use your notes and study sheets as your starting points. In the process of making new study sheets, you will effectively review the material. If you made self-tests for each chapter, use them again to find out what you already know and what you still need to learn.

STAY MOTIVATED

As you prepare for each of your finals, use strategies to stay motivated. If you get tired or discouraged, give yourself a pep talk. Plan rewards that will help you stay on task. Surround yourself with other motivated people. Join a study group or check in with friends who also have made a commitment to work hard during finals week. One of the worst things you can do is hang around with other students who don't have very many exams or who don't plan to study for the exams that they do have. They'll constantly distract you and may, without meaning to, tempt you to forget your studies and "party" with them. Even though it's hard to say no to your friends, you have to. Remember that your academic goals must come first. If you have a heavy exam schedule, save the partying for when you're finished. Many students don't realize that partying every night after they study can be very harmful. Memory interference and too little sleep may nullify all your hard work. Don't drink during finals preparation; hangovers interfere with your ability to concentrate during exams and with your ability to stick to your study schedule.

PUT FORTH YOUR BEST EFFORT ON EACH EXAM

Work hard during each of your exams. Stay in the testing room for the entire time period. Review your answers and use test-wise strategies to try to figure out the correct answer for any question that you're not sure about. Concentrate on only one exam at a time. Don't think about the exam that you had yesterday or the one that's coming up tomorrow. If you feel anxious, use one of the relaxation strategies that you learned. Focus all of your energy and all of your effort on the exam. After the exam, take a break before beginning your next study session. Don't allow your performance on one exam to interfere with your ability or commitment to prepare for another one. If you leave an exam angry or upset about your performance, accept the fact that you may not achieve your goal in that class, but don't give up on all of your other classes. You may be able to do even better than you expected on one of your other exams.

MONITOR YOUR PROGRESS

After the exam is over, evaluate your performance. Write down a few notes about how you thought you did on the exam. Note any areas where you think you had difficulty and then review your notes or study sheets to check your answers. At the beginning of the next semester, visit your professor and ask to look at your exam. If you had problems with some areas, ask your professor to go over them with you. Even though the course is over and your grade is already assigned, you still may benefit from reviewing your final exam. You can decide whether or not the plan that you set up or the strategies that you used were effective. If they were, you may want to use those strategies again in a similar class. If they weren't effective, you should revise them for future exams.

ACTIVITIES

1. Write a paragraph that describes how you prepared in previous semesters or how you think you will prepare for final exams this semester. Be as specific as possible in describing both how you planned your time and what strategies you used.
2. List up to ten strategies that you think you might be tempted to use in preparing for your final exams.
3. Make a list of all the assignments, exams, and projects that you need to complete before the end of the semester.

Figure 14.4 Final Exam Planning Calendar

	Wednesday	Thursday	Friday	Saturday	Sunday	Monday	Tuesday	Wednesday	Thursday	Friday	Saturday
9:00											
10:00											
11:00											
12:00											
1:00											
2:00											
3:00											
4:00											
5:00											
6:00											
7:00											
8:00											
9:00											
10:00											
11:00											

4. List the grades that you have in each of your classes and total your points earned. Then decide which grade you think you could earn in the course and determine what grade you would need to get on the final. Finally, decide which of your courses should be a priority.
5. List some of the obstacles that you'll have to overcome during finals week, along with the strategies or resources that you plan to use to overcome them.
6. Complete the Final Exam Planning Calendar shown in Figure 14.4.
7. After your final exams are over, make some notes about what worked and what didn't. Include information on how effectively you set priorities, how well you stuck to your plan, and how you felt before, during, and after each of your exams. Refer to these notes when you begin to plan for your finals next semester.

POSTTEST

Where Are You Now?

Now that you have completed Chapter 14, take a few minutes to answer *yes* or *no* to the following questions. Compare your answers with those in the pretest.

	YES	NO
1. Do you work ahead before finals to free up study time?	_____	_____
2. Do you tend to give up at the end of the semester and spend little or no time preparing for finals?	_____	_____
3. Do you usually score lower on final exams than on the other exams given during the semester?	_____	_____
4. Do you set up a plan to prepare for your finals?	_____	_____
5. Do you put most of your effort into the course in which you have the lowest grade?	_____	_____
6. Do you generally spend a lot of time partying at the end of the semester when you know you should be studying?	_____	_____
7. Do you review all of your old exams before your final?	_____	_____
8. Do you use a four- or five-day plan to prepare for each of your finals?	_____	_____
9. Do you put so much effort into one exam that you don't have the time and/or energy to prepare for one or more of the others?	_____	_____
10. Do you realistically consider your chances of success before preparing for final exams?	_____	_____

Give yourself one point for each *yes* answer to questions 1, 4, 7, 8, and 10, and one point for each *no* answer to questions 2, 3, 5, 6, and 9. Now total up your points. Compare your score on this posttest with the score that you got on the pretest. In what areas do you still need to improve?

CHAPTER 15

Writing College Papers

"I found that if I follow the five steps in the writing cycle, I have better results. I used to just write a rough draft, go over the mistakes, and then write the final copy. Now I follow the writing cycle, and my papers have really improved. Not only have my grades improved, but my writing skills have also improved. As long as I continue this process, I know my grades will show how well I can do."

Stephanie Weiss

BASIC STRATEGIES CAN HELP

Many college students dread the thought of having to write reports, essays, and term papers. What's so bad about writing a college paper? Nothing, really, if you know how to go about it. Why, then, do so many students dread writing papers? For some students, getting started is the biggest problem. Finding a good topic, writing the first paragraph, or figuring out what to do when you feel as though you've said all you can but you have only one page written are all common stumbling blocks. Some students know what to do but have difficulty motivating themselves to begin their papers early enough to gather the information, write the paper, and then

PRETEST

Where Are You Now?

Take a few minutes to answer *yes* or *no* to the following questions.

	YES	NO
1. Do you usually sit down and just write your paper without planning first?	_____	_____
2. Do you often find that your topic is too broad?	_____	_____
3. Do you have difficulty organizing your ideas when you write papers?	_____	_____
4. Do you correct errors in spelling and grammar only when you revise a paper?	_____	_____
5. Do you know how to develop an introductory paragraph?	_____	_____
6. Do you have problems with supporting your thesis?	_____	_____
7. Do you use transitional devices to identify main ideas and show connections to supporting ideas?	_____	_____
8. Do you develop some type of outline before you write?	_____	_____
9. Do you generally understand why you got the grade that you got on a paper?	_____	_____
10. Do you start long-term paper assignments early in the semester?	_____	_____

Give yourself one point for each *yes* answer to questions 5, 7, 8, 9, and 10, and one point for each *no* answer to questions 1, 2, 3, 4, and 6. Now total up your points. A low score indicates that you need to develop some new skills for writing college papers. A high score indicates that you already are using many good strategies.

revise it. Although this chapter cannot substitute for an entire course in writing, it should provide you with some basic strategies for successfully writing college papers.

WRITING IS A PROCESS

Writing is a work in progress. Several years ago I was reading a book that seemed somewhat familiar to me. I did some checking to see if I had purchased a book I had read before that had been given a new cover design (something I have often done). I found that I never had read this very same book. What I previously had read, however, was an earlier version of the same novel. The author wrote the first version before she became "accomplished," and she decided to rewrite the entire novel, improving on the story line and technique. After I finished reading the new version, I spent several hours going back and forth from the old version to the new version, looking at the changes that were made. Seeing how another person's writing style and technique developed over time was kind of exciting.

You may want to look back at some old papers that you wrote and compare them to some more recent ones. You may be surprised by what you find. Theoretically, you could probably go back to just about any paper or essay answer that you wrote and improve on it, because each time you write you develop more skills. Perhaps after you complete this chapter, you will decide to rewrite one of your old papers to see how much you can improve it.

You may be wondering how writing is a process. If you think about all the steps you must go through in order to "create" a paper, though, it becomes more obvious. Can you think of any other creative efforts that involve a process? The first thing that comes to my mind is a photograph. In order to create a photograph, you must go through many steps. First, you must decide on a subject. Then you must decide how you want to capture that subject and compose the picture in such a way that you achieve your desired result. You then must process the film into a negative and then go through even more steps to print the picture. If you don't follow all of the steps in the process, your finished product — the photograph — will be disappointing. Writing is this same sort of process. Unfortunately, some students try to "print the picture" before they "develop the film." They try to produce the finished product without going through the necessary steps.

Many writing experts have defined the steps in the writing process. Hans Guth describes five stages in the writing cycle: Explore, Focus, Organize, Draft, and

Revise.[1] Others use variations of Guth's stages, but all of them include activities to do before, during, and after writing. These stages often are referred to as *prewriting, writing,* and *rewriting.* In this chapter, you will learn to use the following steps in the writing process: *getting started, getting organized, drafting, revising,* and *evaluating.*

Getting started includes brainstorming for ideas, limiting your topic, and focusing your thoughts and ideas. Getting organized includes listing and selecting ideas, formulating a tentative thesis, and outlining your paper. When you draft your paper, you transform the ideas from your outline into sentences and paragraphs in order to develop an introduction, body, and conclusion. Revising is an active process that may involve improving the development, coherence, and unity of your paper as well as correcting errors in spelling, grammar, and sentence structure. Finally, evaluating your writing involves looking critically at your paper after it's returned as well as during the various stages of its development.

Many students see these steps as distinctly different and linear in nature — in other words, when one step is completed, you simply move on to the next step. However, writing is somewhat different from developing a photograph. Not every piece of writing develops in exactly the same way. Instead, writing can be thought of as a cycle. During the writing process, you may complete one stage, begin the next, and then return again to the first stage. In other words, you may gather information, limit your topic, and then realize that you need to gather additional information. You may organize your ideas and, in the process, realize that you need to limit or narrow your focus again. Look at the diagram in Figure 15.1. You can see that the writing cycle comes full circle; it's a series of stages or steps that often lead back to the beginning. In many ways, it's similar to the cycle of concentration that we discussed earlier in the text. In this case, however, moving backward may improve your performance rather than interfere with it. As you learn about each of the five stages in the writing cycle, remember that you can and should move back and forth through them as you prepare your paper.

GETTING STARTED

Getting started often is the most difficult step for students who are inexperienced writers. In fact, it often is the most difficult step for experienced writers. Many

[1]Guth, H. P., *Words and Ideas: A Handbook for College Writing*, 4th ed. (Belmont, CA: Wadsworth, 1975).

Figure 15.1 Steps in the Writing Process

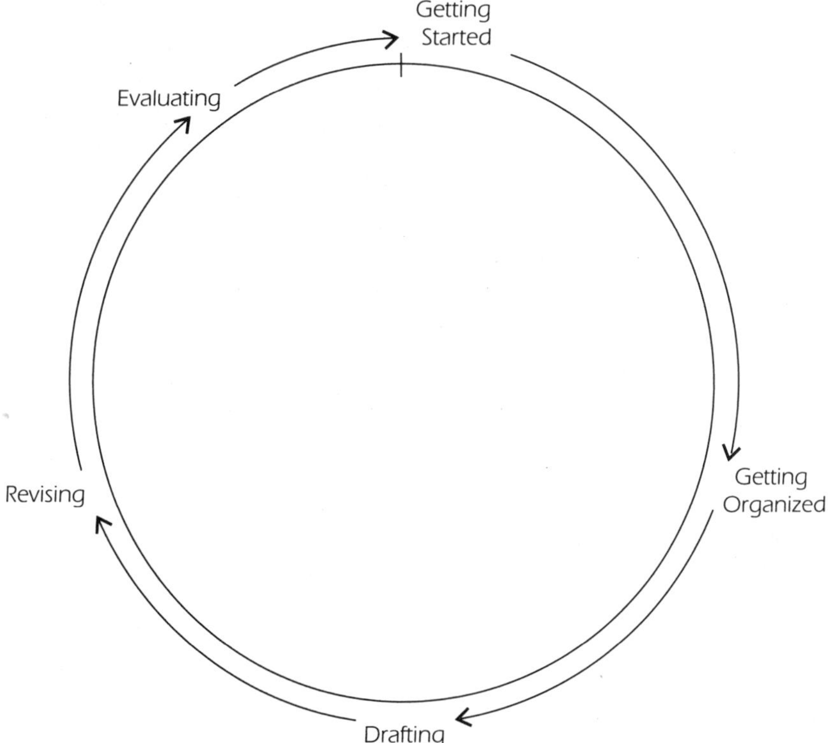

students spend hours staring at a blank piece of paper or computer screen trying to decide what to write. Before computers became so popular, crumpled sheets of paper strewn around the room were often a sign that a student was starting to write a paper. Now of course, many students compose their papers directly on the computer and only the bare screen, the blinking cursor, and fingerprints on the "delete" key bear the telltale signs of the failure of the composing process. Learning to brainstorm for ideas and learning to focus your topic will help you get started on your assignments without becoming stalled or frustrated.

BRAINSTORMING

Brainstorming can be thought of as a way of getting all of the ideas that you have in your head onto paper, where you can use them. A number of brainstorming techniques can help you get started on your assignments. In this chapter you'll learn to use journaling, listing, mapping, and questioning strategies.

Journaling

One of the easiest ways to get started on a writing project is just to start. After writing a topic at the top of a piece of paper, just start writing anything that comes to mind. Write for five or ten minutes without stopping. Don't worry about spelling, grammar, or even sentence structure. Your goal is to get ideas on paper. If you get stuck, write about the last idea that you had. Even if you get a good idea early in your brainstorming, keep writing, because you may come up with an idea that's even better. After you finish putting your ideas on paper, circle or underline the ones that you think are the best.

Look at the example of journaling in Figure 15.2. The topic was "Writing." In just five minutes this student generated two ideas for a paper topic. Although you won't always come up with a great idea through brainstorming, with a little practice you will learn to generate good ideas.

Listing

Although some students find that journaling works very well for them, others prefer listing their ideas in order to generate a paper topic. Rather than writing ideas in sentence or paragraph form, you can make lists of words or phrases that pop into your head. As with journaling, write the general topic at the top of a sheet of paper. This time, though, jot down your ideas in list form. If you get stuck or run out of ideas, go back and reread your list. You may think of more ideas after

Figure 15.2 Example of Journaling

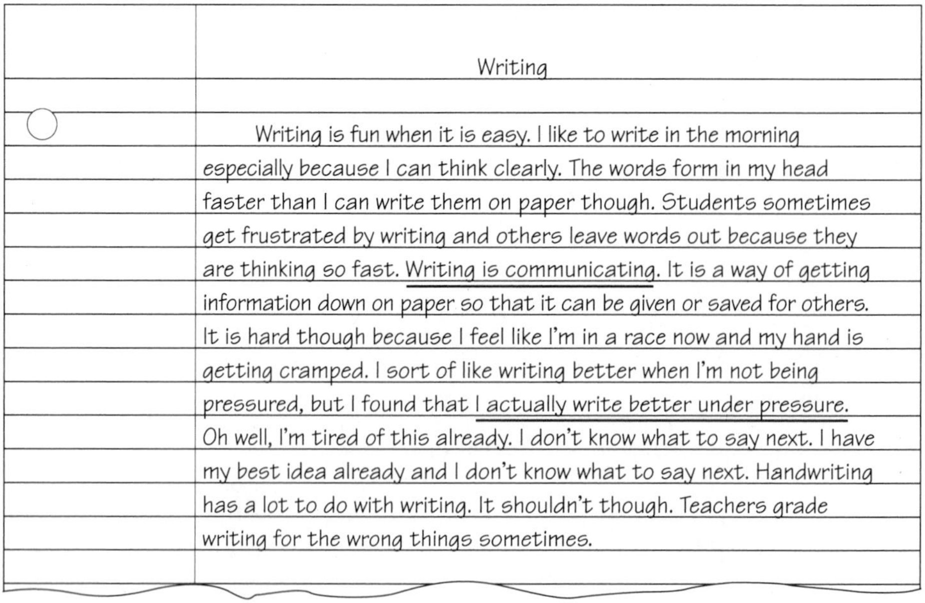

Writing

Writing is fun when it is easy. I like to write in the morning especially because I can think clearly. The words form in my head faster than I can write them on paper though. Students sometimes get frustrated by writing and others leave words out because they are thinking so fast. Writing is communicating. It is a way of getting information down on paper so that it can be given or saved for others. It is hard though because I feel like I'm in a race now and my hand is getting cramped. I sort of like writing better when I'm not being pressured, but I found that I actually write better under pressure. Oh well, I'm tired of this already. I don't know what to say next. I have my best idea already and I don't know what to say next. Handwriting has a lot to do with writing. It shouldn't though. Teachers grade writing for the wrong things sometimes.

reading an earlier entry; you may form different associations this time. Try to generate at least forty ideas. Then circle or underline your three or four best ideas. Many students find that several of their best ideas — the most original and creative ones — occur in the middle or toward the end of their brainstorming sheet; the ideas that are generated first frequently are common or overused. An example of listing to brainstorm the topic "Advertising" is shown in Figure 15.3. Which ideas do you think are the best? Circle three or four. Where are they located in the list?

Mapping

If you already are using one of the mapping techniques for taking text notes or preparing study sheets, you may find that mapping works just as well for generating paper topics and ideas. If you haven't tried mapping yet, try it now. Some students find that the visual display provided by mapping helps them get started on their writing assignments. Figure 15.4 contains an example of mapping used to brainstorm for ideas on the broad topic "Natural Disasters."

Figure 15.3 Example of Listing

Advertising

Ads on TV	sells products
in magazines	Jerry Lewis movie–get it now
books are advertised on talk shows	cereal boxes used
persuasion	toys
motivate to buy	I want a
manipulate	consumer policies
focus on product	regulations
Raisin commercial	15 second spots
win an award	4 per minute
music on ads	Betty Crocker–changed image
high pressure	high salaries
low pressure	Darren from Bewitched
no bargain	Dog food instead of stew
expensive	Tuna ad on movie, Mr. Mom
1000's per spot	appeal to consumer
Super Bowl–cost per shot	aimed at certain markets
journalism	soap operas
no alcohol ads	different kinds of ads in daytime vs. evening
smoking	test media

Figure 15.4 Example of Mapping

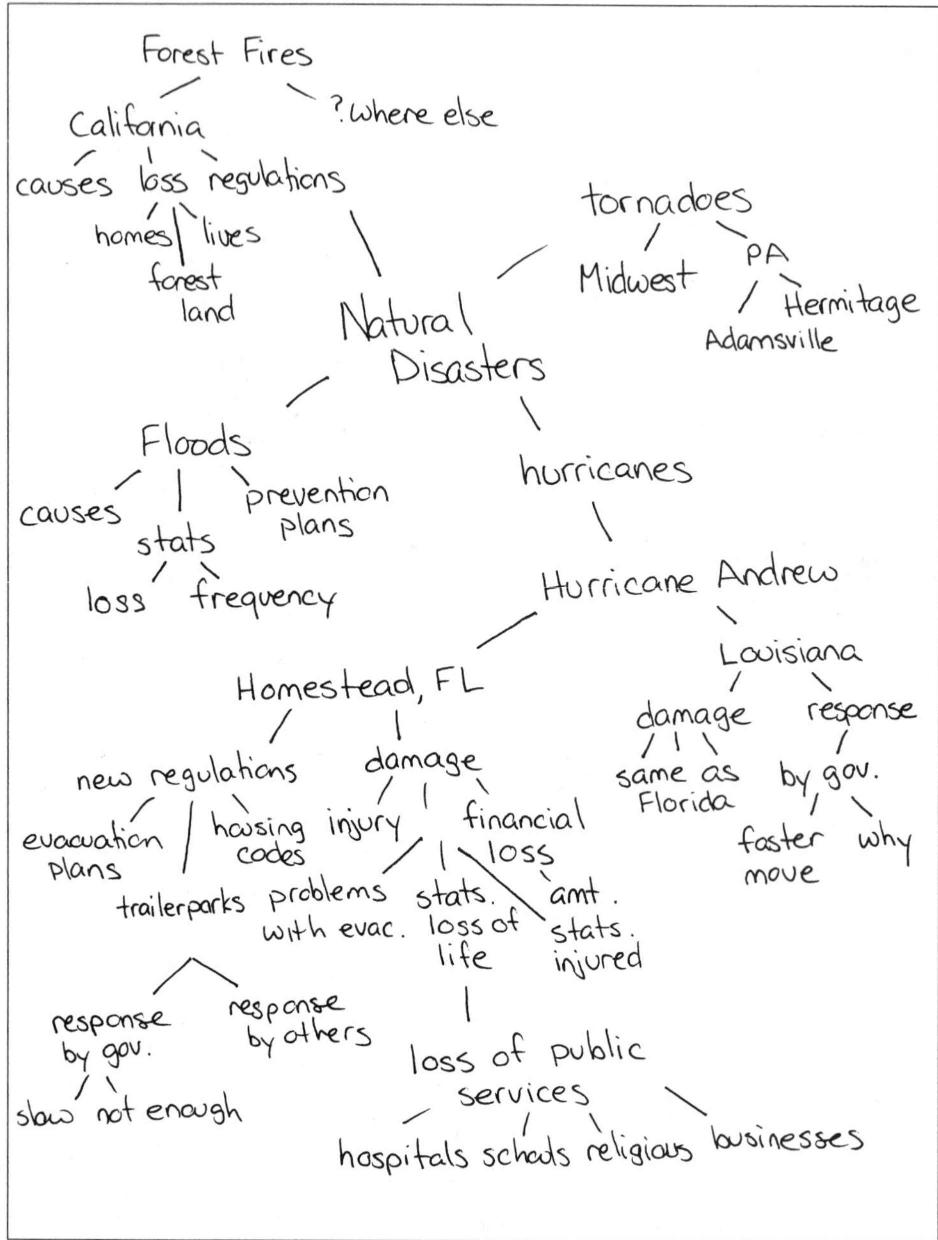

Questioning

If you're writing a paper on a topic that's relatively unfamiliar to you, you may find it difficult to brainstorm for ideas. It's hard to write for five or ten minutes about something you don't know much about. Many students experience this type of difficulty when they begin a research paper. Just as you generate ideas by listing what you know, you may find it helpful in some cases to list what you don't know. One way to do this is by questioning. You can get ideas for a paper or get started on your research by generating a list of questions about the topic. As an exercise in questioning, jot down at least five questions on the topic "Amniocentesis." (Hint: Amniocentesis is a test that is given to pregnant women.)

If you have some general idea about what the topic refers to, you will find it easy to generate questions. On the other hand, if you have never heard the word, you may find it difficult to begin. You may need to check at least one resource in order to find out something about the topic. Once you know even a little bit about it, you can generate questions that can help you determine which direction you want to take in planning your paper or your research. Look at the questions that were generated by one class on the topic of amniocentesis (see Figure 15.5). Circle the ideas that you think could lead to a good paper on this topic.

You can develop a number of questions by thinking of yourself as a reporter and asking questions that begin with the words *Who, What, Where, Why, When,* and *How.* These types of questions can be very effective in exploring a topic. However, don't be satisfied with only one "What" question or only one "Why" question. Ask as many of each type of question as you can think of.

GETTING FOCUSED

After you develop some ideas, you also need to limit your topic. You couldn't write a well-developed short essay or research paper on any of the topics that you used in the brainstorming activities, because they were all too broad. One of the reasons to circle your best ideas after brainstorming is to help focus your writing, to help narrow your topic. It would be impossible to write about the broad topic "Natural Disasters" in a five-paragraph essay or even in a five-page paper. It even would be difficult to discuss everything that related to hurricanes or to Hurricane Andrew in a paper of that length. However, you might be able to develop the topic of "relief efforts" or "damage to schools" in a short paper.

Many students believe that the broader the topic, the easier it will be to write the paper. In some ways this may be true, but often the result tends to be a rather

Figure 15.5 Questioning

AMNIOCENTESIS

What is amniocentesis?	When is it needed?
What is it used for?	Is it practical?
Where did it originate?	Is it accurate?
How was it developed?	Is it safe?
Does it help?	Do all women need it?
Who discovered it?	What does it show?
How does it work?	What negative effects are associated with it?
Does it hurt?	Why was it developed?
Is it harmful?	What improvements have been made?
Does it cost a lot?	
Is it a must?	

general discussion with little depth or insight. In most cases, by narrowing the topic, you actually increase your ability to write a good paper. By dealing with a more focused, specific topic, you can communicate your information more clearly.

There are a number of ways to narrow your topic in addition to the brainstorming techniques mentioned above. One method that seems to be particularly effective is to make the topic more specific. Think of one example, one person, one time, or one event to write about. Ask yourself who, what, where, when, why, or how questions again, but this time use the specific answer to one of them as your topic. If you were assigned the topic "Vandalism," you might brainstorm to get ideas. In the process of brainstorming you might narrow or limit your topic to one better suited to a short writing assignment. (You also could narrow the topic prior to doing your brainstorming.) Several broad topics, including vandalism, have been limited in Figure 15.6.

Figure 15.6 Limiting the Topic

Vandalism
At colleges
In dormitories
Caused by students
When drinking
Leads to increased fees

Occupations
Teachers
College Teachers
Teaching English Composition
Rewards of Teaching English Composition

Pollution
In cities
Air pollution
Auto exhaust
Pollution control regulations for autos
Effectiveness of pollution control regulations for autos in major cities

Remember, if a topic is so broad that entire books are written on it, it's too broad for a two- or three-page paper. You may, however, be able to limit the topic by using the library to locate a general resource book or article that will help you identify specific aspects or parts of the topic that would be more suited to a short paper. You may get an idea for a topic from one of the chapter titles, from one of the headings, or even from one of the examples used in a longer work. Doing this preliminary research may help you select a more suitable topic.

You also may find that other people can be a great source of information to you. Ask your professor, your friends, your classmates, or even your relatives if they have any ideas for you. You also can develop ideas for how to limit a topic by using yourself as a resource. Think about what you know about the general topic, think about what you find interesting about the topic, think about what concerns you about the topic.

Once you have chosen your topic, you may find that you need to brainstorm again for more ideas. Write your limited topic in the center or at the top of a piece of paper and brainstorm again. Now you are brainstorming for *support* that you can use to develop your topic into a paper. You may find that you develop a number of new ideas on the topic that you didn't think of before.

If you are writing a research paper, you will need to locate a number of sources such as books, journal articles, or government documents in order to gather information for your paper. Use the resources that were described in Chapter 1 to prepare a working bibliography for your paper. This list of possible sources on the topic should provide you with most of the information that you will need to write the paper. As you read each of the books or articles, make notes on information that you think will be useful in your paper. You may want to refer to the style manual or handbook that you are using in your writing course for more information on how to take notes and create your bibliography.

GETTING ORGANIZED

After you've brainstormed for a topic, focused the topic, and generated ideas to use in your paper, you need to organize your ideas before you begin to write. Except for mapping, which allows you to group your ideas as they develop, the brainstorming techniques don't have a built-in method of organization. By listing and selecting ideas, you may find that you can easily organize the points that you want to make. You also may find that this strategy helps you decide which ideas to use in your paper and which to omit. In addition, at this stage of the development of your paper, you may realize that you need to add more information to some parts of your paper. Developing a tentative thesis statement helps you organize and structure your outline. Finally, outlining the paper provides you with a framework in which to write.

LIST AND SELECT IDEAS

The next step in the writing process is to select which ideas to use and which to throw away or save for another paper. Some of the ideas generated during your brainstorming session may not be appropriate to your limited topic. Many students try to use all of their ideas or research in their paper just because they think they should. Unfortunately, this often results in a paper that lacks unity of purpose. Look at the list of ideas that students generated on the limited topic, "Why Walk?" (Figure 15.7). You may notice that many of the ideas are related or seem to revolve

Figure 15.7 Listing Ideas

WHY WALK?

everyone walks	lower cholesterol level
ages 5 to 75	show off
relaxation	makes wife happy
good exercise	lower insurance rates
improves circulation	get fresh air
builds endurance	saves gas
strengthens legs	healthy
relieves tension	live longer
get rid of anger	keep trim
relaxes emotions	helps respiratory system
start at slow pace	cardiovascular
look younger	tones muscles
lose weight	looking good
feel better about self	sense of accomplishment
mental rest	burn energy
clears senses	cute outfits

around the same basic headings. After listing and selecting from the brainstormed ideas, the class developed three groups of ideas (shown in Figure 15.8).

One method that you can use to group or organize your ideas involves four steps. First, look at your list of ideas. Pick out the idea that you like the best. Second, look through the list for other ideas related to it. Third, circle or underline all of them. Fourth, decide which to use first, second, and so on before beginning to write the paper. You also may want to try a second method that involves labeling each idea with a letter or number. Look at the first good idea that you have on your brainstorming list. Put an "A" in front of it. Now go through the list and identify any other ideas that seem closely related to it. Mark each of these with an "A" also. Repeat with the next good idea and mark all of these with the letter "B." Continue until all groups of ideas are matched. Then list each group on a separate piece of

Figure 15.8 Grouping Ideas

Physical Health	Physical Fitness	Mental Health
cardiovascular	lose weight	release tension
respiratory	build endurance	clears senses
improves circulation	tone muscles	relaxation
strengthens legs	look younger	get rid of anger
lower cholesterol level	keep trim	feel better about self
live longer	looking good	mental rest

Other possible category titles:

- Feeling good
  - Physically—Health
  - Mentally—Emotions
- Looking good
  - appearance due to fitness

Tentative thesis: Walking is beneficial because it improves one's physical fitness, physical health, and mental health.

paper and decide which group or groups can be used for your writing assignment. After selecting the appropriate groups of ideas, go back and add a heading and make sure that each of the ideas supports that heading. Finally, decide whether you need more ideas for one or more of the groups, and brainstorm to complete your list. If you are writing a research paper, refer again to your working bibliography for additional support. If necessary, you may need to search for additional sources that will provide you with the information that you need.

DEVELOP A TENTATIVE THESIS

After you list and select your ideas, you need to develop a tentative thesis statement. Developing a thesis statement at this point in the writing process will help you determine how to organize your information. It also will help you determine whether you need additional information in order to write an effective paper. Your thesis is simply one sentence that tells your reader the main point or points that you are going to make in the paper. A good thesis statement shows your point of view or attitude about the topic. Look at the sample thesis statement that was developed for the essay on "Why People Walk" (Figure 15.8). The thesis shows that the writer views walking as useful or beneficial. It also tells the reader that there are three reasons that the writer believes walking is a beneficial activity. Your thesis can help you, the writer, know where you are going. As you develop an outline and write your first draft, you may decide to modify your thesis. That's fine. However, having some idea of what you plan to discuss in the paper can help you organize it more clearly.

OUTLINE YOUR PAPER

Outlines help you structure your ideas before you begin to write. They allow you to check each main section to make sure that it includes sufficient support and is well organized. If you find that some areas of your topic are not well developed, you may decide to gather additional support through brainstorming or library research. You also may decide to switch paragraphs around, move supporting ideas from one main topic to another, or even change your thesis. All of these changes are much more easily made in the outlining stage than after you already have written the paper.

You can develop an informal outline by asking yourself why you believe your thesis is true. For example, when you were in high school, did you ever ask your parents to loan you the car or ask them for an advance on your allowance? If you did, you probably had a list of reasons ready to support your request. That is the same kind of list that you should develop to back up your thesis statement.

DRAFTING YOUR PAPER

For many students, writing a paper begins and ends with the drafting stage; they simply write the paper once, and that's that. No brainstorming, focusing, or organizing occurs before they write, and no revision or evaluation occurs afterward. Although some students actually can produce a good paper without going through the prewriting steps, most cannot. Their papers lack focus, organization, adequate development, or all three. By completing the prewriting steps, however, it's easy to write a first draft.

Essays, reports, and term papers generally contain an introduction, body paragraphs, and a conclusion. A typical five-paragraph theme will contain an introductory paragraph, three body paragraphs, and a concluding paragraph. Similarly, a five-page paper may contain several introductory paragraphs, a number of body paragraphs, and one or more concluding paragraphs. Once you understand how to write a five-paragraph theme, you should be able to use the same basic ideas in preparing longer papers. Let's look at the basic format for each part of the essay.

THE INTRODUCTION

Many students have a hard time starting a paper because they don't know how to write the first paragraph. Before we even begin to discuss some strategies for composing introductory paragraphs, you should know that you don't have to write the introduction first. As long as you have written your thesis statement and your outline, you can begin with the first body paragraph, the first main point, and write the introduction after you complete the rest of the paper.

The introduction gives you the opportunity to do several things. First, it allows you to capture the reader's interest. You can use a catchy phrase or quotation, a startling statistic, a brief story, or even a question to get your reader interested in your topic. Second, the introduction provides you with a convenient "slot" in which to place your thesis statement. Once you get the reader's attention, you need to present the topic or subject of your paper and your position or attitude toward your topic. Finally, the introduction allows you to tell your reader what main points you intend to discuss in order to support the position that you took in your thesis statement. Introductory paragraphs, then, are used to get your reader interested in your topic, to state your thesis, and to show the method of development that you intend to use in your paper.

Introductions can be three or four sentences long or three or four paragraphs long, depending on the length of the writing assignment. If you are writing a five-hundred-word paper, your introduction should be about four to eight sentences long. If your introduction is much longer, you may find that it loses some of its impact. Some students make the mistake of discussing one or more of their main points in the introduction, which weakens the introduction and takes the reader's attention away from the paper's thesis.

THE BODY PARAGRAPHS

The body paragraphs are the most important part of the paper. However, they are often the hardest paragraphs to write. Basically, all you have to do is write a topic sentence and back it up with details, reasons, examples, or facts. Sounds easy, doesn't it? However, it's not; entire books and courses are devoted to helping students learn to write body paragraphs. In this text, we can't go into the detail that is necessary to fully examine this topic. However, some basic strategies may help you begin this process.

Once you develop your thesis statement, you need to ask yourself why you believe the view that it expresses. By answering that question, you'll generate the main points for each of your body paragraphs. If you've developed your paper by completing the prewriting stages suggested earlier, you already may know what you want to say to back up or support your thesis. In either case, these main points each will become a topic sentence (one topic sentence for each body paragraph). In developing the topic "Why Walk?" students generated three categories of ideas: physical health, physical fitness, and mental health. Each of these categories or main points must be developed into a topic sentence.

Just as the thesis statement provides the controlling idea for the essay or paper as a whole, the topic sentence expresses the overall, controlling idea of one body paragraph. If you recall, the class generated the following thesis statement for the paper on walking: "Walking is beneficial because it improves one's physical fitness, physical health, and mental health." If you were developing topic sentences for each of the body paragraphs based on this thesis, you might use the following:

1. Walking improves one's physical fitness because it is an excellent form of aerobic exercise.
2. In addition to building physical fitness, walking provides long-term benefits to a person's physical health.
3. Walking also is beneficial because it improves one's mental health.

Although there are many other ways that you could formulate a topic sentence for each of your body paragraphs, your topic sentence must include the topic that you are discussing and the point of view (or position) that you are taking. Good topic sentences should take one position or one side; they should be positive, in favor of the subject, or negative, against the subject. If your topic sentence doesn't take a stand about the topic, you won't be able to back it up with supporting sentences.

After you develop your topic sentences, you need to refer to your outline for supporting points to make your case. Each of the ideas that you listed under the main headings can be developed into separate sentences. Some students make the mistake of listing all of their reasons or examples in one sentence to back up their main point. By doing this they forfeit the opportunity to convince the reader that their position is the correct one. When you wanted an advance on your allowance, you probably went into great detail about the ski trip or concert that you wanted to attend. You might even have talked about how you would never get a chance to go again or how important it was to attend. You probably thought up several excellent arguments to use to convince your parents to give you the money. You need to use the same strategies when writing a body paragraph. You need to include excellent reasons, examples, and/or facts to convince your reader that the points you are making are sound.

If you're writing a research paper, the information that you find in reference materials generally can be used as secondary support. You still need to make your own points as you write the paper and use the information from your research notes to back up those points, though.

Be careful when you use reference material in your paper. Many students unintentionally are guilty of plagiarism when they write research papers. Plagiarism is a difficult concept but can be described in laymen's terms as taking someone else's ideas or words and using them as if they were your own. The easiest way to avoid plagiarizing is to carefully document all of the information that you take from reference sources. One method of documenting information involves putting quotation marks around any information that you copy directly from a book, periodical, or other source. Another method involves paraphrasing information from source materials. Many students think that as long as they put the information into their own words, they don't have to cite (indicate the source) the information. Unfortunately, in most cases, even paraphrased information must be documented, too. The only time you really don't have to document reference material is in the case of common knowledge. Information that is included in every source or many sources that you referenced may be considered common knowledge. On the other hand, information that is contained in only one of your sources is considered the unique idea(s) of the author of that book or article. This information must be documented in order to give credit to the person who developed it. If you aren't sure whether or not you need to document information, check with your professor.

You can cite a source by including the publication information of the article or book or other work in a footnote, endnote, or reference list. Since many different citation styles are used in college, you should check with your professor to find out which format he or she expects you to use and then use your style manual or handbook to verify the proper form for each reference work you are using.

Adequate Development

Some students weaken their argument by failing to develop their topic sentence. Without enough evidence, you can't really persuade your reader that you're making a reasonable and plausible point. Trying to drive home your point with only one supporting idea is a common problem for beginning writers. Listing a number of points without really explaining them often is just as much of a problem. Try to include several reasons or examples to support your main point, and then explain why you think they are relevant in one or two sentences.

Unity

Lack of unity within a body paragraph can be another problem. A paragraph has unity when each sentence contributes to the single idea expressed in the topic sentence. If one or more of the supporting sentences is "off the topic," the paragraph lacks unity. A paragraph that is unified helps convince the reader to agree with the point that's being made. It doesn't allow the reader to move away from the argument.

Coherence

Students who begin writing without planning or outlining often have problems with coherence in body paragraphs. We say that a paragraph has coherence if each sentence follows logically from the one before. Papers that lack coherence often are hard to read or seem disorganized. You can improve the coherence in your paragraphs by planning your primary and secondary support before you write and by deciding which points should be made first, second, third and so on. In addition, you can let your reader know where you're going in the paragraph by using transitional devices. You can introduce each main point with a transition word like *first, second, next,* or *finally.* Drawing your reader's attention back to the main point is another method of adding continuity to the paragraph or paper.

THE CONCLUSION

Just as your introduction should capture the reader's attention, your conclusion should leave the reader thinking about the issues that you presented in your paper. Your concluding paragraph should bring your paper to a logical end. Without a conclusion, some papers appear unfinished. Your reader may wonder whether he or she lost the last page. Restating your thesis or main points in the concluding paragraph can help convince your reader that your position is a valid one.

Although restating the main points provides an effective conclusion for many papers, several other strategies also may be useful. You may be able to move or inspire your reader with a striking quotation, a dramatic example, or a startling statistic. If you begin your paper with a question, you might decide to answer that question in the concluding paragraph. You could offer suggestions for how to solve the problem, or you could urge the reader to take action about the issue that you discussed in the paper.

The conclusion is not, however, the appropriate place to discuss additional points that were not developed in the body paragraphs. Some students introduce supporting details in the conclusion because they don't seem to fit anywhere else. Rather than helping to build the argument, they often detract from it because the points seem almost "thrown in."

REVISING YOUR PAPER

For many students, revising a paper means correcting spelling errors, recopying (or typing) the paper, and fixing a word here and there. Revision, however, is much more involved than that. Revision may include adding further support, eliminating ideas that disrupt the unity of a paragraph or the essay as a whole, or rearranging information to improve the coherence of the paper. Revision can be undertaken at almost any point in preparing your paper, but students often do a "formal" revision after completing the first draft.

Many students try to get a first draft of their paper done several days before it's due so that they can set it aside for a day or two. You may find that you're more aware of problems in your paper after you have been away from it for a few days. If you try to evaluate the paper immediately after you've finished drafting it, you may be reading what you expect to see rather than what is really there. Similarly, you may think that you have developed your thesis adequately or properly organized the ideas when really you are so familiar with the material that you know what you mean even if others won't.

Your professor may require you to revise your paper after it is returned. Many professors believe that students learn the most about writing papers by correcting the errors that they have made. Although they assume that you will correct spelling errors, fix grammatical mistakes, and improve sentence construction, that is not all that will be expected in your revision. Your revision may require a reworking of your entire paper, beginning perhaps with a more specific or focused thesis. If the thesis is too broad, you may have had difficulty supporting it in a short writing assignment. You may need to rethink or reexplore your topic for ideas on how to develop the points that you have made. Some professors may expect you to go into more detail or provide more support from outside sources. You may need to examine each paragraph individually to determine whether you provided convincing evidence or support for the point that you made in your topic sentence.

How much you change or how many times you make changes in your paper before you hand it in is really up to you. If you spent a lot of time planning your paper before you wrote the first draft, you may find that you need to make only minor improvements during the revision stage. On the other hand, if you just sat down and wrote the paper "off the top of your head," you may need to go back to the prewriting stages in order to properly develop your topic.

Revision is difficult when you know that something is wrong with your paper, but you don't know what it is or how to fix it. Many students make the mistake of waiting until their paper is done to ask someone to look at it. You may find that it saves you a lot of unnecessary frustration and extra work if you ask someone to help you in the planning stages. Once you have a tentative thesis and an informal outline, ask a friend who will be honest with you, a tutor, or your professor to take a look at it. Problems with development, coherence, and even focus can easily be spotted in your outline. At this point, you may be able to make some revisions in your plan that will save you hours of drafting and revision.

DRABBLE reprinted by permission of UFS, Inc.

EVALUATING YOUR PAPER

Evaluating your paper is the final stage of the writing process. Unfortunately, many students neglect this important step. Once they've written the required number of words, they assume the job is done. Good writers, however, take time to analyze and evaluate the finished product. Try to put yourself in the place of your professor. Look critically at the paper, and then grade the paper as if you were the professor. In order to do this effectively, you need to know what criteria your professor is planning to use to evaluate papers. If you are not told how your paper will be evaluated, ask.

Most professors grade papers according to a combination of criteria. For many professors, the content of the paper is the most important factor. They base their evaluation on how well the paper answers the question or develops the topic that was assigned. Depending on the course, the next criteria for evaluation may be the writing style or writing ability of the student. Organization, paragraph development, or even sentence construction and variety are some of the factors that may be considered. Finally, the last set of criteria for grading includes errors in mechanics, spelling, and paper presentation (neatness, format, and so on).

If this paper is your second, third, or fourth piece of written work for a certain class, you should have a pretty good idea of what your professor expects. Use your other papers to help you determine the merits of the newest one. Ask yourself the following types of questions.

1. What types of errors did I make on my previous papers?
2. Have I corrected the errors that my professor noted on the previous papers?
3. What were the strengths of my previous papers?
4. Is this paper better than my previous papers? Why?
5. Am I satisfied with this paper?
6. What grade would I give this paper?

Write out your answers to these questions so that you can review them after your paper is returned and compare your own responses to those of the professor. If your professor uses a grade sheet or check sheet for each of the papers that you write, complete one yourself before you turn in the paper. Until you develop your own evaluation sheet, you may prefer to use the Paper Evaluation Sheet shown in Figure 15.9.

Figure 15.9 Paper Evaluation Sheet

PAPER EVALUATION SHEET

Introduction

What is the attention-getting device? ______________________________

What is the thesis statement? ______________________________

____

____

What are the three (two, four) ways the topic will be discussed?

____

Is the introduction well organized? ______________________________

Is the introduction well written? ______________________________

Body Paragraphs

How many body paragraphs are there? ______________________________

What are the topic sentences of each?

____

____

____

____

____

____

Does each topic sentence support the thesis? yes ____ no ____

If not, why not? ______________________________

(continued)

Figure 15-9 (continued)

Is each topic sentence well supported by primary supporting sentences? yes _____ no _____

If not, which one is not well supported? ____________________

Does each body paragraph have a concluding sentence? ____________________

Is each body paragraph well organized, _____ unified, _____ and well written _____?

Conclusion

How many sentences make up the conclusion? ____________________

Does the conclusion bring the essay to a logical end? ____________________

What technique is used in the conclusion? ____________________

Is the conclusion well written? ____________________

General Comments

What grade would you give the paper? _____ Why?

____

____

____

What major changes or improvements did you make in this paper compared to your previous paper?

____

____

____

If you could do the paper again, what would you do differently?

____

____

____

Once your paper is returned, look at the comments and suggestions that the professor has made rather than just at the grade. If your evaluation of the paper was similar to the professor's, you know that you have a pretty good idea now of what the professor expects. If, however, the two evaluations differ, don't be discouraged. Go talk to your professor about the paper. Take the notes or check sheet that you completed with you so that you can discuss your own efforts at evaluation, and ask your professor to explain why you were incorrect in one or more areas. Learning what the professor expects is a critical step in effectively writing the next paper. On the other hand, showing the professor why you thought the paper was a good effort may help him or her view the paper in a new way. If you had difficulty with organization, the paper may have appeared to be poorly developed even though it contained good support. Discussing the paper in a rational and realistic way with your professor may help you gain some points, but, more important, you may learn how to write a better paper.

ACTIVITIES

1. Write for five or ten minutes on the topic "Smoking." Start with the words "Smoking is." Then circle or underline your three best ideas.
2. In five or ten minutes, create an idea map on the topic "Education." Circle or underline your best ideas.
3. Develop a list of questions to generate ideas on the topic "Termites."
4. Use one of the methods described in the chapter to select and group the ideas that you would use if you were going to write a short essay on one of the topics that you brainstormed. (Hint: Look for three or four groups of ideas.)
5. Use the Paper Evaluation Sheet to evaluate a paper that you recently completed. What are your strengths and weaknesses?

POSTTEST

Where Are You Now?

Now that you have completed Chapter 15, take a few minutes to answer *yes* or *no* to the following questions. Compare your answers with those in the pretest.

	YES	NO
1. Do you usually sit down and just write your paper without planning first?	_____	_____
2. Do you often find that your topic is too broad?	_____	_____
3. Do you have difficulty organizing your ideas when you write papers?	_____	_____
4. Do you correct errors in spelling and grammar only when you revise a paper?	_____	_____
5. Do you know how to develop an introductory paragraph?	_____	_____
6. Do you have problems with supporting your thesis?	_____	_____
7. Do you use transitional devices to identify main ideas and show connections to supporting ideas?	_____	_____
8. Do you develop some type of outline before you write?	_____	_____
9. Do you generally understand why you got the grade that you got on a paper?	_____	_____
10. Do you start long-term paper assignments early in the semester?	_____	_____

Give yourself one point for each *yes* answer to questions 5, 7, 8, 9, and 10, and one point for each *no* answer to questions 1, 2, 3, 4, and 6. Now total up your points. Compare your score on this posttest with the score that you got on the pretest. In what areas do you still need to improve?

Index

W

To the owner of this book:

I hope that you have been significantly influenced by *Orientation to College Learning*. I'd like to know as much about your experiences with the book as you care to offer. Your comments can help me make it a better book for future readers.

School: ______________________ Instructor's name: ______________________

Address of school (city, state, and zip code): ______________________

1. What I like most about this book is: ______________________

____

____

____

2. What I like least about this book is: ______________________

____

____

____

3. Specific suggestions for improving the book: ______________________

____

____

____

4. The name of the course in which I used this book: ______________________

____

5. In the space below—or in a separate letter, if you'd care to write one—please let me know what other comments about the book you'd like to make. I welcome your suggestions!

Optional:

Your Name: ______________________________ Date: ________________

May Wadsworth quote you, either in promotion for *Orientation to College Learning*, or in future publishing ventures?

Yes: ______ No: ______

Sincerely,

Dianna L. Van Blerkom

FOLD HERE

NO POSTAGE NECESSARY IF MAILED IN THE UNITED STATES

BUSINESS REPLY MAIL
FIRST CLASS PERMIT NO. 34 BELMONT, CA

POSTAGE WILL BE PAID BY ADDRESSEE

Dianna L. Van Blerkom
Wadsworth Publishing Company
10 Davis Drive
Belmont, CA 94002

FOLD HERE